The American History Series

SERIES EDITORS
John Hope Franklin, *Duke University*
A. S. Eisenstadt, *Brooklyn College*

D1365066

David W. Southern
Westminster College

The Progressive Era and Race
Reaction and Reform, 1900–1917

Harlan Davidson, Inc.
Wheeling, Illinois 60090-6000

Visit us on the World Wide Web at www.harlandavidson.com.

Library of Congress Cataloging-in-Publication Data

Southern, David W. The progressive era and race : reaction and reform, 1900/1917 / David W. Southern.
    p. cm. — (The American history series)
Includes bibliographical references and index.
ISBN 0-88295-234-X (alk. paper)
1. African Americans—Politics and government—20th century.
2. African Americans—Social conditions—To 1964. 3. African Americans—Economic conditions—20th century. 4. United States—Politics and government—1901–1909. 5. United States—Politics and government—1909–1913. 6. United States—Politics and government—1913–1921.
7. Progressivism (United States politics)—History. 8. United States—Race relations. 9. Racism–United States—History—20th century. I. Title.
II. Series: American history series (Wheeling, Ill.)
    E185.6.S68 2005
    305.896'073'009041—dc22
                           2004031093

Cover photo: Booker T. Washington posing with some of the teachers and trustees, including Andrew Carnegie, of the Tuskegee Institute, April 1906. Photographs and Prints Division, Schomburg Center for Research in Black Culture, The New York Public Library, Astor, Lenox, and Tilden Foundations.

Manufactured in the United States of America
08 07 06 05 1 2 3 4 5 VP

To Barbara

FOREWORD

Every generation writes its own history for the reason that it sees the past in the foreshortened perspective of its own experience. This has surely been true of the writing of American history. The practical aim of our historiography is to give us a more informed sense of where we are going by helping us understand the road we took in getting where we are. As the nature and dimensions of American life are changing, so too are the themes of our historical writing. Today's scholars are hard at work reconsidering every major aspect of the nation's past: its politics, diplomacy, economy, society, recreation, mores and values, as well as status, ethnic, race, sexual, and family relations. The lists of series titles that appear at the back of this book will show at once that our historians are ever broadening the range of their studies.

The aim of this series is to offer our readers a survey of what today's historians are saying about the central themes and aspects of the American past. To do this, we have invited to write for the series only scholars who have made notable contributions to the respective fields in which they are working. Drawing on primary and secondary materials, each volume presents a factual and narrative account of its particular subject, one that affords readers a basis for perceiving its larger dimensions and importance. Conscious that readers respond to the closeness and immediacy of a subject, each of our authors seeks to restore the past as an actual present, to revive it as a living reality. The individuals and groups who figure in the pages of our books ap-

pear as real people who once were looking for survival and fulfill-
ment. Aware that historical subjects are often matters of controversy,
our authors present their own findings and conclusions. Each volume
closes with an extensive critical essay on the writings of the major
authorities on its particular theme.

The books in this series are designed for use in both basic and
advanced courses in American history, on the undergraduate and graduate levels. Such a series has a particular value these days, when the
format of American history courses is being altered to accommodate
a greater diversity of reading materials. The series offers a number of
distinct advantages. It extends the dimensions of regular course work.
Going well beyond the confines of the textbook, it makes clear that
the study of our past is, more than the student might otherwise understand, at once complex, profound, and absorbing. It presents that past
as a subject of continuing interest and fresh investigation. The work
of experts in their respective fields, the series, moreover, puts at the
disposal of the reader the rich findings of historical inquiry. It invites
the reader to join, in major fields of research, those who are pondering anew the central themes and aspects of our past. And it reminds
the reader that in each successive generation of the ever-changing
American adventure, men and women and children were attempting,
as we are now, to live their lives and to make their way.

John Hope Franklin
A. S. Eisenstadt

CONTENTS

ACKNOWLEDGMENTS

My greatest debt is to Andrew J. Davidson, the publisher. He stuck with me through a personal crisis and generously extended the deadline for this book. Andrew also meticulously edited the book, raising insightful questions, improving the clarity and flow of the text, and excising many errors, thereby saving me from many embarrassing lapses. My thanks also go to the editors of this series, John Hope Franklin, and Abe Eisenstadt, for entrusting me with this challenging project. In the early stages of the undertaking, Professor Franklin made valuable suggestions on the scope and shape of this book. I also wish to thank an anonymous reviewer who read the manuscript and made valid points. I owe thanks as well to Sam Goodfellow and Butch Lael, my colleagues in the History Department at Westminster College, who read portions of the manuscript and made helpful suggestions for its improvement.

I further want to express my gratitude to Lucy Herz, the production editor at Harlan Davidson, for taking on the task of acquiring the rights for the photographs used in this volume. Finally, I reserve the highest praise for Barbara Alsip, an old and dear classmate from my days at Emory University. She not only read most of the manuscript but she enabled me to get through a very bad time in my life and complete this book. Although many people have assisted me in writing this book, any errors of fact or interpretation in it are solely my responsibility.

INTRODUCTION

When the Progressive Movement swept across the United States in the early twentieth century, oppressed African Americans saw the exuberant impulse toward liberal reform as a glimmer of hope. Led by middle-class, moralistic reformers, the Progressive Movement was a stunningly broad and diverse effort to harness industrialization for the good of the people. Progressive crusaders broke up monopolies, regulated big business and railroads, established the Federal Reserve banking system, legislated progressive taxes, enacted pure food and drug laws, campaigned against vice and corruption, and ushered in women's suffrage and Prohibition. They carried out reforms in virtually every aspect of American life, from the boardroom to the playground. Championing human rights over property rights, progressives spoke fluently the Jeffersonian idiom of egalitarianism and lamented the "betrayal of democracy" that corporate forces had allegedly imposed on the nation. Young, energetic, well-educated progressives believed they had loosed a new interest in social justice and helping the downtrodden. William Allen White, the revered progressive journalist from Kansas, said that his kind felt compelled to reach out to the "have-nots . . . because we felt that to bathe and feed the under dog [sic] would release the burden of injustice on our conscience."

But for all the talk about removing injustices and realizing the democratic promise of America, progressive interest almost always stopped short of the color line. During the Progressive

Era the nation was in fact caught up in a powerful tide of white supremacy at home and imperialism against people of color abroad. Looking back, it is clear that race was the major blind spot of the progressives. Progressive thinkers and politicians became ensnared in a web of "scientific racism." Incredibly, the best science of the time told them that blacks were innately inferior and deserved to remain at the bottom of society as a despised caste. Even those whites who believed in black rights often became defeatist on the race issue because of the overwhelming opposition to racial equality.

Indeed, Americans in the Progressive Era were obsessed with race. Race explained historical development and human society not only for white-supremacist intellectuals such as Theodore Roosevelt and Woodrow Wilson but also for black leaders such as W. E. B. Du Bois. White progressives used their belief in the racial inferiority of blacks to justify the exclusion of African Americans from American democracy. One can even trace the racial sentiment that militated against the inclusion of blacks in the thinking of two future liberal icons in the Progressive Era: Franklin D. Roosevelt and Harry S. Truman. As a Har-vard student and young Democratic legislator, Roosevelt referred to blacks as "semi-beasts" and wrote in the margin of one of his political speeches, "story of a nigger." In a 1911 letter to his future wife, Truman expressed the limits of his democratic sentiments by saying, "I think one man is just as good as another so long as he's honest and decent and not a nigger or a Chinaman." On the other end of such attitudes, Du Bois declared in 1900, "The problem of the twentieth century is the problem of the color line. . . ."

If academics today insist that race is a mere social construct with no biological meaning, early twentieth-century reformers believed that race was a palpably real biological fact that had ultimate importance. The ideas of race and color were powerful, controlling elements in progressive social and political thinking. And this fixation on race explains how democratic reform and racism went hand-in-hand in the Progressive Era. The most progressive politicians in the South, where almost 90 percent of African Americans lived from 1900 to 1917, led campaigns for legal segregation and disfranchisement of blacks and even vowed to lead lynch mobs against black men accused of raping white women. For their part, the great bulk of northern pro-gressives acquiesced in the consolidation and maintenance of southern white supremacy.

In *The Negro in American Life and Thought: The Nadir, 1877–1901* (1954), the black historian Rayford W. Logan placed the low point of black life in the post-Reconstruction period. In a later edition of his book, however, Logan extended the concept of the "nadir" into the Progressive Era. Rightly so. It was particularly dispiriting for the most oppressed group in the nation to be excluded from a reform movement that espoused democracy and social justice. The emotions of African Americans boiled because white progressives seemed so indifferent to, even supportive of, the racial staples of the Progressive Era: segregation, disfranchisement, peonage, lynching, and race riots. Nothing aroused the anger of blacks more than the racist policies of the federal government, such as President Woodrow Wilson's segregation of the federal bureaucracy. As the historian Richard Weiss summed it up, "[A]s the Progressive movement reached its peak, and the nation prepared to embark on a war to save the world for democracy, the black man found himself more threatened, more despised, and more discriminated against in his own land than at any time since emancipation."

One of the reasons for so much belligerent anti-black discourse and action in the Progressive Era was the advent of the "New Negro." E. L. Doctorow described one of the new militants, Coalhouse Walker, in his celebrated novel *Ragtime* (1975). The fictional Walker was a dapper young jazz musician who proudly owned a shiny new Ford. Resentful white firemen in the area soiled the seats of Walker's prized car with human excrement and forbade him to pass on the road. Doctorow conveyed the black man's thoughts as follows, "He was not unaware that in his dress and as the owner of a car he was a provocation to many white people." The novelist added that the defiant Walker "had created himself in the teeth of such feelings." Not surprisingly, the reaction of Walker to rampaging racism was dramatic and explosive—the stuff of novels and movies. But Walker's steadfast resolve to achieve and advance was emblematic of the New Negro of the Progressive Era. And the specter of such a black man proved exceedingly provocative to whites, thus explaining the pervasive racial violence of the time.

The history of African Americans always has two sides. One side relates what whites have thought about and done to blacks, as much of this book does. The other side traces the aspirations and strivings of blacks to make a life for themselves in a hostile white world. If one focuses only on the first aspect, blacks appear as no more than victims. As the black scholar Cornel West observed, "While black people have never been simply victims, wallowing in self-pity and begging for white giveaways, they have been—and are—*victimized* [emphasis in original]." The guidelines of this series do not, for considerations of length, permit me the space to discuss all the social and cultural ways that blacks avoided victimization and carved out a social harbor for themselves in church, education, music, fraternal orders, sports, and the like, but Chapter Five demonstrates in some detail how African Americans forged their own Progressive Movement and fought doggedly and courageously against the ideology and practice of white supremacy.

In this study I have chosen as the chronological boundaries of the Progressive Era the years 1900 to 1917. Some historians place the start of the era in the late nineteenth century, usually at 1890, where progressivism obviously had its roots. I use the more traditional starting date of 1900, for I believe that the Progressive Movement did not achieve any significant cohesion or momentum until early in the twentieth century; indeed, there was little or no sense of a Progressive Movement before 1900. In 1914 the journalist Walter Lippmann said, "The adjective 'progressive' is what we like, and the word is new." Others would extend the Progressive Era through World War I to 1920, for which a good case can be made. But I end my story with the entry of the United States into World War I as, again, the alloted space does not allow an adequate discussion of the racial impact of the military conflict and its ghastly aftermath. I have only hinted at the racial implications of the postwar period in the Epilogue. Finally, I would like to alert the reader that I sometimes use the word "liberal" in this book to distinguish the small minority of progressives who were pro–civil rights from the majority who were either demonstrably racist or indifferent to blacks.

CHAPTER ONE

The Demise of Reconstruction and the Making of White Supremacy, 1865–1900

The vicious, heart-rending conflict that ended slavery proved to be the nation's bloodiest war. The Civil War not only resulted in 620,000 deaths, but it left behind deep resentments, hatreds, and grievances that festered and plagued American society and politics for decades to come. Brooding over the war, slavery, and the "providence of God" in his second inaugural address on March 4, 1865, President Abraham Lincoln marveled that "any men should dare to ask a just God's assistance in wringing their bread from the sweat of other men's faces." Lincoln prayed for a speedy end to "the scourge of war" but bowed to a higher power on the matter of the price for the sin of slavery:

> Yet if God wills that [the war] continue, until all the wealth piled by the bond-man's two hundred and fifty years of unrequited toil shall be sunk, and until every drop of blood drawn with the lash, shall be paid by another drawn with the sword, as was said three thousand years ago, so still it must be said "the judgments of the Lord, are true and righteous altogether."

In a religious sense, none understood better than Lincoln the transcendent evil of slavery and the tragic cost of its abolition.

But in time many seemed to forget the tragedy of the war so deeply felt by Lincoln. In *The Era of Reconstruction, 1865–1877* (1965), the historian Kenneth M. Stampp observed, "The Civil War, though admittedly a tragedy, is nevertheless often described as a glorious time of gallantry, noble self-sacrifice, and high idealism." When Stampp wrote his influential, revisionist account about Republican racial reform after the Civil War, most Americans believed that Reconstruction, not the war, constituted the real tragedy of American history. For almost a century, Stampp complained, historians had painted Reconstruction as "The Tragic Era," "The Dreadful Decade," "The Age of Hate," and "The Blackout of Honest Government." White historians, both North and South, indicted influential Republicans who supported civil rights and fought for economic and educational assistance for the freed slaves, portraying the so-called Radicals as hate-driven politicians and hopelessly misguided egalitarian activists. White racism best explains the formation of this popular but distorted view of Reconstruction. Typical of his time, the esteemed historian William A. Dunning charged in 1901 that Reconstruction inevitably failed because Republican views about "the political capacity of the blacks had been irrational." That is, Republicans erred fatally in thinking that they could make black men into responsible voting citizens.

Then, in the 1950s and 1960s a new wave of Revisionist historians began to undermine the Dunning school of thought by pointing out the benign aspects of the Republicans and stressing the positive, even courageous side of Reconstruction. In tune with the civil rights movement of the time, the Revisionists characterized Republicans as principled and far-sighted believers in equal rights. They emphasized beneficial things, such as the lasting constitutional and educational changes of Reconstruction that prepared the way for the more successful "Second Reconstruction" of the 1950s and 1960s.

Then the historical thinking shifted again. Today a group of historians, sometimes called post-Revisionists, think that Reconstruction failed, but for very different reasons from those cited by Dunning and his adherents. The post-Revisionists generally argue that Reconstruction failed not because the Republicans tried to do too much, but because they did not go far enough. They claim that the federal government shortchanged African Americans by not distributing land and by not promoting sufficiently black education and protecting suffrage for an extended period of time. Keen to the presence of racism, the post-Revisionists charge that the Republican party, including Lincoln, believed in white supremacy and therefore did not have the will to see Reconstruction through to its rightful end. And as a result of the failure of the first Reconstruction in the 1860s and 1870s, they lament, the nation had to undergo a tumultuous Second Reconstruction, nearly one hundred years later.

In *Lincoln and Black Freedom* (1981), the Revisionist LaWanda Cox argued that the post-Revisionism had gone too far in blaming Republicans for the failure of Reconstruction. She further contended that the Second Reconstruction was a faulty model by which to judge the First. Accentuating the "limits of the possible" in history, Cox doubted whether a true Reconstruction had been achievable given the social, political, and constitutional obstacles to racial equality in the 1860s and 1870s. She suggested that when the people in a democratic system overwhelmingly reject a public policy, the government is helpless to enforce it, no matter how just the cause.

Like the work of Cox, the first few pages of this chapter stress factors that led to the defeat of Radical Reconstruction in the South. The remainder of the chapter describes the deteriorating status of African Americans in the post-Reconstruction era and characterizes the racial dilemmas that black and white American reformers faced at the dawn of the twentieth century, typically seen as the beginning of the Progressive Era.

Why Radical Reconstruction Started and Why It Faltered

In retrospect, Radical Reconstruction, which made former slaves into voting citizens, appears more as an aberration than the logical or inevitable outcome of the Civil War. As shown below, only through a series of highly unusual postwar circumstances and events did a small group of revolution-minded Republicans come to wield enough power to initiate what was called "Radical Reconstruction." Only this tiny minority of Republicans thought it essential to undertake a sweeping agenda of new legislation and policies that included the passing of civil rights bills, amending the United States Constitution to secure racial equality, granting blacks land and suffrage, integrating public places, denying the ballot and officeholding to large numbers of former

Confederates and confiscating the land of southern leaders, and stationing for an extended period of time large numbers of federal troops—some of them black—in the South to occupy the land and enforce the law. On the other hand, it is clear that at the end of the war a majority of Republicans and most northern whites had no desire to elevate blacks to first-class citizenship, and it is equally apparent that southern whites were willing to risk their lives and use any means necessary, including fraud, intimidation, and murder, to overthrow any form of Reconstruction that empowered blacks. As it was, Radical Reconstruction was too radical for the American people and yet not radical enough to ensure the lasting rights and security of African Americans. This was the real tragedy of Reconstruction.

The Civil War freed approximately 4 million slaves in the South and border areas. The reactions of blacks to emancipation varied greatly. Some persons appeared stunned, confused, or scared when informed they were free. Most of them, however, remembered the advent of freedom as the central event of their lives. A former Georgia slave recalled: "I felt like a bird out of a cage. Amen. Amen. Amen. I could hardly ask to feel any better than I did that day. . . ."

Many of the former slaves moved about the countryside just to demonstrate that they were free of white control, while others sought lost husbands, wives, daughters, sons, and various relatives who had been separated by family-busting masters or vanished in the fog of war. African Americans strove to formalize their marriages, which had no legal standing under slavery, and reestablish families. The freedpeople knew that they also needed education, land, and political power if they were to rise; and they sought these objectives with courage and resolve. Many believed their years of unpaid labor entitled them to a plot of land. Some simply claimed land they squatted on, and others hopefully waited for Yankee officials to award them "forty acres and a mule."

At mass meetings throughout the South, emancipated slaves and free blacks further demanded equal rights, including the right of manhood suffrage. The following petition from a convention of South Carolina blacks at the end of the war was typical:

We simply ask that we be recognized as men; that there be no obstructions placed in our way; that the same laws which govern white men shall govern <u>black men</u>; that we have the right of trial by jury of our <u>peers</u>; that schools be established for the education of <u>colored children</u> as well as <u>white</u>. . . . that no impediments be put in the way of our acquiring homesteads for ourselves and our people; that, in short, we are dealt with as others are—in equity and justice [emphasis in original].

Slavery obviously had not rendered most African Americans docile. Certainly, however, 250 years of forced, unpaid labor left former slaves in a precarious social and economic position. In 1865 most blacks were landless and lived in abject poverty, and 95 percent of them were illiterate. Many twentieth-century scholars, black and white, have argued that slavery also inflicted psychic damage on African Americans. In the 1960s and 1970s, however, many black activist scholars denied that the ordeal of slavery had created an impaired "Sambo" personality in blacks. They rejected the association of any kind of pathology with black culture—past or present—and argued that the strength of the "slave community" had since colonial times protected the psyches of enslaved persons and allowed them to develop healthy personalities.

But prior to the 1960s, black leaders had shown no hesitation in claiming that slavery had left a lasting and harmful effect on the black personality. In 1892 James Weldon Johnson, a poet, novelist, musician, diplomat, and the first African American to serve as executive director of the NAACP (in 1920), said that slavery had severely damaged black "manhood, intelligence, and virtue" and had engendered "vice, superstition, and immorality" among African Americans. In more recent times, several black analysts also have bewailed the ill effects of slavery. The psychiatrists William H. Grier and Price M. Cobbs said in *Black Rage* (1968) that "pathology as seen in black people [today] had its genesis in slavery." In *Southern History* (2002), the historian Nell Painter, who described human bondage as "soul murder," assailed those who denied the psychic damage of slavery to blacks. The civil rights leader and historian Roger Wilkins argued in *Jefferson's Pillow Talk* (2001) that slavery inflicted "enormous psychic costs" and "resulted in the mangling of far too many souls of black folk. . . ."

Whatever the psychic damage of slavery to African Americans, the racism of the white establishment did far more than anything else to retard their progress in society. Well before the Civil War the over-whelming majority of white Americans, North and South, viewed African Americans as a degraded race, one held back not by slavery but by biology. In the notorious *Dred Scott* case of 1857, Chief Justice Roger B. Taney undoubtedly spoke for a majority of whites when he declared that African Americans constituted "an inferior order" and "were altogether unfit to associate with the white race, either in social or political relations; and so far inferior that they had no rights which the white man was bound to respect."

And the fate of some 250,000 free blacks in the antebellum North suggested how the freed people might expect to fare. Laws in north-ern states legally denied the vote to 90 percent of blacks. Most north-ern blacks could not serve on juries or as witnesses in court, and they were either segregated or excluded from such public places as schools, trains, ships, hotels, restaurants, libraries, and theaters. Many states in the Midwest plus the new state of Oregon (1858) forbade blacks from crossing their borders in the 1850s. Only the most menial, low-paying jobs were open to African Americans, resulting in widespread misery and poverty.

Even abolitionists taught that Africans were fundamentally dif-ferent from whites. In *Uncle Tom's Cabin,* the history-making, anti-slavery novel of 1852, Harriet Beecher Stowe described blacks as "an exotic race, whose ancestors, born beneath a tropical sun, brought with them, and perpetuated to their descendants, a character so essen-tially unlike the hard and dominant Anglo-Saxon race, as for many years to have from it only misunderstanding and contempt." Stowe depicted Africans as emotional, artistic, hedonistic, and, like Uncle Tom, passive before whites. She believed the God-given mission of African Americans was to export Christianity and civilization to Af-rica.

Like Stowe, Lincoln detested slavery, but he believed that Afri-can Americans could not be assimilated into American society. In his famous 1858 debates with the Democrat Stephen Douglas, the future president proclaimed that he was not "in favor of bringing about in any way the social and political equality of the white and black races." Lincoln further specified that he was opposed to "making voters or jurors of negroes, or of qualifying them to hold office...." The physical differences between the races, he claimed, were so great that blacks and whites could never live "together on terms of social and political equality." Lincoln therefore declared, "I as much as any other man am in favor of having the superior position assigned to the white race." When Douglas expressed horror at the thought of interracial marriage, Lincoln rejoined, "A thousand times agreed."

Some have argued that the "Great Emancipator" only resorted to racist language to get elected, but subsequent comments and actions by him suggest otherwise. Even after Lincoln had issued the preliminary Emancipation Proclamation in the fall of 1862, he explained to a black delegation visiting the White House that racial differences and past prejudices and discrimination meant that the two races could never live together in friendship and peace. "It is better for us both, therefore, to be separated," Lincoln told the delegation. Finally, Lincoln was a strong advocate of "colonization," and tried to persuade American blacks to emigrate to Africa or some other suitable place.

Frederick Douglass, the most important black leader in nineteenth-century America, considered Lincoln a friend and a great man, but he did not equivocate when he assessed the late president's true interest. In 1876, in the presence of President Ulysses S. Grant, the Cabinet, and several Congressmen at the dedication of the Freedmen's Memorial Monument in Washington, D.C., Douglass declared that Lincoln was "entirely devoted to the welfare of white men" and that he was, first and last, a white man "[i]n his interests, in his associations, in his habits of thoughts, and in his prejudices." Looking out over the white audience, the black orator proclaimed: "You are the children of Abraham Lincoln. We are at best his step-children; children by adoption; children by force of circumstances and necessity."

If such a magnanimous, slavery-hating man as Lincoln treated blacks as stepchildren, it is not difficult to predict how defeated, pro-slavery Confederates viewed them and their Yankee friends. The bitter hatred of defeated Southerners for their Northern conquerors ran deep. Edmund Ruffin, an eccentric Virginia planter and an early fire-eating secessionist, was one of many white Southerners who could not face defeat and northern occupation. Before Ruffin shot himself in the head at the end of the war, he proclaimed in the final entry of his diary his hatred for "the perfidious, malignant and vile Yankee race." As many as ten thousand slaveholders moved to foreign countries rather than remain in the occupied South. Planters insisted that blacks would not work without coercion, and they feared that crime and chaos would engulf the South after the demise of slavery. If some planters were once paternalistic toward blacks, they now tended to ignore the needs of the weak, the sick, and the aged among their field hands and worried more about their bottom lines. As one Louisiana planter said after the war: "When I owned niggers, I used to pay medical bills and take care of them. I do not think I shall trouble myself much now." Planters felt frustration in the new order, and according to the historian James L. Roark, "Most adjusted merely enough to make their way, rarely enough to make real peace."

Taking out one's frustrations on well-armed Yankee troops could be dangerous, so most white Southerners projected their anger onto blacks. And now that blacks were no longer property worth $500 to $1,000 apiece, their lives had little value to whites. Freedom, ironically, exposed freed blacks to the wrath of all whites, not just the master. After the war southern whites plundered, raped, and murdered African Americans with impunity. Local militia units, often composed of former Confederates still in their gray uniforms, terrorized blacks. Texas courts, for example, indicted five hundred whites for the murder of blacks in 1865 and 1866 but did not convict a single one. In 1865 whites massacred hundreds of African Americans in Louisiana. Throughout the South, they harassed, physically attacked, and sometimes killed white Unionists and Yankee volunteers who came to teach the freed slaves.

Despite southern white attitudes toward the blacks, Lincoln, to the dismay of abolitionists and radicals in his party, offered a very generous peace plan to the defeated Confederates in December 1863, one that afforded little protection for blacks. Although every former Confederate state had to abolish slavery under Lincoln's plan, each one could temporarily assign blacks a status "consistent . . . with their present condition as a laboring, landless, and homeless class." When Congress passed a more rigorous plan of Reconstruction in 1864, Lincoln vetoed the bill. If blacks would not return to Africa as Lincoln urged, they were faced with being a voteless, landless mass of peasants under the thumb of their former masters. Lincoln's 1865 plea for "malice toward none" and "charity for all" has forever given him the image of a great and humane statesman. But if the North had practiced Lincoln-like charity toward defeated Confederates, it would have been at the expense of the rights and livelihood of blacks.

Since Lincoln's plan for Reconstruction was tentative, one can argue that he might have adopted a harsher policy had he not been assassinated. Indeed, he hinted at such during his final days. As a humane man, Lincoln probably would not have tolerated the wholesale murder of blacks. As a political man who believed in a strong federal government that supported economic development, he probably would have done everything possible to prevent the highly racist, states' rights Democrats from taking control of the federal government. A practical politician, Lincoln most likely would have followed his party in doing whatever was deemed necessary to continue its modernizing rule, including the granting of suffrage to blacks.

But President Andrew Johnson, Lincoln's vice-president and successor, was not a flexible, tactful politician who had sympathy for former slaves. The southern Unionist was a Republican in name only. He was, in fact, a crude racist with a prickly and stubborn personality who believed in states' rights and limited government. When the Republicans passed civil rights bills in 1866, Johnson, a former slaveholder from Tennessee, raised the specter of the "Africanization" of the South and warned about interracial sex and marriage. In his annual message to Congress in 1867, the president claimed that blacks had less "capacity for government than any other race of people" and charged that whenever blacks were free from white control they had shown "a constant tendency to relapse into barbarism."

Under Johnson's guidance, the southern states enacted the infamous Black Codes during the summer and fall of 1865. Although these codes generally gave blacks the right to marry, own property, enter into contracts, and sue and testify in court, the main thrust of these laws was to control black labor and restore a kind of plantation discipline in the South. For example, the codes dictated that blacks who quit work before the termination of their annual labor contracts (which most were forced into if they hoped to get any work) had to forfeit all pay. Some of the codes forbade blacks to hold any job outside farm or domestic work. The state governments quickly broadened the definition of *vagrancy* in order to entrap more blacks and subject them—either as full-fledged convicts or in order to "pay-off" their fines—to forced plantation labor, and they apprenticed many black minors to whites, without pay. Codes in many states forbade blacks to own guns or to hunt and fish.

Northern journalists stationed in the South reported on the Black Codes, the atrocities they had witnessed against blacks and white Unionists, and the troubling election results. By the fall of 1865 southern whites had elected and sent to Congress many former Confederate military and civilian officials. For instance, Georgia elected Alexander Stephens, who had been vice president of the Confederacy, to the U.S. Senate. Northern newspapers and Republican politicians accused the defiant South of trying to evade completely the consequences of military defeat in a horrendous war that had cost the nation so dearly.

When Congress convened in December of 1865—it had been in recess since March—outraged Republicans refused to seat the elected representatives from the former Confederate states, and in early 1866 they passed two major bills. One act continued and enlarged the functions of the Freedmen's Bureau, the main welfare, educational, and service agency for blacks in the South, and the other conferred citizenship on African Americans. Johnson caustically declared both bills unconstitutional and vetoed them. Two months later Congress approved the Fourteenth Amendment, constitutionally granting blacks citizenship with the rights of due process and equal protection of the law. Johnson advised the southern states not to ratify the amendment. The president's harsh rhetoric, tactlessness, and uncompromising attitude, combined with a series of bloody race riots in the South in 1866, drove Republican moderates into the arms of the radicals and aroused much of the northern population to demand that defiant Southerners be punished. And firmly.

These unique circumstances and events resulted in a Republican landslide victory in the election of 1866, greatly increasing the strength of the radicals and securing a veto-proof Congress. Accordingly, in

January 1867, "Radical Reconstruction" began. Now Congress passed a series of Reconstruction acts that nullified the Johnson state governments in the South, invalidated the Blacks Codes, and put the former Confederate States under military rule until they drafted and approved new constitutions, enfranchised blacks, disfranchised many former Confederates, and ratified the Fourteenth Amendment. After Johnson vetoed several civil rights bills, spoke out vehemently against the ratification of the Fourteenth Amendment, and liberally used his pardoning power and prerogatives as commander-in-chief to undermine the Republican plan of Reconstruction, an angry and frustrated House impeached him in 1868; he escaped conviction in the Senate by a single vote. By 1870 all of the former Confederate states had met the basic requirements and been readmitted to the Union, and for a time the dominant force in the reconstructed South was a biracial Republican party.

Indeed, Radical Reconstruction constituted a daring experiment in biracial government. The Fourteenth Amendment of 1868 granted citizenship to African Americans, and the Fifteenth Amendment of 1870 promised suffrage to black men. In 1875 Congress passed a Civil Rights Act that banned segregation of public places. In cooperation with the Freedmen's Bureau, church-related organizations in the North and African Americans in the South established hundreds of black schools and colleges. Throughout the South black men organized, voted in mass, and got elected to high office. During Reconstruction sixteen African Americans sat in Congress, two as Senators. More than six hundred blacks served as state legislators, and over one hundred held statewide offices such as lieutenant governor—P. B. S. Pinchback served briefly as governor of Louisiana—treasurer and secretary of state. Others held local offices such as superintendent of schools, justice of the peace, sheriff, and alderman.

Unfortunately for blacks, Radical Reconstruction was badly flawed and short-lived. A major defect of the policy stemmed from the failure to enact land reform. Deprived of land, most blacks had nothing to sell but their labor. Few blacks had any means to accumulate enough capital to buy land. In 1876 Georgia blacks, who composed nearly half of the state's population, controlled only 1.3 percent of the land. Most blacks therefore became landless sharecroppers, tenant farmers, and wage laborers largely under white control. An oppressive system of debt, one-crop farming, soil exhaustion, high interest rates, declining cotton prices, and exploitive landlords trapped most southern blacks in grinding poverty. When black sharecroppers, who for all their toil were granted only one-third to one-half of the crop they produced, settled with their white landlords at the end of the year—their only pay check—they realized the near futility of getting ahead. If any money was left after the black farmer sold his share of the crop and paid his debts, often carried by the local merchant at usurious interest rates of up to 20 percent, the white landlord regularly cheated the illiterate, powerless farmer out of some or all of his meager profits. As an African American folk song put it: "Niggers plant the cotton/Niggers pick it out/White man pockets money/Niggers does without."

Under Radical Reconstruction, blacks also had to forego integration and, after 1870, federal aid to education as well. The belated Civil Rights Act of 1875, which outlawed segregation in transportation and public places such as theaters and restaurants, but tellingly not in schools and cemeteries, was never seriously enforced, and the Supreme Court declared it unconstitutional in 1883. Even under Radical Reconstruction the southern states, with two exceptions, segregated public schools, as did the Congress-controlled District of Columbia. African Americans generally faced not a choice between integration and segregation, but between exclusion and segregation. The majority of blacks (who had eagerly withdrawn from white denominations into all-black churches) and their white Republicans allies settled for the hollow compromise of separate but equal facilities. The Freedmen's Bureau ceased to operate in 1870, abruptly ending the national government's support of black education in the South.

A crucial factor in the failure of Reconstruction was the fierce determination of southern whites to deny blacks any semblance of equality—economic, social, or political. Although southern whites intimidated, physically assaulted, and occasionally killed the white Republican allies of blacks, most of the violence fell on African Americans. No one can say exactly how many blacks died at the hands of whites during Reconstruction, but estimates range from 3,500 (probably much too low) to 12,000. In 1868 southern whites unleashed a new wave of violence to "redeem" the South from the newly installed radical Republican governments. In that year alone in just two Louisiana parishes, whites committed 336 murders and assaults with intent to kill. After the founding of the Ku Klux Klan (KKK) in 1866, it and similar terrorist groups spread rapidly through the South and served as the military arm for local Democrats. After three blacks were charged with making "incendiary" speeches in a small Alabama town, whites killed the Republican judge and two of the defendants. A mob then went on a rampage and killed as many as thirty African Americans, virtually wiping out the entire black leadership of the area.

Many of these bloody events rightly became known as "massacres." In the Colfax, Louisiana, Massacre in April 1873, whites armed with a canon besieged a Republican gathering that was defended by black militiamen. In the assault three white Republicans died along with at least a hundred blacks, half of them killed after they had surrendered. A historic marker erected by the Louisiana Department of Commerce in 1950 states that "150 negroes were slain" in a battle that "marked the end of carpetbag misrule in the South."

In July 1876, in Hamburg, South Carolina, General Matthew C. Butler, a prominent Democrat, led hundreds of whites to disarm what they considered to be an insolent black militia. After the besieged militiamen suffered heavy casualties, twenty-five of them surrendered. On the orders of General Butler, five of the black captives were executed in cold blood. The mob then sacked black homes and businesses in the town.

Participation in the Colfax and Hamburg Massacres and similar atrocities made one a hero in the South. A large marble obelisk in a Colfax graveyard commemorates the deaths of three white heroes "WHO FELL IN THE COLFAX RIOT FIGHTING FOR WHITE SUPREMACY." In 1877 the redeemed legislature of South Carolina rewarded General Butler for his role in the Hamburg atrocity by sending him to the U.S. Senate. Generally, the behavior of southern Democrats and members of the KKK conformed to what the southern journalist W. J. Cash called the "savage ideal," a model that validated honor, manhood, and white supremacy.

Organized groups occasionally fought back against the Democrats and the KKK, but when they did, they almost always got the worst of it. Expert horsemen and marksmen, white Southerners were generally better equipped and armed than blacks. Furthermore, Republicans did not disguise themselves and ride into the night, beating, raping, and killing. Nor did they drive Democrats from the polls. Republicans believed deeply in law and order and democracy. As a black Georgian put it, "We could burn their churches and schoolhouses but we don't want to break the law or harm anybody. All we want is to live under the law."

Another weakness of Reconstruction was the lack of sympathy for the plight of the freed people in the North. At the same time the North was forcing black suffrage on the southern states, referenda in the states of Connecticut, Wisconsin, New York, Minnesota, Ohio, and Michigan denied the vote to blacks. In Michigan in 1868 a vote to legalize black suffrage lost by a margin of 61 percent to 39 percent. Northerners clearly were more interested in punishing defiant ex-Confederates than in empowering blacks.

Also weakening Radical Reconstruction were the early deaths of major radical leaders, including Thaddeus Stevens and Charles Sumner, and the split in the Republican party over corruption, economics, and Reconstruction itself. In 1872 the Liberal Republicans broke with President Grant and campaigned to abandon Reconstruction. In 1873 a crippling depression hit the United States, which distracted the increasingly business-minded Republicans from the problems in the South. A near-lethal blow to Reconstruction came in the 1874 election when the Democrats won a large majority in the House of Representatives. The following year Democrats "redeemed" Mississippi through the use of intimidation and violence. When Mississippi Republicans pleaded for President Grant to send federal troops to protect them, the man who never retreated during the Civil War refused to intervene. Then in two crucial cases handed down in 1876, *U.S.* v. *Reese* and *U.S.* v. *Cruikshank,* the Supreme Court undercut the effectiveness of the Enforcement Acts that had been used against the KKK.

The corrupt and disputed presidential election of 1876 dealt the final blow to Reconstruction. In a very close presidential race between the Democrat Samuel J. Tilden and Rutherford B. Hayes, twenty electoral votes from four states—South Carolina, Louisiana, Florida, and Oregon—were contested, with both sides claiming victory. To solve the impasse, Congress set up a special electoral commission in 1877 that was composed of five Congressmen, five Senators, and five Supreme Court justices. While the commission initially had seven Democrats, seven Republicans, and one Independent on it, the latter resigned and was replaced by a Republican. Not surprisingly, the commission voted 8 to 7 to award all the disputed electoral votes to Hayes, making him president by a single vote, 185 to 184. But to forestall a threatened Democratic filibuster designed to prevent a count of the electoral votes in the House, Republicans bargained with their adversaries and struck what has become known as the Compromise of 1877. Under this agreement, which officially ended Reconstruction, Republicans promised to remove the last few federal troops from the violence-racked South. The bargain further stipulated that the South would receive federal patronage and aid for the construction and maintenance of railroads and internal improvements. In return, southern Democrats pledged to protect black rights.

To be sure, Reconstruction was not a complete failure. It was, as Michael Perman put it in *Emancipation and Reconstruction,* 2d Ed. (2003), "quite probably, the largest program of domestic reform ever undertaken in the history of the United States." Under it, Southern blacks participated in government for the first time in American history. The Fourteenth and Fifteenth Amendments left a constitutional framework that proved to be indispensable for the success of the twentieth-century civil rights movement. Blacks, the federal government, and philanthropic organizations in the North established permanent schools and colleges for African Americans. Blacks also established their own separate churches and reconstituted their families. All of these changes proved crucially beneficial to African Americans in the long run.

Still, Reconstruction was a halfway revolution that went backwards, leaving blacks in a perilous state for almost a century. The demise of Reconstruction was a shocking reversal for black civil rights. W. E. B. Du Bois, the black scholar and civil rights leader, summed up the fate of African Americans in *Black Reconstruction in America* (1935), observing that "the slave went free; stood a brief moment in the sun; then moved back again toward slavery."

The Redeemer Governments and Blacks

In *The Strange Career of Jim Crow* (1955), the historian C. Vann Woodward argued that between the end of Reconstruction and the "capitulation to racism" in the 1890s, race relations were fluid and somewhat benign under upper-class, paternalistic Democrats known variously as Redeemers, Bourbons, and Conservatives. Woodward stressed that under the Redeemers blacks continued to vote and hold office and frequent white-owned public establishments and ride on integrated railroad cars in many places in the South. According to Woodward, the Redeemers allowed "forgotten alternatives" in race relations that would seem unthinkable to white Southerners a few years later.

Several later studies argued that Woodward exaggerated the freedom and security blacks enjoyed and the amount of integration during the Redeemer Era. In *After Slavery: The Negro in South Carolina during Reconstruction, 1861–1877* (1965), Joel Williamson held that segregation had become pervasive by the end of Reconstruction. In *The First New South, 1865–1920* (1992), Howard Rabinowitz demonstrated that under Redeemer rule blacks had their hands full just fighting off exclusion from public places. Whites demanded that no social contact between the races take place that could be interpreted as "social equality." Even before Reconstruction ended, The *Richmond Daily Dispatch* laid down the rules in 1873:

> We want no negro officers and no mixed schools. . . . we do not want to meet him in our box at the theater, by our side at the hotel table, and in our room in an inn, our pew, at church, or our seat on a railroad car.

For those who accepted the Woodward thesis, Wade Hampton served as the model Redeemer. Although this conservative Democrat rode to the governorship of South Carolina in 1876 on a wave of anti-black violence, the former Confederate hero promised that he would "observe, protect, and defend the rights of the colored man. . . ." Many blacks not only voted under Hampton, but as governor he appointed dozens of blacks to state office. Redeemers, however, only allowed blacks to participate in politics when they could manipulate and control them. When they could not, they used fraud, intimidation, gerrymandering, complex voting procedures, and violence to discourage the black vote. When President Hayes withdrew federal troops from the South, he believed that justice for blacks "could be got best and most surely by trusting the honorable and influential southern whites." But after the 1878 election Hayes realized that his faith in the Hamptons of the South had been misplaced, and the president then railed against the fraud, gerrymandering, intimidation, and "violence of the most atrocious character" that had produced a Democratic House that tried mightily to expunge every Reconstruction law on the books.

The fiscally conservative Redeemer governments also hurt blacks economically and educationally. They fortified the oppressive agricultural system with laws that protected the interests of large landowners and worked against sharecroppers and tenant farmers. In the cotton mills, the most successful industrial enterprise of the New South, whites virtually excluded blacks from employment. Under the Redeemers, public schools for both races fell into disrepair, with black education suffering the most. In the first year after Hampton became governor, appropriations for education in South Carolina fell from $250,000 to $100,000. Conservative Democrats in Washington in the 1880s helped defeat the Blair bill, which would have granted federal aid to public schools. Senator John T. Morgan of Alabama complained that the bill would lengthen the school year and remove children from the cotton fields right at the time when they were most needed.

At the city level of government, politicians who spoke of a "New South" deprived the growing black population of services such as water, gas, sewers, and paved roads. Conditions for urban blacks in the rising New South cities were appalling, leading to the formation of squalid slums comprising bad schools, poor health, vice, and crime. The death rate of urban blacks in this period was 60 percent higher than that of rural blacks. As historian Don H. Doyle lamented in *New Men, New Cities, New South* (1990), "The inability to live up to its aims of black uplift . . . was perhaps the most obvious weakness of the New South movement."

Also highly injurious to the health of southern blacks was the convict lease system that flourished under the Redeemers. The southern states not only refused to spend money for the care of black prisoners but they turned a profit on them by leasing them out to planters and businesspeople. Ironically, the convict lease system was integrated, though 90 percent or more of the prisoners under it were black. The states had an incentive to increase the number of convicts under the lease system. Sheriffs not only received a fee for each person arrested, they often got kickbacks from planters and corporations that cheaply leased prisoners. The leased prisoners worked long hours at arduous tasks such as mining and levee building. Planters and mine bosses, with little or no oversight from the states, had the right to punish prisoners physically. Female prisoners routinely suffered sexual assault. Since profit-hungry entrepreneurs were responsible for maintenance of the prisoners, they usually fed and clothed them poorly. Disease spread rapidly through the wretched prisoner camps and exacted an appalling death rate. Almost half the prisoners working for the Greenwood and Augusta Railroad from 1877 to 1879 in South Carolina died on the job. Generally, the death rate of prisoners in the South ranged from 10 to 15 percent while in Iowa, Ohio, and New Hampshire the range was from 0.76 to 1.5 percent. The convict lease system exposed the phoniness of Redeemer paternalism. As C. Vann Woodward said, "The convict lease system did greater violence to the moral authority of the Redeemers than did anything else."

The violence against blacks continued at an alarming rate under the Redeemers. In 1886 in Carrollton, Mississippi, a hundred mounted whites opened fire on a black crowd that had gathered to support the prosecution of some whites accused of racial violence. Without suffering a single casualty, the whites killed twenty blacks. A white spokesman explained that the insolent blacks had needed to learn a lesson. When black sugar workers struck in Louisiana in 1887, white vigilantes, landowners, and the militia put down the strike, killing at least fifty African Americans. Apparently, the "savage ideal" gave every white man a license to punish assertive blacks.

Even though blacks continued to participate in politics during the Redeemer period, their infrequent victories often resulted in deadly counterattacks and the ultimate defeat of their cause. Fusionist movements, in which white Independents and black Republicans challenged the conservative Democrats, provoked racial violence across the South. For example, in Copiah County, Mississippi, a place equally divided between the races, the wealthy white planter-merchant John "Print" Matthews coordinated a black Republican–white Independent coalition that in 1881 had some success against the Democrats. As the 1883 election approached, white vigilantes terrorized Republicans, assaulting several black politicians and killing one of them. Democrats also threatened to kill Print Matthews if he showed up at the polls. They made good their threat. As the brave Matthews was casting his ballot, a Democrat named Ras Wheeler killed him with a blast from a double-barreled shotgun. Wheeler became an instant hero in the area and was rewarded with an appointment as city marshal of Hazelhurst, a major city in the County.

Despite their courage and persistence, blacks steadily lost ground in the Redeemer Era. In 1880 Albion W. Tourgée, a carpetbag lawyer during Reconstruction, informed soon-to-be President James A. Garfield that the racial situation had progressively worsened and that the South was "solidly anti-reconstruction, anti-negro equality, and anti-everything the Republican Party ha[d] done in or toward the South." During the Redeemer Era, African Americans suffered exploitation, brutality, and violence. Even so, the plight of blacks would worsen in the last decade of the nineteenth century.

The 1890s: The Triumph of Racism

The 1890s proved to be a pivotal decade in American history. The previous decades had unleashed forces that propelled the nation toward an urban, industrial society. With astonishing speed, the United States became the world's greatest industrial power in the 1890s. Industrial tycoons formed huge corporations and monopolies, creating millions of jobs and vast, albeit unevenly distributed, wealth along with class conflict, labor violence, and a disastrous depression. The new jobs drew millions of poor immigrants, who filled America's rapidly growing cities and competed with blacks for jobs, even survival. Then, when its new industrial machine led to overproduction, the nation looked abroad for new markets and bases for its new naval fleet. In the 1890s the United States fought an imperialistic war and amassed an empire consisting mostly of nonwhite people. All of these developments impinged profoundly on black-white relations. The 1890s also ushered in the age of Jim Crow (the term *Jim Crow* came from a poor, ragged minstrel character whose name came to symbolize legal segregation in the South), an era that legally disfranchised and segregated blacks even as it subjected them to increasing amounts of humiliation and violence.

The southern black vote had already been greatly reduced by 1890. Still, Democrats, as William Dunning put it, wanted "the termination of equal rights in law as well as fact." Mississippi, one of two states with a majority black population—South Carolina was the other—led the way around the Fifteenth Amendment. In 1890 the Magnolia State disfranchised blacks by adopting a new constitution that required that voters to be able to read and understand the state constitution. (Such tests were selectively administered by white election officials.) The state also enacted a poll tax of $2, a sum most blacks, and many whites, could not afford to pay. Between 1895 and 1908 seven other southern states followed the "Mississippi Plan" and amended their constitutions. The individual states concocted various contrivances to eliminate black voters without completely disfranchising illiterate poor whites. The most famous of these was the "grandfather clause," adopted first by Louisiana. Under this clause, permanent registration to vote was guaranteed to all men whose grandfathers had been eligible to vote prior to 1867, that is, before Radical Reconstruction and the advent of black suffrage.

The decline of black registration and voting in the South was precipitous after 1890. Black voting virtually ceased in Mississippi after it amended its constitution. As in Mississippi, the black vote in Louisiana was virtually erased by the turn of the century. In 1896 more than 95 percent of black men in Louisiana, or 130,344, were registered to vote, but after the state changed its constitution in 1898, the number of registered black voters dropped to 5,320 in 1900—and to less than 1,000 in 1904. In most places in the South the Republican party dwindled into insignificance, and by 1910 the famous one-party South had emerged.

Whites made no secret about the intent of the revamped state constitutions and new laws. James K. Vardaman, an up-and-coming Mississippi politician, volunteered this rationale:

> There is no use to equivocate or lie about the matter. . . . Mississippi's constitutional convention of 1890 was held for no other purpose than to

eliminate the nigger from politics; not the "ignorant and vicious," as some apologists would have you believe, but the nigger.

If Vardaman's rhetoric was unusually crude, his views fairly represented that of most other Southerners. And the candor regarding the intent of southern legislators did not bother the Supreme Court, which in *Williams* v. *Mississippi* (1898) ruled that the state's voting requirements did not violate the Constitution.

But before the black vote was almost totally eliminated, discontented agrarians formed the People's or Populist party in 1892. Struggling farmers hurting from low crop prices, crop-liens, price gouging by monopolies, the unfair practices of the railroads, and high interest rates on the loans they needed to operate showed some willingness to cooperate politically with blacks in order to challenge the all-powerful Democrats. Tom Watson of Georgia, the best known Populist leader, appealed to black voters on the basis of class and economics. "You are kept apart that you may be separately fleeced of your earnings," Watson told black and white farmers. Some historians have praised Watson and the Populists as the greatest hope for racial comity in the South, but others have considered the notion as romantic nonsense. Watson, like the Redeemers, was a manipulator of the black vote. Critics have pointed out that Watson decried any form of social equality and as a state legislator had voted for segregated public transportation and against funds for black schools.

Unfortunately for the Populists, Georgia Democrats proved better manipulators of blacks than the agrarian reformers. Democratic planters and factory owners marched their black employees to the polls and voted them in gangs. Democrats also won black votes with barbecue, whiskey, tobacco, and bribes. When that did not suffice, they stuffed ballot boxes and played the race card, calling the Populists "nigger lovers" who believed in social equality. When all else failed, the conservative Democrats of Georgia employed wholesale violence against blacks. During the 1892 election, fifteen black Populists died at the hand of whites.

The situation in Georgia was not unique among the southern states in the 1890s. The coalition between white Populists and blacks was an unstable marriage of convenience doomed to failure. In the battles between Populists and Democrats, race trumped class every time. Indeed, many of the defeated agrarians soon joined their Democratic foes in disfranchising blacks. Embittered by the Populist debacle, Tom Watson became one of the most notorious race baiters in the Progressive Era. The "Solid South" was briefly tested in the 1890s, but it held and became more impregnable with each passing year.

No group helped solidify the white-supremacist South more than the new breed of colorful demagogues who rose to prominence in the Democratic party after 1890. Benjamin "Pitchfork" Tillman was one of the first and most influential of this group. Elected governor of South Carolina in 1890, he served in the U.S. Senate from 1895 until 1918, dominating politics in his state for more than twenty years. Crude in speech, lacking in good manners, and slovenly in dress, Tillman made his presence felt. A journalist described him as "a sallow-faced, shaggy-haired man with one gleaming, restless, angry eye" (he had lost the other eye to disease, and the eye socket remained creepily empty). Tillman bragged about leading thirty red-shirted gunmen to participate in the 1876 Hamburg massacre. Though a substantial farmer, Tillman pitched his message to the common white man. Unlike the Populist Tom Watson, he did not seek electoral help from blacks, but rather he offered up African Americans as scapegoats on which the white masses might feast.

Tillman gave poor whites empty rhetorical class warfare and racist harangues, effectively destroying Populism in his state. In his inaugural speech in 1890, he hailed his victory as "unparalleled in magnitude and importance" and crowed that it represented the "triumph of democracy and white supremacy over mongrelism and anarchy, of civilization over barbarism. . . ." Tillman, too, played a crucial role in South Carolina's 1895 disfranchisement of blacks, a victory he described as one for "Anglo-Saxon supremacy, good government, and . . . civilization." Although a booster of public education for whites, Tillman declared, "[W]hen you educate a negro you educate a candidate for the penitentiary or spoil a good field hand." Tillman further endeared himself to the white sons of toil when he assured them that he would lead a lynch mob against any black man who raped a white woman.

In his masterful *Ben Tillman and the Reconstruction of White Supremacy* (2000), Stephen Kantrowitz argued that if Tom Watson's life was a tragedy because he failed to forge a biracial democracy in

Georgia, Tillman's life was a tragedy because he succeeded in creating "the violent, repressive world of the Jim Crow South." Tillman reconstructed white supremacy in South Carolina and inspired men to be relentless and savage in its preservation. Race-baiting demagogues multiplied like rabbits throughout the southern states in the early twentieth century, with James K. Vardaman and Theodore Bilbo of Mississippi, Cole Blease of South Carolina, Charles B. Aycock of North Carolina, and Jeff Davis of Arkansas becoming the best—or the worst—of the lot.

As blacks lost political power after Reconstruction, the southern states began to enact some Jim Crow laws. But before 1900 the South was segregated more by custom than by law. In the 1890s a few southern states began to pass legislation mandating the racial segregation of railroad cars and streetcars, but most of the Jim Crow laws came in the early twentieth century (see Chapter Three). Despite rhetoric about equal facilities for each race, accommodations for blacks were almost always decidedly inferior to those for whites. The "colored" railroad cars, invariably hitched right behind the foul-smelling, coal-fueled engines, were run-down and filthy. Blacks described the restrooms in the cars as unspeakable, and Du Bois complained that his meals were served through "a dirty and ill-attended hole in the wall." At the railroad station the Jim Crow car came to rest outside the canopy, so that blacks were exposed to the weather as they disembarked.

These stigmatizing laws reflected the increasing white hysteria about the behavior of younger blacks. By this point racial demagogues ranted constantly about the dangerous new generation of blacks who had never been disciplined by slavery. Thomas Nelson Page, a Virginian who wrote popular romantic novels about the Old South, reported "a general depravity and retrogression of the Negro . . . closely resembling a reversion to barbarism." White officials and social analysts alleged that black crime was spiraling out of control. For many whites, the answer to allegedly antisocial behavior by blacks was a greater degree of racial separation.

In *Plessy* v. *Ferguson* (1896), the United States Supreme Court upheld an 1890 Louisiana law that required segregated railroad cars. Legal briefs for the plaintiffs argued that the law denied blacks equal rights guaranteed by the Fourteenth Amendment and that its intent was "to humiliate and degrade" and reduce blacks to a "subject race." However, the court's opinion, written by Henry Billings Brown of Massachusetts, maintained that racial segregation was within the police powers of the state to keep public order. Segregation laws passed muster as long as the facilities were "separate but equal." In a rousing dissent Justice John M. Harlan of Kentucky, the half-brother of a former slave, lectured that the Constitution was "color-blind" and that the majority decision assigned blacks to a "condition of legal inferiority." Although *Plessy* merely confirmed decisions of the lower federal and state courts and was uncontroversial at the time, the decision was still disastrous for blacks. It firmly planted in constitutional law for more than half a century the right of the individual states to discriminate with abandon on the basis of race.

As Justice Harlan predicted in his dissent, the racist rhetoric that saturated the campaigns for segregation and disfranchisement intensified racial violence. The torrid pace of lynching between 1890 and 1920 attested to that sorry fact. As Joel Williamson observed in *The Crucible of Race* (1984), "The sudden and dramatic rise in the lynching of black men . . . after 1889 stands out like some gigantic volcanic eruption on the landscape of Southern race relations." Lynching occurred rarely under slavery, and it was considered more of a western or frontier phenomenon until the 1890s. From 1882 to 1888, 595 whites died at the hands of lynch mobs, as compared to 440 blacks. In the 1890s, however, almost three-fourths or 1,110 of the lynch victims were black, and 82 percent of the lynchings occurred in the South. Lynching peaked in 1892, during which 230 people were lynched, 161 of them black. Women did not escape this epidemic. Between 1882 and 1927, mobs lynched 92 women, 76 of them black. Moreover, juries hurriedly handed down hundreds of guilty verdicts that amounted to "legal lynchings." That is, the courts carried out quick, sham trials before mobs proceeded to lynch black defendants.

The lynching of a black person almost always entailed more than just an unlawful hanging. Although the white victims of lynch mobs usually got a quick, clean hanging, black victims often suffered prolonged torture and grisly mutilation. Many blacks were burned at the stake, but not before mobs cut off their fingers, ears, noses, and genitals and extracted hunks of flesh with corkscrews. Adults and children alike scrambled, in what sometimes was a carnival-like atmosphere, to retrieve body parts to hail as proud souvenirs. Large crowds of whites thrilled to the agony of blacks in their death throes. In 1893 in Paris, Texas, special excursion trains brought perhaps 10,000 people to see Henry Smith lynched. To the excitement of the crowd, the lynchers set upon the man accused of murdering a young white girl and gouged out his eyes with a hot poker before slowly roasting him to death.

Any sign of resistance to the mob could be deadly. When Mary Turner, in her eighth month of pregnancy, threatened to swear out warrants against the lynchers of her black husband in Valdosta, Georgia, the mob hanged her upside down in a tree and lighted her gasoline-soaked body. While she was still alive, a member of the mob ripped her unborn baby from the womb and crushed its head with his heel. And if a drunken mob could not quickly find the accused person or persons, it often killed any hapless blacks or "bad niggers" in the area. Relatives of the hunted were always at risk, especially if they showed any resentment or resistance to the mob. When Daniel Barber was arrested for bootlegging, members of his family allegedly resisted the authorities. As a result, the mob forced Barber to watch his son and two married daughters hanged to death before he suffered the same fate.

Newspapers reported on lynchings in gory detail, creating a body of what some have called "folk pornography." The killers and the onlookers came from all classes, with women and men often attired in their Sunday best. Members of the mob openly posed for photographs, which they sometimes used as postcards to commemorate "Negro barbecues." A nine-year-old boy commented to his mother, "I have seen a man hanged, now I wish I could see one burned."

Obviously, little risk attached to this kind of racially motivated murder. Although some southern states passed anti-lynching laws in the 1890s, they were weak and seldom enforced. And all-white juries generally declined to indict or convict members of a lynch mob, lightheartedly specifying that the victims "died at the hands of persons unknown."

Even the most influential members of southern society justified lynching for at least one crime: the rape of a white woman by a black man. They declared that sex-crazed African American males could not resist white women. The demagogue Tillman raved that he would rather have one of his virgin daughters killed by a wild beast "than to have her crawl to me and tell me the horrid story that she had been robbed of the jewel of her womanhood by a black fiend." Rebecca Felton, a Georgia feminist and wife of a Congressman, cried out against sexual assaults, "If it takes lynching to protect woman's dearest possession from drunken, ravening human beasts, then I say lynch a thousand a week if it becomes necessary."

Despite the obsessive rape complex of southern whites, only about a quarter of the blacks lynched were even accused of rape. A greater number of those lynched were accused of murdering whites, and about one-fourth of the blacks swung for minor offenses such as theft, sassiness, or other breaches of racial etiquette. Most historians agree with Ida B. Wells, the militant journalist from Memphis, about the primary purpose of racial lynchings. After being forced to flee her hometown in 1892 because of her condemnation of lynching—three of her best friends were lynched in Memphis that year for running a grocery store that competed too successfully with a white-owened business—Wells moved to New York City and then to Chicago (she married a Chicagoan in 1895 and became Wells-Barnett). Continuing to publish strident tracts against mob violence from the North, she charged that lyching was "an excuse to get rid of Negroes who were acquiring wealth and property and thus keep the race terrorized and 'keep the nigger down.'" Lynching was ultimately about power and perpetuating white dominance through terror; and it was clearly effective. Richard Wright, the noted black writer from Mississippi, recalled that lynching haunted black men, even children. At the age of ten Wright developed "a dread of white people" based on his precocious realization that a white person could end his life at will, and with impunity.

Another element adding to the distress blacks lived with in the 1890s was the "Lost Cause" mania. The Lost Cause represented a resurgence of southern nationalism that spawned an orgy of adulation for the Confederacy and its heroes. Organizations such as the United Confederate Veterans (1889), the United Daughters of the Confederacy (1895), and the Sons of Confederate Veterans (1896) waxed nostalgically about the loyal, happy, and compliant "Old Negro" of slavery days and stridently condemned the new generation of insolent blacks who, they insisted, were pushing the region toward a racial cataclysm.

Something close to that happened in the 1890s. In 1898, for example, the appointment of Frazier B. Baker, a black man, as the postmaster of Lake City, South Carolina, incited a mob to set his house afire. When Baker's wife and four children fled the burning house, three of them were wounded and the baby was killed in her mother's arms. Baker died in a hail of bullets inside his burning house. The Spanish-American War further inflamed racial tensions. In early 1898 the U.S. Army transferred highly seasoned and decorated black troops, the so-called Buffalo Soldiers, from the western frontier to the South to prepare for action in Cuba. When white troops nonchalantly used a black child for target practice, black soldiers intervened, causing a brawl that left twenty-seven blacks and four whites wounded. While still in Florida awaiting deployment, at least three black soldiers lost their lives for refusing to obey Jim Crow laws on streetcars.

Later in the same year an election set off a racial conflagration in North Carolina. From 1894 to 1898 white supremacists in that state had chafed under the rule of a Populist-Republican fusionist government in which blacks played a key role. In the election of 1898 the Democratic leaders Charles Aycock, Furnifold Simmons, and Josephus Daniels resolved to restore white rule to North Carolina. Reminiscent of Reconstruction, Democrats formed White Government Leagues and staged "White-Supremacy Jubilees" in which hundreds of armed men paraded the streets to intimidate Republicans and Populists. Tillman sent 300 Red Shirts from South Carolina to help the Democrats to the north. Aycock, Daniels, and other Democratic leaders fabricated tales about black men raping white women. Democratic newspapers called for "Proud Caucasians" to rise up and protect their wives and daughters from black beasts.

An editorial that appeared in a black newspaper shortly before the election stoked the sexual fears sweeping the state. Alexander L. Manly, the editor of the *Wilmington Record,* responded to the false rape charges. The light-skinned Manly, the son of a former governor of North Carolina, not only rejected the accusations against black men, but he also claimed that many white women willingly had sex with black men and that white men regularly violated black women without punishment. Angry Democrats picked up the story and circulated it widely. When Tillman came up from South Carolina to rally North Carolina Democrats, he asked, "Why didn't you kill that damned nigger editor who wrote that?"

The Manly affair helped galvanize Democrats to terrorize the opposition and carry the election of 1898. Alfred M. Waddell, a former Confederate colonel and a fiery white supremacist, made sure that the Democratic party carried Wilmington, the largest city in the state and one with a black majority. On the eve of the election, Waddell instructed hundreds of his armed cohorts, "If you find a Negro out voting, tell him to leave the polls, and if he refuses, kill him, shoot him down in his tracks." Waddell told his followers that they had to win the election, "even if we have to choke the Cape Fear River with [black] carcasses." But the election of 1898 did not immediately restore Democratic rule in Wilmington. The Republican-controlled city government, which included three black aldermen, had been elected in 1897 and would therefore serve most of 1899.

Waddell, however, demanded a regime change immediately. Right after the election his private army used threats and force to banish all of the Republican office holders from the city, along with some prominent black businessmen. Soon after the coup d'état, a frenzied mob, some of them soldiers back from the war with Spain, invaded the black sections of Wilmington, killing between 24 and 300 blacks (estimates vary greatly). It also looted and torched homes, causing over a thousand blacks to flee the city. The bloody event in Wilmington was not really a race riot, but a one-sided massacre like those of Colfax and Hamburg. For his service in redeeming the city, Waddell became the mayor of Wilmington. In 1900 North Carolina followed other southern states and disfranchised blacks and segregated its trains and streetcars. Top Democrats proudly announced that "political niggerism" was at last dead in North Carolina.

The Abandonment of Blacks by the North

Only forceful, conscientious, and sustained action by the federal government could have afforded African Americans some protection in the South. But the national government, even when controlled by

Republicans, gradually lost interest in the "southern question." After the Compromise of 1877 the Republicans steadily retreated from their support of southern blacks. The election of the Democrat Grover Cleveland to the presidency in 1884 and in 1892 and the frequent control of the House of Representatives by the party of states' rights after 1874 further eroded the federal protection of civil rights.

In the election of 1888, however, the Republicans gained control of the White House and Congress. Furthermore, Republicans inserted a plank in their 1888 platform that hailed "the supreme and sovereign right of every lawful citizen, rich or poor, white or black, to cast one free ballot in public elections and to have that ballot duly counted." President Benjamin Harrison also spoke out forcefully against lynching, supported the Blair bill to provide federal aid to education, and declared that voting rights had to be protected. In 1890 Republicans introduced the Federal Elections Bill, which authorized federal officials to police elections across the nation. Dubbed the "Force Bill" by opponents, the Federal Elections Bill passed the House but failed in the Senate. In the end, strong public opinion against the act in the North, a lengthy filibuster by white supremacist Democrats in the Senate, and disunity among the Senate Republicans spelled defeat for the federal policing of elections. Northern Republicans in the Senate sacrificed the elections bill for the passage of the Sherman Anti-Trust Act of 1890, and western Republicans abandoned the issue in order to secure legislation calling for an increase in the coinage of silver, which was abundant in their region. Henry Cabot Lodge of Massachusetts, the sponsor of the elections bill in the House, admitted that the proposed act had been "sold for dishonest money," pieces of silver rather than gold.

At this point northern Republicans realized that removing blacks from southern politics could actually help the party. They found that southern whites would more likely join a Republican party purged of blacks. By the 1890s the party's racial work consisted primarily of dispensing a few federal jobs to elite blacks such as Frederick Douglass. It is unclear how much the Republican attempt to pass the federal elections bill hurt the party, but it is clear that the Democrats came roaring back in the elections of 1890 and 1892. The Democrats first captured the Congress and then the White House, causing a further erosion of black rights. By the time the Republicans won the elections of 1894 and 1896, making them the majority party for the next generation, the party of Lincoln and Sumner was firmly in the clutches of big business. The party that initiated Reconstruction found that it no longer needed the South and its black voters to win national elections.

The Republican party naturally reflected its electoral base in the North and Midwest, where people had lost any faith they might have had in the ability of African Americans to rise in society on their own merits. More and more, Northerners excluded blacks from restaurants, theaters, hotels, and other public places. States such as Ohio, Indiana, Kansas, and Nevada segregated public schools. The yellow press sensationalized black crime, and even the pricey genteel magazines such as *Harper's, Atlantic Monthly,* and the *North American Review* were saturated with the caricatures of blacks penned by popular southern writers such as Thomas Nelson Page and Joel Chandler Harris. The northern literati routinely referred to African Americans as "niggers," "coons," and "pickaninnies."

Such words stung, but no discrimination hurt more than the prejudice that excluded blacks from virtually every job in the North that paid a living wage. Most labor unions excluded blacks, and white workers often struck rather than work alongside African Americans. As the eminent black educator Kelly Miller lamented, "The Negro is compelled to loiter around the edges of industry." Blacks were virtually absent from such professions as law, medicine, and dentistry.

By the 1890s the white North seemed to crave reconciliation with the white South. A "New North" devoured the copious plantation literature coming from the South. The press played up its coverage of marriages between white northern men and southern belles. Northern and southern families now vacationed together in such watering holes as White Sulphur Springs, West Virginia. Accepting the myths of the Old South, Northerners were now ready to embrace the South at its racial worst. The former abolitionist Anna Dickinson assailed the new amity between the North and South as the "grasping of hands across the prostrate body of the negro."

Even many of the old abolitionists recanted their earlier beliefs about racial equality. In 1877 the *New York Herald Tribune* confessed that Reconstruction proved that blacks "as a race . . . are idle, ignorant, and vicious." Daniel Chamberlain, the former carpetbagger governor of South Carolina, admitted his belief in the inherent inferiority of blacks and apologized for the "frightful experience" and the "shocking and unbearable misgovernment" that Radical Reconstruction had forced on southern whites. Lyman Abbott, an idealistic clergyman who assisted blacks in the South during Reconstruction, wrote in his memoirs forty years later, "It is easy . . . to see that men of that generation blundered egregiously and brought upon the country, especially the South, and most of all upon the negro race, tragic disaster of their blundering."

Most educated Northerners employed some sort of "science" to support their racial views, science that went back to such renowned Enlightenment thinkers as Georg Wilhelm Friedrich Hegel, Immanuel Kant, and David Hume, all of whom taught the superiority of "civilized" Europeans over "uncivilized" Africans and Asians. Many of the most influential thinkers in the nineteenth-century West believed in a fixed heredity that naturally relegated blacks to the lowest caste. The renowned English scientist Thomas Huxley proclaimed, "I am a firm believer in blood . . . I believe in the immense influence of the fixed hereditary transmission which constitutes a race." Physical anthropologists measured brains of the different races and concluded that the cranial capacity of blacks was smaller than that of whites. The world fairs in Chicago, Atlanta, and Nashville in the 1890s served as a kind of anthropological laboratory where the cultures of exotic and savage dark people were juxtaposed beside the scientific and technological developments of the West. Frederick Douglass fumed because the inhabitants of the African Dahomey Village at the Chicago World Fair were presented as "repulsive savage[s]."

Although Americans at the time were obsessed with race, they used the term with colossal imprecision. In the late nineteenth and early twentieth centuries, they labeled many national and ethnic groups as races, including the Irish, Italians, Poles, Mexicans, and Slavs, none of which they considered truly white. American intellectuals and government leaders constantly proclaimed the superiority of Anglo-Saxons over other kinds of whites, and this theory of Anglo-Saxon superiority saturated instruction at every level of education. Teachers and professors taught that Anglo-Saxons (or closely related Germanic or Teutonic people) had an inherent tendency to excel in science, technology, law, government, and martial conquest. To them, the study of history revealed that Anglo-Saxons were destined to dominate the globe. As Senator Albert J. Beveridge of Indiana bellowed in his "March-of-the-Flag" speech in 1899:

> God has not been preparing the English-speaking and Teutonic peoples for a thousand years for nothing but vain and idle self-contemplation and self-admiration. No! He has made us master organizers of the world to establish [order] where chaos reigns. He has given us the spirit of progress to overwhelm the forces of reaction throughout the earth.

Beveridge's racial chauvinism justified American rule over the allegedly savage and genetically challenged Filipinos who, the Senator declared, were not fit for self-government.

The cult of Anglo-Saxonism received support from the work of Charles Darwin and the interpreters thereof. Applying Darwin's theory of evolution to human society, the British philosopher Herbert Spencer gave natural selection a deep social meaning that was majestically captured in a phrase of Spencer's creation, "survival of the fittest." The foremost American Social Darwinist, William Graham Sumner of Yale, scoffed at romantic sentiments about equality and insisted that legislation could not change natural laws or make inferior races equal. The Supreme Court smuggled Sumner's dogma into the *Plessy* verdict when it ruled that legislation was "powerless to eradicate racial instincts based on physical differences. . . ." Most Social Darwinists held that blacks were so far back on the evolutionary scale that it would take them centuries to catch up with whites.

Indeed, many social analysts took seriously Darwin's belief that the "civilized races" would most likely exterminate "the savage races." Frederick L. Hoffman used statistics to show that African Americans had a death rate 62.1 percent higher than that of whites. As a New York executive of the powerful Prudential Insurance Company, Hoffman established race-specific benefit tables that resulted in higher premiums for blacks. In *Race Traits and Tendencies in the American Negro* (1896), arguably the most influential work on race in America in this period, Hoffman concluded that the biological and social de-

generacy of blacks "must lead eventually to the[ir] extermination."
The race problem would thus solve itself.

Only a few social analysts predicted the extinction of blacks, but
many influential Northerners agreed with white Southerners that blacks
had regressed dangerously after the end of slavery. They also agreed
with the white South that the chances of assimilating blacks into white
society were practically nil. By the turn of the new century, the old
abolitionist spirit in the North had reached its low point.

Blacks React to a Revolution Gone Backwards

The overthrow of Reconstruction and the triumph of white supremacy
in the South left African Americans stunned and demoralized. Around
the turn of the century, several noted blacks described the gloomy
outlook. T. Thomas Fortune, the editor of the *New York Age,* complained "that Southern white men had educated Northern white men
so that they have no faith whatever in black men." Anna J. Cooper, an
eminent black educator in Washington, D.C., observed, "The colored
people of America find themselves today in the most trying period of
all their trying history. . . ." Charles W. Chestnutt, a black writer from
Cleveland, observed that "the rights of the Negroes are at a lower ebb
than at any time during the thirty-five years of their freedom, and the
race prejudice more intense and uncompromising."

The deepening racial crisis evoked a variety of responses from
African Americans, one of which was to leave the South and migrate
to the North, as the talented Chestnutt did in the 1880s. But leaving
the South was not very practical for poor, illiterate farmers, especially
when employers and unions in the North shunned black workers.
Blacks found better prospects in the West. From 1879 to 1890 more
than 30,000 blacks voted with their feet by migrating to Kansas and
the Oklahoma Territory.

Some doubted that blacks could ever enjoy justice in the United
States and sought refuge abroad. The most important promoter of
migration to Africa was Henry McNeal Turner, a bishop in the American Methodist Episcopal Church. Embittered by his participation in
the Reconstruction of Georgia, Turner grew to detest America. He
explored parts of Africa and depicted what he had seen as an Eden.

Not many African Americans, though, answered Turner's invitation to join him in paradise. Only around five hundred blacks emigrated to Liberia in 1895 and 1896, and most of those who went there in the 1890s found it more like hell. Many of the emigrants died of diseases and many others became disillusioned and returned to the United States.

Another response to the bitter plight of African Americans was the intensification of protest. Frederick Douglass continued to agitate and work for an integrated society until his death in 1895. In 1890, however, T. Thomas Fortune established the most notable protest organization of the time: the National Afro-American League. At the founding meeting of the League in Chicago, Fortune told about one hundred delegates: "It is time to face the enemy and fight him inch by inch for every right he denies us. . . . Let this League be a race League." Fortune hoped to plant a militant chapter of the League in every village in the South.

The Afro-American League drafted an extremely broad agenda that mixed several different strategies, including self-help, political activity, and promotion of economics and education. An early defector from the Republican party, Fortune had for several years preached self-reliance and "Race first, then party." Although the League professed to be a self-help and an apolitical agency, it nevertheless supported civil rights and black suffrage and denounced segregation laws, exclusion of blacks from public places, convict lease, and lynching. While Fortune believed in peaceful methods, he put whites on notice that "if others use the weapons of violence to combat our peaceful arguments, it is not for us to run away from violence. A man's a man, and what is worth having is worth fighting for."

Despite the League's noble goals and soaring rhetoric, it was, for a number of reasons, short lived. First, Fortune, though journalistically brilliant, was mercurial and lacked the qualities necessary to provide stable and lasting leadership. Second, the extreme breadth of the League's program and its confusion over methods caused it to splinter into quarreling factions. Third, planting a militant civil rights organization in the South in the 1890s, where Tillman's ruthless and violent white supremacy had emerged triumphant, bucked all the odds. The *Atlanta Constitution* warned the League, "There is no conceivable direction in which an organization can do the Negro race any good, and it might do great harm." By the mid-1890s, the Afro-American League was dead.

Although many blacks gave up on politics, others continued to protest. African Americans held meetings in major southern cities to condemn the segregation of railroad cars and streetcars. In Arkansas in 1891 eleven black legislators argued eloquently against a law to segregate railroad cars. In several southern cities blacks boycotted segregated streetcars, and in Nashville some entrepreneurs established a short-lived, black-owned trolley company. These protests, however, hardly slowed down the implacable march of Jim Crow.

In the 1890s Ida Wells-Barnett conducted a heroic campaign against lynching, which she called "color line murder." Between 1892 and 1900 she wrote three accusatory pamphlets about racial murder. Wells also armed herself and proclaimed that "a Winchester rifle should have a place of honor in every black home, and it should be used for that protection which the law refuses to give." Some blacks heeded her advice, and on rare occasions, armed blacks prevented lynchings.

Women such as Wells-Barnett also felt compelled to protest the widespread slander of black women. Whites charged that black women were congenitally immoral and as mothers were incapable of instilling sexual morality in their sons and daughters. From this perspective, whites argued that black women could not be "ruined" by white men. "As far as sexual relations go," Ben Tillman said, black women were "little better than animals" and always ready to satisfy white lust. The drive to restore the reputation of black women was one of the important factors that led to the women's club movement of the 1890s. In 1896 black women founded the National Association of Colored Women (NACW), and by 1900 it had 300 clubs comprising about 18,000 members. Although the NACW consisted primarily of middle-class women engaged in polite teas and moral uplift, it also evolved and later exhibited the animating reform impulses of the Progressive Era (see Chapter Five).

Black protest nonetheless had seriously declined in the South by 1900. In 1879 a national black conference held in Nashville captured the emerging mood of African Americans to seek compromise with whites and promote self-help. The delegates at the conference concluded that "we are to a great extent the architects of our own fortune, and we must rely mainly upon our own exertion for success." For black success the convention recommended "strict morality, temperate habits, and the practice of the acquisition of land, the acquiring of agriculture, [and] of advancing to mercantile positions. . . ."

In 1895, the year of Douglass's death, Booker Taliaferro Washington, a former slave, delivered a speech at the Atlanta Cotton States and Industrial Exposition that artfully articulated and expanded on the direction blacks had taken at Nashville in 1879. Washington's timely oration and his rags-to-riches life story as told in his autobiography, Up From Slavery (1901), made him the most famous and powerful black leader in America until his death in 1915. Washington carefully prepared his "Atlanta Compromise" speech to produce an effect that would please southern whites, northern capitalist-philanthropists, and African Americans—an improbable challenge but one he accomplished magnificently. With southern whites in mind, Washington referred to Reconstruction as a failure in which blacks foolishly "began at the top instead of at the bottom," and he declared, "The wisest of my race understand that the agitation of questions of social equality is the extremest folly. . . ." Washington advised blacks to stay in the South and work hard in "common occupations." He insisted that the two races could cooperate economically and remain apart socially. As Washington held his hand aloft, he uttered the words that brought the most applause, "In all things that are purely social we can be [spreading his fingers] as separate as the fingers yet one as the hand [closing his fist] in all things essential to mutual progress." To the delight of southern whites, he offered a racial settlement under which blacks acquiesced in the disfranchisement and segregation and asked for little in return. In addition, Washington assured the New South leaders that the black labor force would constitute "the most patient, faithful, law-abiding and unresentful people that the world has seen." His emphasis on industrial education at the Tuskegee Institute, a school for young blacks that he ruled as his fiefdom from 1881 to 1915, also endeared him to the ruling classes.

To northern capitalists such as Andrew Carnegie and John D. Rockefeller, who generously contributed funds to Tuskegee and its leader, Washington offered cheap, menial labor that would build railroads and work in factories "without strike and labour [sic] wars." William H. Baldwin, director of the Southern Railway and an enthusiastic Tuskegee supporter, explained that the black man "will willingly fill the more menial positions and do the heavy work, at less wages than the American white man or any foreign race which has yet come to our shores." In a word, Washington had allied himself with some of the most conservative people in the North, ones who crushed labor, made huge profits, and preached the "survival of the fittest."

The reaction of blacks to Washington's speech was varied. The fawning adulation of Washington by powerful whites made the Tuskegee master irresistible to many oppressed blacks. Even Du Bois, later Washington's primary foe, initially thought the Atlanta Compromise might serve as a basis for racial progress and peace. Yet several among the black elite lambasted Washington's speech. John Hope, an eminent Atlanta educator, said, "I regard it as cowardly and dishonest for any of our colored men to tell white people or colored people that we are not struggling for equality." Bishop Turner of Atlanta charged that Washington "will have to live a long time to undo the harm he has done our race." In most cases, the line between the Bookerites and the anti-Bookerites was not so clear-cut in the 1890s, but during the Progressive Era the two factions engaged in bitter ideological and organizational combat—a subject for later discussion.

The next step, though, is to explore what progressive sages thought about race and the worsening race problem in the first two decades of the twentieth century. Labeled the Progressive Era, this period has long been hailed for its democratic idealism, its governmental innovations, and its quest for social justice. But since triumphant white supremacy and progressivism strode in simultaneously at the dawn of the twentieth century, one may well wonder how the two phenomena were related. Did the progressive mind envision equal rights for African Americans? If so, did it have a realistic plan to effect it?

CHAPTER TWO

Tough-Minded
Progressives and Race

The ravaging forces of white supremacy that triumphed in the late
nineteenth century left blacks and whites more separate, hostile, and
unequal. At the beginning of the new century, however, a number of
black leaders expressed renewed hope for racial change. One reason
for that hope was the ascendancy of the Republican party after the
1896 election. The party that preserved the Union, ended slavery, and
engineered Reconstruction took control of the federal government in
the first decade of the twentieth century. Moreover, for most of the
decade Theodore Roosevelt held the presidency. When the young,
energetic, and activist president took office in 1901, he seemed to
embody the very spirit of progressivism, and, furthermore, the New
Yorker appeared favorably disposed toward blacks. Even the skepti-
cal W. E. B. Du Bois acknowledged that "a renaissance of civic virtue" was sweeping across the nation.

But would this rebirth of civic virtue challenge the racial status
quo? What did the best progressive minds and the most idealistic reformers think about blacks and the race problem? Did they formulate
realistic and sincere plans for achieving racial justice? To put progressive thought about race relations in context, one needs first to

explore the general nature and promise of progressivism. Since progressivism was a majority grassroots movement that percolated up
from the local and state levels to the national government and since it
cut across region, party, and class, it was incredibly broad, diverse,
and complex. The first part of this chapter will shed some light on the
tendencies of progressivism and suggest its potential for addressing
the worsening race problem.

The Shape and Promise of Progressivism

Basically, the Progressive Movement was a response to industrialization and its troublesome by-products: the immense increase in corporate power, the problems of rapid urban growth and large-scale immigration, widening class conflict and labor violence, and wholesale
political corruption. This broad movement consisted of hundreds of
differing interest groups with an impulse toward change. Some of
these contending groups came to a meeting of the minds often enough
to pass mountains of reform legislation at the local, state, and federal
level.

Despite their many differences, progressives had some meaning-
ful commonalities. First, the great bulk of the progressives were pragmatic and moderate, not ideological and radical. They wanted to preserve the American system, not overthrow it. Second, they believed
that larger government was necessary to solve the problems created
by industrialization. Almost all progressives, whether agrarians or
middle-class urbanites, called for more government regulation of big
business, often demanding the breakup of monopolies. Middle-class
progressives feared that seemingly unbridled corporate influence was
undermining the autonomy of the individual and the power of their
groups, whether they were teachers, lawyers, physicians, ministers,
or small businesspeople. Third, because progressives believed that
larger government posed threats to liberty, they also sought to make
government more democratic and answerable to the people. Fourth,
scientific-minded progressives harped incessantly on "efficiency."
Champions of efficiency undertook time-and-motion studies to determine how to increase human productivity and even tried to apply these
ideas to civic and political functions. Fifth, a large number of progressives stressed the idea of social justice, meaning they favored laws

that protected the poor, the oppressed, and the helpless—minimum-wage laws and limits on working hours for children and women are some examples. Finally, most progressives were moral reformers who wanted to eliminate greed, vice (especially the use of illegal drugs and alcohol, gambling, and prostitution), and political corruption. And once they exposed a wrong, the progressive reformer invariably proposed a law to squelch it. Indeed, the flood of legislation passed by progressives attested to their faith that new laws could effect social harmony and justice. Progressives enacted statutes that touched on every area of American life, from city hall to the Oval Office, from the union hall to the boardroom. At the national level, progressives—coalitions of Republicans, Democrats, Socialists, and Independents—passed laws that regulated railroads and corporations and broke up monopolies such as Standard Oil and the American Tobacco Company. During the Progressive Era, the federal government began the regulation of food, drugs, alcohol, child labor, and business competition, establishing regulatory oversight agencies such as the Food and Drug Administration and the Federal Trade Commission. Progressives enacted legislation that preserved natural resources and set aside millions of acres of land for the creation of national forests and parks. Progressives also passed the Federal Reserve Act, which established a modern banking system. Under the guidance of progressives, the federal government aided education and subsidized the building of highways. In 1916 Congress established an eight-hour day for railroad workers and awarded them pensions; and it exempted labor unions from anti-trust laws, which had been used by the courts to stifle the organization of workers.

If one does not count the Bill of Rights, progressives set a record by passing four amendments to the Constitution in seven years: the Sixteenth, giving Congress the right to enact income taxes, the Seventeenth, allowing people to elect U.S. Senators directly, the Eighteenth, outlawing the manufacture and sale of alcoholic beverages, and the Nineteenth, giving women the right to vote. Cities and states passed even more legislation that often affected more directly the health, education, and welfare of the people.

Early historians of progressivism praised the first two decades of the twentieth century as vital years of modernizing reform, a precursor of New Deal liberalism. After World War II, however, a new generation of historians criticized the inconsistencies, the conservatism, and the failures of the Progressive Movement. In the 1960s New Leftist historians castigated progressives for failing to redistribute wealth and reign in the excesses of big business. These revisionist historians sneered at the middle-class "corporate liberalism" of the Progressive Era. The title of Gabriel Kolko's provocative book on progressivism, *The Triumph of Conservatism* (1963), conveyed the radical view that big business had shaped progressivism to its own ends. While revisionists may have exaggerated the defects of progressivism, they proved that many of the progressive laws were weak, poorly enforced, and had unintended and often reactionary consequences. Prohibition comes to mind.

Still, for every negative assessment of progressivism, positive, if critical, accounts of the phenomenon have continued to appear. With liberalism coming under such scathing attacks in the 1980s and 1990s, some Democrats, such as Bill Clinton, Al Gore, and Bill Bradley (and even the Republican John McCain), began to use the term *progressive* to describe their ideas and programs. In an article in the *Journal of the Gilded Age and the Progressive Era* in 2002, the historian Robert D. Johnson observed that the Progressive Movement was being rehabilitated and "its democratic promise" was once again being recognized. He argued that "the progressive impulse at its best had trust in the people, a respect for small-scale solutions, and healthy moral imperative that many today find difficult to kindle in their political souls."

Though messy and flawed, progressivism did inspire millions of Americans because of its democratic promise of equality and justice. In *The New Democracy* (1912), the progressive journalist Walter E. Weyl asserted, "The basis of democratic striving . . . is an ethical belief in the sanctity of human life, and the desire for an equality in this universal possession." Speaking at the Progressive party convention in 1912, Senator Albert J. Beveridge of Indiana proclaimed: "We stand for a nobler America. We stand for a broader liberty, a fuller justice. We stand for social brotherhood against savage industrialism." William Allen White, a progressive journalist from Kansas, rejoiced that a new interest in the downtrodden "was manifest in the land."

But for all its good intentions, the progressive conscience never seriously challenged the color line. Most progressive intellectuals in fact acquiesced in the consolidation of Jim Crow in the South or simply ignored the race problem. All but a tiny handful of white progressive thinkers subscribed to either biological or cultural racism, or some combination thereof. The question, then, is not whether a white progressive thinker was a racist, but what kind of racist was he: mild, strong, or even vicious? Research over the last thirty years has bolstered Rayford Logan's idea that the Progressive Era marked the "nadir" of African American life after emancipation. If judged by race alone, the Progressive Era should be called, in the words of the historian Pete Daniel, the "Regressive Era."

Scientific Racism and the Progressive Mind

The typical progressive intellectual thought in terms of racial hierarchy because the young, well-educated, middle-class activist was exposed to a steady diet of racist literature and teaching from birth. As Donnarae MacCann, a prolific writer on racism in youth literature, demonstrated in *White Supremacy in Children's Literature* (1998), "There was little reason for the white American child to doubt his or her racial superiority because the storybooks, periodicals, schools, churches, and government authorities were all sending the same signal." That is, children learned early that whites were the instigators of high civilizations while blacks were lazy, emotional, clownish, instinctual, and incapable of restraint and logic. White authors made black children into cartoon characters, generally referred to as "pickaninnies." Even the stock Mammy figure, ever gentle and understanding with white children, had little patience with rowdy black youths. In one scene of a children's story, a black Mammy chastised one of her own, "[L]ook er hyear, yer kinky-head nigger, whar's yer manners?" A white child from any region or class could scarcely escape such malignant racial conditioning.

At college, budding progressives not only read exposés of capitalistic barons and attacks on laissez-faire economics by muckraking journalists, they also read racist tracts that drew on the latest anthropology, biology, psychology, sociology, genetics, eugenics, and medical science. Everything in the education of progressives militated against them treating blacks as equals. In 1909 the *Nation* sounded an early alarm against "The Science of Race Hatred," also known as "scientific racism."

For most ordinary white Americans, innate black inferiority was a given. This belief was, as the Swedish economist and Nobel-Prize winner Gunnar Myrdal observed in his classic work on race relations in the United States, *An American Dilemma: The Negro Problem and Modern Democracy* (1944), "totally independent of rational proofs" and embraced "in a deep mystical sense." But educated progressives did not easily tolerate obvious contradictions in their hallowed democratic creed, which necessitated the generation of elaborate theories of black inferiority. Ironically, the more democratic the nation, the more its thinkers needed an ideology of racism. Put another way, scientific racism was, as Myrdal argued, "a function of egalitarianism."

The scientific racism of the Progressive Era borrowed heavily from Darwinism, which profoundly influenced American intellectuals. Those who cited Darwin's work to divine historical development insisted that the theory of evolution easily explained why Anglo-Saxons stood at the apex of white civilization. This kind of thinking surfaces in the work of the sociologist Edward A. Ross. A Ph.D. from Johns Hopkins University, Ross wrote dozens of books of social analysis and was a major advisor to the progressive Wisconsin governor and Senator, Robert M. La Follette. In a 1901 article in the *Annals of the American Academy of Political and Social Science,* Ross declared, "The superiority of a race cannot be preserved without *pride of blood* and an uncompromising attitude toward the lower races [emphasis in original]." Ross advised progressives to discard the sentimental, religious equalitarianism of the old abolitionists and base their ideas of reform on hard science.

Professor John R. Commons, a political economist, was also a distinguished member of Governor La Follette's brain trust at the University of Wisconsin. Commons drafted a civil service law for the governor, helped to reorganize the government of Milwaukee, and served on the United States Immigration Commission under President Roosevelt. As a champion of the common man and labor, Commons opposed unlimited immigration on the grounds that it tended to drive down wages and weaken unions. But instead of opposing immigration on strictly economic grounds, Commons, like many other progressives, rejected the newcomers on the basis of race. In *Races and Immigrants in America* (1907), he aimed his venom primarily at immigrant "races" from southern and eastern Europe, but as an aside he declared that all tropical races were "indolent and fickle." The only way blacks could adapt to the strenuous regimen of the Anglo-Saxons, he posited, was by some kind of coercion.

Commons further argued that democratic institutions simply did not work when controlled by inferior races. Comparing the corruption and disorder in Reconstruction with that of urban corruption in the Progressive Era, he arrived at the disturbing corollary that America might have to "despotize [its] institutions" in order to control them, writing that "Race differences are established in the very blood and physical constitution. . . . They are most difficult to eradicate, and they yield only to the slow processes of the centuries."

As Reform Darwinists, Ross and Commons believed that some human beings had evolved to the point that they could use their brains to devise laws that would curb the excesses of unregulated capitalism and ameliorate the Darwinian struggle in order to effect a fairer and more democratic society. They contributed significantly to progressive reform by attacking laissez-faire economics, the steel chain of ideas that anchored the status quo. But their pessimistic views on race stood strangely at odds with their optimistic ideas about reforming society in general.

Psychology was another social science that was just coming into its own in the early twentieth century, and it, too, influenced racial thought. Psychologists of the period generally concluded that blacks were mentally feeble and unable to cope with modern civilization. In the early twentieth century psychologists developed a new "scientific" tool that supported many of their racial and ethnic assumptions: I.Q. tests. American psychologists seemed to consider intelligence tests an infallible measurement of human potential. In *The Measurement of Intelligence* (1916), Lewis Terman, one of the primary advocates and developers of I.Q. tests in America, found that native whites scored far above immigrants and blacks, the latter being at the bottom. Massive testing of draftees during World War I by Terman and others showed that blacks averaged about 25 points lower than whites on I.Q. tests, and 80 percent of blacks were graded as mentally "inferior." Social scientists have since exposed the unreliability and the cultural biases of these early tests.

Physicians also engaged in much racial speculation, and always to the detriment of African Americans. Like physical anthropologists, physicians put much stock in physical differences of races and linked biology with psychological theories about the black mind and temperament. Like Ross and Terman, medical doctors preached that humanitarian notions about equality must not be allowed to cloud racial thinking. For example, Professor James Bardin, a teaching physician at the University of Virginia, lectured in 1913 that racial differences were biological and therefore "ineradicable as long as the strain of blood remains unimpaired." Since the mind was linked to the body, Bardin argued, certain races had "peculiar mental characteristics" that limited their social and political progress. Nothing would change, Bardin sighed, "as long as a Negro is a Negro." In 1906, after a lengthy study comparing the brain sizes of different races, Dr. Robert Bennett Bean expressed his opinion in the *Century Magazine*—in an article excerpted from the *American Journal of Anatomy*—that it was futile to try to educate African Americans.

Adding to the racist material that Americans of the Progressive Era fed on was the new field of eugenics. Francis Galton (1822–1911), the founder of eugenics and a cousin of Charles Darwin, advertised his work as the use of Darwinism to improve human stock. Although eugenics was not about race per se, it was nonetheless similar to racism in its stress on heredity. After publishing *Hereditary Genius* in 1869, Galton judged that blacks were "childish, stupid, and simpleton like." Galton's movement spread across Europe—in Germany it eventually folded into Nazism—and ultimately to America, where it thrived in the Progressive Era. Eugenics built naturally upon established Darwinism and utilized intelligence tests and the work of the behavioral sciences to spin a wide and sticky web of scientific racism that few escaped. Eugenics appealed to tough-minded progressives because it was reformist, involved the use of government, and was, seemingly, based on cutting-edge science. Before the Nazis gave eugenics a bad name, it was a kind of secular religion in America. Between 1910 and 1914 more articles appeared on eugenics than on slums and poverty.

Leading the surge of eugenics in America was Charles B. Davenport. Davenport received a Ph.D. in zoology from Harvard in 1892 and in 1904 became the head of the Station for Experimental Evolution at Cold Spring Harbor on Long Island, New York, a project financed by the steel magnate Andrew Carnegie. For many years Davenport brought the leading scientists and social scientists to Long Island to determine how best to apply genetics to eugenics, which he defined as "the science of improvement of the human race by better breeding." Though Davenport was not preoccupied with blacks, he clearly was a racist. He decried the mulatto as an inferior mongrel, and he constantly urged white citizens "to keep the blood of the race pure."

Better breeding was, of course, difficult to legislate, but the state could and did sterilize allegedly inferior and dangerous people for the good of society. From 1907 to 1917 seventeen states adopted legislation that allowed sterilization of "unfit individuals." Fearing that inferior people were outbreeding superior stock, Davenport and his circle set off a near panic in the first decade of the twentieth century over the possibility of "race suicide" by Anglo-Saxons, an idea that haunted Theodore Roosevelt and loomed large in Madison Grant's best-selling racist polemic, *The Passing of the Great Race* (1916).

In the late nineteenth and early twentieth centuries, the rash of American world fairs spread the vogue of scientific racism to the masses. After world fairs in Chicago, Atlanta, Nashville, and Omaha in the 1890s, the popular extravaganzas continued in Buffalo (1901), St. Louis (1904), San Francisco (1915), and San Diego (1915–16). The fairs attracted millions of Americans from all sections, classes, and races. In his *All the World's a Fair: Visions of Empire at American International Expositions, 1876–1916* (1984), historian Robert W. Rydell maintains that the fairs not only entertained, but sold Americans on capitalism, imperialism, and white supremacy. As Rydell illustrated, "the idea of technological and national progress" at the exhibitions was "laced with scientific racism." The fairs not only reflected American views, they enhanced them with science. The Filipinos Village became a key exhibit at Buffalo and St. Louis. By contrasting a primitive Asian village with Western exhibits that featured advanced science and technology, the fairs demonstrated that the primitive Filipinos were unfit for self-rule and in need of the benign supervision of advanced Americans. All of the fairs, Rydell demonstrated, depicted "white supremacy as a utopian agency" and "left an enduring vision of empire."

The 1901 Buffalo fair also featured an African Village and an Old Plantation concession that displayed blacks as primitive creatures, a race of people given to fun and frolic. The fairs also reeked of minstrel shows, ragtime bands, and "coon songs" from Broadway. At San Diego in 1915 the Science and Education Building dedicated five rooms to an anthropology exhibit designed to explain "Man's Evolution." Exhibits such as this one linked biology and race with displays of human skulls arranged according to genetic typology and cranial capacity. The San Diego Fair featured a Race Betterment Booth designed by eugenicists. Race science was everywhere on display at the fairs, justifying white economic and political control of dark-skinned people at home and abroad.

Meanwhile, an unprecedented flood of racist books and articles drawing on the various sciences appeared in the early twentieth century, much of it printed by the best publishing houses in the North. For example, in *The Negro A Beast* (1901), Charles Carroll argued that blacks were not human beings but higher apes put on earth by God to do menial work for whites. In *The Negro, A Menace to American Civilization* (1907), R. W. Shufeldt offered a final solution to the race problem, which was "to emasculate the entire negro race . . . and effectually stop the breed right now and thus prevent any further danger from them, and the horrors of their crossing continually with the Anglo-Saxon stock."

Ironically, William Hannibal Thomas, an educated mulatto who fought in the Civil War and participated in Reconstruction politics, wrote one of the most racist books of the period, *The American Negro* (1901). Soured by his political and financial setbacks and wracked by pain from physical disabilities, Thomas turned his anger on African Americans. Published by Macmillan of New York on the advice of Franklin H. Giddings, a distinguished professor of sociology at Columbia University, *The American Negro* argued that the only contribution blacks had made to American development was "a pretentious imitation of civilization, a veneering over barbarous instincts." The

"Black Judas," as African Americans of all stripes called Thomas, charged that 90 percent of black women were "lascivious by instinct and in bondage to physical pleasure." The race-baiting "Pitchfork" Ben Tillman happily distributed a hundred copies of *The American Negro* to his South Carolina constituents.

The two most important popularizers of scientific racism were the aforementioned Madison Grant and Lothrop Stoddard. Both authors sounded the familiar progressive theme that Americans should dispense with sentimental ideas about equality and soberly apply scientific knowledge to questions about immigration and race. Grant, a wealthy New York lawyer, self-taught naturalist, and felicitous writer, published *The Passing of the Great Race* in 1916. It went through many printings and was in its fourth revised edition by 1921. Although Grant thought blacks a "stationary species," he was primarily concerned with the "new immigrants." He believed the Melting Pot theory of immigration was pushing the nation toward a "racial abyss." Adolf Hitler called *The Passing of the Great Race* "his Bible."

Grant's book also impressed Stoddard, a Harvard Ph.D. who became perhaps the most effective writer in the crowded field of anti-black literature. Proud of his illustrious Anglo-Saxon ancestors who dated back to Puritan Massachusetts, Stoddard, unlike his mentor Grant, focused on black-white relations. Stoddard gained widespread attention in 1920 with *The Rising Tide of Color Against White World Supremacy,* a book that inspired the leaders of the second Ku Klux Klan. He continued to churn out his racist barrage of books in the 1920s and 1930s. After praising Hitler's eugenics experiments in *Into the Darkness* (1940), Stoddard received and accepted an invitation from the German leader to enjoy the rare privilege of observing the Eugenics Courts of the Third Reich.

Perhaps no academic group was more monolithic in its racism than historians. Although not scientists, American historians who came of age in the Progressive Era were trained in the scientific method of history. They believed in objectively letting copious, documented facts recreate the past exactly as it was. Several prominent professors combined so-called scientific history with scientific racism to plant anti-black sentiments in the minds of a generation of students. Professor Herbert Baxter Adams led the way by mentoring graduate students at prestigious Johns Hopkins University in the late nineteenth century. Trained in Germany in the scientific method of history, Adams harped on Teutonic superiority. John W. Burgess, a Tennessean who studied law, history, and political science at several German universities, disseminated theories of Teutonic superiority at Columbia University from 1880 until his retirement in 1912. His influential books *The Civil War and the Constitution* (1901) and *Reconstruction and the Constitution* (1902) explicitly taught the inferiority of blacks and lent support to white southern racial policies. He assured the South that the North would never "again give themselves over to the vain imagination of the political equality of man."

As noted previously, no one was more influential in spreading anti-Reconstruction and anti-black views than William Archibald Dunning, a native of New York. Between 1886 and 1922 Dunning trained a legion of historians at Columbia University, who then produced numerous state studies of Reconstruction. His own *Essays on the Civil War and Reconstruction* (1897) and *Reconstruction, Political and Economic, 1865–1877* (1907) established a template for what became known as the Dunning School of historians. Denigrating "the trite generalities of the Rights of Man," Dunning justified the notorious Black Codes of 1865 as necessary to control an inferior and savage race. And he excused violence against blacks on the basis that "the coexistence in one society of two races so distinct in characteristics" made biracial government impossible. Generally, Dunning and the Dunningites skewered the abolitionists as sentimental idealists and praised Andrew Johnson for fighting against the "Africanization" of the South. Unfortunately, the racist themes of the Dunning School soon permeated school textbooks, popular nonfiction, best-selling novels, and the new medium of motion pictures.

Out of the Progressive Era also came *American Negro Slavery* (1918), which became the standard work on slavery until the late 1950s. The author, U. B. Phillips, was a Georgian who received his higher education in the North and taught at the Universities of Wisconsin and Michigan, and at Yale. His well-researched and sophisticated book on slavery depicted blacks as naturally docile and happy. To Phillips, slavery was a benign "school constantly training and controlling pupils who were in a backward state of civilization."

Even some historians who had once shown sympathy for African Americans fell prey to the racist predilections of the time. A good example is Albert Bushnell Hart, the son of an Ohio abolitionist, a Harvard professor, and one of the most prominent members of his profession. Hart directed Du Bois's dissertation on the slave trade, saw to its publication, and remained friendly with his brilliant black student. Although Hart's early writing condemned slavery and the cruelty of Southerners toward blacks, he increasingly sympathized with southern whites. In 1908 he confessed, "I feel more sympathy with the Southerner than I did five years ago." In 1910 he published *The Southern South,* which was scholarly in tone but devastating to African Americans of the day. In this work Hart concluded, "Race measured by race, the negro is inferior, and his past history in Africa and America leads to the belief that he will remain inferior in race stamina and achievements."

To be fair, not everyone joined the chorus singing the praises of white supremacy. During the Progressive Era, Franz Boas (1858–1943) founded the school of cultural anthropology at Columbia University, which by mid-century had undermined the dominance of racist thought in the American academy. A social and political activist, Boas stressed environment over heredity and found equal intellectual potential among the races. His seminal work, *The Mind of Primitive Man* (1911), has been hailed as the Magna Charta of the darker races.

In addition to Boas, a small number of other academicians seemed to have resisted the ubiquitous racism of the period. The work of W. I. Thomas, a distinguished sociologist at the University of Chicago, appeared to have no hint of racism. The pioneering progressive sociologist Lester Frank Ward, a debunker of Social Darwinism, opined that intelligence was distributed equally between the different classes and races. Recent research, however, shows that these liberal thinkers had tendencies of thought that tainted their egalitarianism. For example, while Boas believed in the equal potential of the races, he thought that the physical differences between blacks and whites indicated mental differences as well. For his part, Thomas believed that race prejudice was instinctual and therefore impervious to education and anti-discrimination laws. And Ward claimed that the rape of white women by black men resulted from "the imperative voice of nature." Put an-

other way, black men were following a biological imperative to elevate their race by wishing to have sex with white women. With friends
such as these, African Americans faced a daunting future.

Progressive Activists and the Race Problem

A close look at various elements of the Progressive Movement reveals that the race problem overwhelmed and muddled even the thinking of reformers most inclined to support the underprivileged and
oppressed. Perhaps the views of no other progressives were more revealing than those of former abolitionists. As noted earlier, Lyman
Abbott represented many erstwhile abolitionists who lost their cru-
sading belief in racial equality. After Reconstruction, the Reverend
Abbott became an influential member of the Social Gospel in New
York. As the editor of the *Outlook* magazine, a progressive journal
with a circulation of 100,000, Abbott was a faithful ally of Theodore
Roosevelt and an important voice in the Progressive Movement.

During Reconstruction, Abbott favored black suffrage and integrated schools and proclaimed that the progress blacks had made since
the Civil War had refuted "slavery's accusations of idleness and incapacity." By the 1890s, though, Abbott opposed the Federal Elections
Bill (that had proposed the oversight of elections across the nation)
and acquiesced in the disfranchisement of blacks. Now an apologist
for the South, Abbott declared, "Any man can vote, black or white, if
he can read the English language, owns three hundred dollars' worth
of property, and pays his poll tax." He characterized blacks as a dependent and inferior people who could rise slowly, if at all, through
hard work, improved morality, and industrial education. Nothing
alarmed Abbott more than the specter of race-mixing. "For my part,"
he announced, "I thoroughly and heartily sympathize with the passionate resolve of the Southern people that this intermarriage shall
not go on in their borders. . . ." Once persona non grata in the South,
the New York editor became a popular lecturer in Dixie.

Abbott won accolades from Booker T. Washington, but Du Bois
insightfully criticized him as having a "singular gift in sensing the
popular side of any great social question and discovering deep and
esoteric reasons for supporting that side." According to Du Bois,

Abbott "had joined the slander of mulattoes, misrepresented and helped disfranchisement, and used every art of his remarkable gift of casuistry to put the religion of Jesus Christ into the service of color caste." Abbott's respectability and influence made him, Du Bois said, one of "the most subtle and dangerous enemies of the Negro in America."

In a study of an abolitionist stronghold, *Boston Confronts Jim Crow, 1890–1920* (1997), the historian Mark R. Schneider found that racial liberals in Massachusetts gave up the fight for racial equality after the defeat of the Federal Elections Bill (the election oversight bill) in 1891. Adding to black woes in Boston, Irish immigrants, known for their antiblack attitudes, began to exert political power in the state capital. Boston increasingly segregated blacks and discriminated against them economically. White Bostonians, Schneider concluded, came to treat blacks "with paternalism at best and violence at worst."

One of Boston's finest citizens was Charles Francis Adams, Jr., a railroad executive in the Gilded Age, the grandson of the antislavery advocate John Quincy Adams, and the son of Charles Francis Adams, Lincoln's minister to Britain. Adams viewed the Civil War as a humanitarian crusade. A colonel in the United States Army, Charles Francis Adams, Jr., led black cavalry troops into Richmond in 1865. His experience with black soldiers gave him confidence that African Americans could advance if given the opportunity. In his later years Adams became a crusader for railroad regulation and honesty in business and government, and he lectured widely and wrote about the history of New England. By 1900, however, the Boston Brahmin's view of blacks had been transformed. After a trip to Africa, he expressed his complete disillusionment with African Americans in a 1906 article in the *Century Magazine*. In it, he expressed his regret that Reconstruction had been carried out "in utter ignorance of ethnological law and total disregard of unalterable fact." At the sight of Africa, he declared, "the scales fell from my eyes." Gazing on the ancient city of Omdurman, he had an epiphany: "As Omdurman is to London, so is the African to the Anglo-Saxon. Distinctly, the difference is too great to admit of measurement." In 1908 Adams returned to Richmond to speak to the members of the Academy of Music. The Yankee historian captured his audience by opining that the race question should be left to white Southerners to solve. Adams told his hosts that all the glittering rubbish about "the equality of men" that resonated during Reconstruction now seemed "strangely remote, archaic even."

Most former abolitionists did not travel as far down the road to hardcore racism as did Adams, but even those who still believed in racial equality often threw up their hands in despair. In 1913 Alfred R. Hussey, a former abolitionist who retained a sincere concern for the civil rights of blacks, confided to a friend that on the race question he was "in a condition of grave bewilderment." "Frankly," he sighed, "I do not see the way out." Like Hussey, many progressives became defeatists on the race problem.

The muckrakers were inclined to remain optimistic about solving social problems. Playing a vital role as a catalyst for reform, this new wave of investigative journalists exposed, even if sensationally, every conceivable flaw in American democracy. And they invariably proposed legislation to cure whatever they felt hindered social and economic justice. Muckrakers, according to one estimate, published more than two thousand articles between 1903 and 1912. Yet the muckrakers and the journals that employed them showed little interest in African Americans.

The only muckraker who examined the race problem in any depth was Ray Stannard Baker, a native of Michigan. When his employer sent Baker to cover a lynching in 1904, he knew nothing about blacks. Once engaged, though, Baker plunged into the race issue, traveling throughout the North and the South, digging up copious facts and recording the unvarnished opinions of whites and blacks. He published most of his findings in a series of articles in the *American Magazine,* which were later collected and published as *Following the Color Line* (1908).

Baker's study rendered a grim picture of African American life. It found southern blacks living under constant insult and the threat of violence and having no chance of receiving justice in the courts. Baker related the story of how a handsome black man, after accidentally bumping into a white woman on the sidewalk, raced off wildly down the alley, fearing such an accident might well get him lynched. In his articles Baker described several fiendish lynchings and gave an account of the bloody Atlanta race riot of 1906. He also discussed the ghettoization of blacks in the North and showed how race discrimination in that region denied blacks economic opportunity and resulted in their living in wretched housing and appalling poverty.

But Baker's articles also accented the "animal-like ferocity" of African Americans and the large and growing black criminal class. He charged that most blacks were "still densely ignorant, and have little or no appreciation for the duties of citizenship." He attributed the achievements of mulattoes to their infusion of white blood, and he showed strong distaste for the militant "New Negro." In the end, Baker favored disfranchisement and segregation. Though he condemned lynching (because he said it brought whites down to the level of savage blacks), he accepted the southern myth that lynching occurred because of the inefficiency of the southern justice system. Sadly, if not surprisingly, the Yankee muckraker concluded that the white man "with his higher civilization, his keener sensibilities, his memories of departed glory had suffered far more [than blacks]."

Uncharacteristic of a muckraker, Baker proposed no legislation to right the wrongs of racism, not even an antilynching law. Instead he counseled that time and education alone could improve the racial situation. More education, he added, would bring less miscegenation. He argued that blacks had to accept a subordinate status indefinitely because of the shortcomings of their race. Stunned by the hostility of whites in both the North and the South to fairer treatment of blacks, Baker, too, turned defeatist. He advised that "the less they [race relations] are talked about the better," and at the Sagamore Sociological Conference in 1909, he admitted that "most of us in the north do not believe in any real democracy between white and colored men."

If much of the muckraking press was cool to the plight of blacks in America, some of it was downright hostile. Even though the *American Magazine* published Baker's articles, its editor instructed him not to offend the South. S. S. McClure, the owner of the most popular muckraking magazine, *McClure's*, was a white supremacist who believed that eastern and southern Europeans and blacks caused all the major problems in the United States. In *McClure's* time of glory, Thomas Nelson Page, the southern romantic novelist, wrote long articles for the magazine that portrayed blacks as inferior, oversexed, and morally depraved. According to Page, equality meant only one thing to a black man: the right to share a bed with a white woman. In 1904

James Boyle, a professor at the University of Wisconsin, expressed in *The Arena* an attitude about blacks that was typical of the muckraking journals. "They gave the members of the inferior race a fair trial, and then disfranchised them," Boyle said. "They were found unfit, even after years of freedom to participate in the administrations of the high functions of a republican form of government." In the *Forum* in 1911, the journalist Walter Winston Kenilworth singled out ragtime music as proof of black immorality. "How could it be different," he asked, "when the music had its birth through the sensuously sonorous larynx of the negro and was first voiced from his sensuously formed mouth?" Kenilworth maintained that the sexual seductiveness of barbarous blacks was a threat to white civilization. After all, he said, "Marc Anthony [sic] is not the only instance—and it is said that Cleopatra was an Ethiop."

Among the muckraking sheets, the *Independent* alone advocated black equality. Founded in 1848 in New York City, the *Independent* was an old abolitionist journal that became a muckraking beacon on the "southern problem" in the Progressive Era. Under the editorship of William Hayes Ward, a brilliant classical scholar who turned down a chair at Harvard to become a journalist, the *Independent* was the most passionate ally of blacks in the Progressive Era. The magazine supported federal aid to black education and railed against lynching, disfranchisement, segregation, convict lease, peonage, and anti-miscegenation laws. Although critics maligned the journal for its pro-black positions, Ward answered them forcefully and at length. He explained that America's largest minority, one-ninth of the population, was the "worst oppressed" group in the nation. He therefore advised progressives not to focus on lesser problems until the all-important race problem had been settled. Ward also opened the pages of his magazine to militant black writers such as Du Bois. Like William Lloyd Garrison's *Liberator,* the *Independent* consistently stood its ground on the issue of racial equality.

As a group, the less sensational, more intellectual writers of the period usually had no more concern for blacks than did the muckrakers. An examination of Herbert Croly, Walter Lippmann, and Walter Weyl is revealing in this regard. In 1914 these cerebral men established the *New Republic* (a weathervane for liberalism for decades to come), advised Presidents Roosevelt and Wilson, and wrote many influential political works. In 1909 Croly published *The Promise of American Life,* a book from which Roosevelt drew much of the New Nationalism that served as his platform for the 1912 election. In this long book, Croly attempted to reconcile the opposing threads of Jeffersonian and Hamiltonian government in order to achieve the requisite amount of "national cohesion" to solve the pressing problems of industrialization. Yet he spoke only fleetingly of African Americans, and then only while discussing the Civil War. As an afterthought, Croly noted that blacks constituted "a race possessed of moral and intellectual qualities inferior to those of the white man." Apparently, Croly believed that was enough said on the subject.

Lippmann, who advised every president from Theodore Roosevelt to Richard M. Nixon and was one of the most influential newspaper columnists in American history, dispensed his progressivism in *A Preface to Politics* (1914). Just out of Harvard, the precocious, left-leaning writer laced his book with Freudianism, Bergsonianism, and Jamesian Pragmatism. Although he discussed many of the major problems facing the nation, he barely acknowledged that American blacks were not really free. But he put forth no plan to remedy this problem of democracy, saying only that the fight for black equality would depend on the changes in the "character and social customs of the nation." From Lippmann's pragmatic treatise, one could scarcely tell that the United States had a deep, violent, and deteriorating race problem.

Walter Weyl, however, was not the type of person to evade the race question. In *The New Democracy,* the release of which was timed to influence the presidential race of 1912, Weyl anguished over the vexing race question. Unlike Croly and Lippman, he considered the problem thoroughly and put the issue in the context of his time. On the issue of black suffrage, Weyl argued that disfranchisement was only permissible "if we can honestly believe that the denial of the Negro vote is advantageous, not only to us, but to him." Looking at the corruption of the black vote in Cincinnati and Philadelphia, he wondered whether the vote in Atlanta or Charleston was worth fighting for. Despite his doubts about black suffrage, he advised that the question must remain open in a society that believed in democracy.

Recognizing the oppression and anger of African Americans, Weyl warned that a prolonged evasion of the race issue might result in a savage race war: "There may arise a Negro consciousness, a dark sense of outraged racial dignity. There may come a stirring of a rebellious spirit among ten, or as it soon will be, twenty or thirty million black folk." In the end, though, he presented no new programs or proposed no new laws, and he held out little hope for improvement in the status of African Americans. Weyl grimly concluded: "The South is psychologically cramped. The North is bewildered. The Negro problem is the mortal spot of the new democracy."

Among progressive reformers, white social workers seemed most inclined to include blacks in the new democracy. As the historian Allen F. Davis argued in *Spearheads for Reform* (1968), idealistic social workers such as Jane Addams, Florence Kelley, and Lillian Wald served as the shock troops of progressivism. The first of their kind in America, they worked tirelessly for laborers, immigrants, women, and children. They constructed settlement houses, playgrounds, schools, and kindergartens and campaigned for the passage of protective legislation. Davis also stressed that as a group, social workers extended their compassionate hands to blacks. He noted that Lillian Wald welcomed blacks to the Henry Street Settlement House in New York City and that several prominent social workers played a central role in the founding of the National Association for the Advancement of Colored People (NAACP).

Although Davis conceded that some social workers held racist views, he nevertheless exaggerated the pro-black proclivities of these reformers. Recent studies by historians Thomas Lee Philpott, Elisabeth Lasch-Quinn, and others have revealed that social workers were far more sensitive to the needs of European immigrants than to those of blacks. Even though settlement workers often thought of the various nationalities and ethnic groups from southern and eastern Europe as "lower races," they considered them more redeemable than African Americans. In most cases, settlement houses segregated blacks and whites, and many of the social workers held stereotypical views of African Americans. Frederick Bushee, for instance, described the typical Boston black as "low and coarse, revealing much more of the animal qualities than the spiritual." Jane Addams thought that blacks were "unique and spontaneous" and naturally humorous and rhythmic, but she also believed that blacks were uniquely inferior to other groups in their lack of social control and family stability.

Although social workers like Addams tended to cite environmental factors as the cause of black pathology, they sometimes gave biological explanations. Addams spoke of the "lack of inherited control" by blacks. Almost all social workers found blacks more socially deficient than European immigrants. John Daniels, a Boston settlement house worker and Harvard-educated Iowan, made this point in his study of Boston blacks, *In Freedom's Birthplace* (1914). In his book Daniels stressed black cultural deficiencies such as excessive emotionalism that allegedly stemmed from "a shortage in the power of restraint and self-control." He contended that the black man lacked "fundamental moral stamina" and had "an intrinsic weakness or flabbiness at the very root and core of his make-up." Indeed, he argued that self-induced black failings explained white prejudice.

The historian Axel Schäfer suggested that the attitude of social workers toward blacks resulted from the model of reform they chose. In "W. E. B. Du Bois, German Social Thought, and the Racial Divide in American Progressivism, 1892–1909," published in the *Journal of American History* (2001), Schäfer argued that the evasion of the race issue, the "notorious blind spot of progressivism," eventuated in part from the fact that many American progressives, including Du Bois, studied in Germany and brought back to the United States a reform model that stressed the institutional and ethical development of national and ethnic groups rather than the inalienable rights of individuals enshrined in the American Constitution. In judging blacks as a group, social workers—and virtually all white Americans—believed African Americans much less amenable to social and political improvement than other minority groups. The German model thus marginalized blacks in regard to reform priorities and put little stress on constitutional rights such as suffrage and equal protection of the law.

Nor did mainstream white churches seriously seek to improve the civil rights of African Americans. Most Protestant leaders were in fact very much in tune with the new industrial order and the racial subordination that reigned at the turn of the twentieth century. In the

South the white churches, even the most liberal ones, fiercely defended segregation, disfranchisement, and the generally shabby treatment of African Americans, basing their arguments on the Bible. The other-worldly Protestant churches throughout the nation concerned themselves primarily with individual salvation and gaining entrance of their parishioners into heaven, showing little concern for the plight of urban industrial workers and the rights of African Americans. The oil tycoon John D. Rockefeller, a regular Sunday school teacher in the Baptist church, once said, "God gave me my money." The conservative churches seemed to agree that the Lord had judiciously sanctioned the vast riches of the plutocracy, and just as surely the dismal poverty and misery of those at the bottom of society. Traditional religious leaders often attributed poverty and the social pathology that accompanied it to moral failings and character defects, not to the social and economic system. Not surprisingly, secular reformers and historians of reform have held the church complicit in the injustice of the social order in the late nineteenth and early twentieth centuries.

The rapidly growing Catholic church proved no more effective than Protestants in achieving equal rights for African Americans. Ignoring its creed of universalism and color-blindness, the Catholic church segregated its schools, colleges, seminaries, and churches, in both the North and South. Revealing is the fact that only four black priests received ordination during the Progressive Era. Paternalistic and racist white priests ministered to African Americans as if they were on a foreign mission. The Reverend John R. Slattery, who headed the Josephites, the only Catholic congregation devoted to the welfare of blacks, tried to increase the number of black priests, but racist bishops opposed him at every turn. After Slattery left the church in disgust, he told the *Independent* in 1906, "If anything in this world is certain, it is that the stand of the Catholic Church toward the negroes is sheer dishonesty."

But what about the Social Gospel, the liberal movement within the Protestant church that conspicuously called for social and economic reforms? Starting in the late nineteenth century, a minority of Protestant ministers worked to change the focus of the church from other-worldly goals to the mounting social and economic problems in the United States. Prominent ministers such as Washington Gladden in Ohio and Walter Rauschenbusch in New York City, who wrote the influential *Christianity and the Social Crisis* (1907), blamed poverty and urban pathology not on the moral defects of industrial workers, but on the depraved economic system. Working in the notorious neighborhood Hell's Kitchen in New York City, Rauschenbusch preached that it was not reasonable to expect common laborers to adhere to high moral standards until their basic material needs were met. To ensure that such needs were satisfied, the Social Gospelers supported such measures as child labor laws, compulsory education, work safety laws, and a "living wage" for all workers. Their goal of Christian unity was partially fulfilled when these liberal clergymen formed the Federal Council of Churches in 1908 (it included only Protestants as the Catholic church had not yet embraced ecumenicalism). At the height of the Progressive Movement, the Social Gospel therefore marched arm-in-arm with social workers, forming another "spearhead for reform."

But several studies of the Social Gospel by historians showed that many Social Gospel ministers also were either apathetic about or blind to racial injustice. In *White Protestantism and the Negro* (1965), David M. Reimers charged that liberal preachers "turned away from concern for the Negro" in favor of more general industrial and urban problems. George M. Fredrickson concluded in his magisterial book, *The Black Image in the White Mind* (1971), "For the most part, Gladden and other Northern proponents of 'social Christianity' ignored the Negro. . . ."

Two subsequent historical studies of liberal Christianity, *Liberty and Justice for All: Racial Reform and the Social Gospel* (1990) by Ronald C. White and *The Social Gospel in Black and White* (1991) by Ralph E. Luker, argued that Social Gospelers did care for blacks. To be sure, White and Luker demonstrated that some less-known members of the Social Gospel fought for racial justice. White also suggested that by 1900 Gladden had moved closer to Du Bois and had finally developed the racial implications of his belief in the "fatherhood of God and the brotherhood of man." Still, both White and Luker counted as friends of blacks many ministers who favored disfranchisement, segregation, and racial purity. Luker largely rescued the Social Gospel by including several black ministers in the movement and playing down the paternalism of many white preachers. Like most social workers, Social Gospelers believed that voting was a privilege, not a right, and many held the pessimistic belief that race prejudice was instinctual. In 1907 Gladden was so dispirited by the race problem that he advocated setting aside three or four southern states for blacks. In 1914 Rauschenbusch, the leading intellectual of the movement, felt compelled to explain his long silence on the race question. "For years, the problem of the two races in the South," he said, "has seemed to me so tragic, so insoluble that I have never yet ventured to discuss it in public." Although several white members of the Social Gospel movement were members of the NAACP, few got involved in its everyday work; and the Federal Council of Churches, as White conceded, did not commit to civil rights for African Americans until the 1920s.

Nor did the women's rights movement prove friendly to blacks. The National American Woman Suffrage Association and the General Federation of Women's Clubs, both formed in 1890, generally excluded blacks. Leading suffragists such as Susan B. Anthony and Elizabeth Cady Stanton bitterly resented the fact that the Fifteenth Amendment enfranchised black men but not women. Seeking not to offend the South, northern women advocated an "educated suffrage," and southern white women argued that their vote would help maintain white supremacy. A 1917 issue of the *Suffragist* headlined the injustice of "Refined, Intelligent Women," that is, suffragists, being thrown in jail "With Negroes and Criminals."

In *White Women's Rights* (1999), the historian Louise Michele Newman arraigned white women reformers for claiming racial and cultural superiority. As Anglo-Saxon, middle-class women assumed a broader role in society, they essentially placed a racial modifier before the word "woman" and billed themselves as "civilizers of inferior peoples." Frances Willard, the founder of the Women's Christian Temperance Union, believed that backward, immoral blacks hindered the push for Prohibition and lectured that alcohol increased the black man's tendency toward rape. Charlotte Perkins Gilman, one of the most radical feminists of the era, also accepted southern beliefs about rape and said that African Americans were so "dissimilar and in many respects inferior" that their "present status is to us a social injury. . . ."

Like so many progressives, Gilman and many of her feminist colleagues considered blacks to be, as the historian Fred H. Matthews put it, "a permanent clot in the social bloodstream" of American life.

Literary and Popular Culture and Race

The elite literary set, often thought of as the champions of the oppressed, proved as racist as any group in America. Popular writers such as Owen Wister, Frank Norris, and Jack London expressed contempt for blacks and portrayed them as cowardly, venal, and deceitful in their popular fiction. In *The Jungle* (1906), a widely read novel whose nauseating descriptions of conditions in the meat-packing plants of Chicago spurred the passage of the Meat Inspection Act, Upton Sinclair detailed the plight of immigrant workers and espoused Socialism. Yet Sinclair, the champion of the voiceless, referred to blacks as "wooly heads" and "buck negroes" and warned that "ignorant country negroes" had "nameless diseases" that tainted the meat they processed. He described black Chicago as a "saturnalia" of "human beasts," fighting, stabbing, and shooting one another.

Another jaundiced view of American blacks could be seen in Vachel Lindsay's 1914 poem, "The Congo." For sixteen years Lindsay recited this popular poem on the lecture circuit. Having read Joel Chandler Harris's *Uncle Remus,* Henry M. Stanley's *In Darkest Africa,* and Joseph Conrad's *Heart of Darkness* as a child, Lindsay was primed to produce a three-part poem on Africans, which served as a prism through which to view African Americans. The first part of the poem, "Their Basic Savagery," described Africans as "fat bucks" and "tatooed cannibals" who worked themselves up into a "blood-lust." In the second part, "Their Irrepressible High Spirits," Lindsay painted a picture of "high minstrelsy" adorned with "wild crap shooters" and "cake-walk royalty." In the final part, "The Hope of Their Religion," he suggested that, with the help of well-intentioned whites, Africa could be redeemed through Christianity. Still, Lindsay warned whites that bringing civilization to Africa carried the risk that the "Mumbo-Jumbo, God of the Congo . . . will hoo-doo you."

If foreign lands carried risks, many American writers nonetheless believed that white males, softened by modern life, had to prove their manhood by venturing into distant and uncivilized worlds. In *Manliness and Civilization* (1995), the historian Gail Bederman demonstrated the felt need of Anglo-Saxon writers to prove that white manliness was superior to that of other races. In the novel, *Tarzan and the Apes* (1914), Edgar Rice Burroughs gave America and the white world an icon for masculinity. Burroughs, who left Chicago as a child to grow up as a cowboy in Idaho, created a highly muscled white man and set him in Africa to tame the savage jungle. The king of the jungle not only slew killer gorillas but he also killed Kulonga, a fierce African warrior who had murdered his ape mother. Tarzan actually strung Kulonga up in a tree before plunging a knife into his heart. Apparently, like real-life whites in the American South, the fictional Tarzan believed it his duty to lynch dangerous blacks.

Despite the rhetoric of white supremacy, many Caucasians feared that African Americans and other people they deemed as lower might not just outbreed them but best them in physical competition. As a physical fitness craze swept America in the 1890s, whites had begun to exclude blacks from most professional sports. Until they were banned from the major leagues in that decade, blacks routinely played professional baseball with whites. African American jockeys not only rode thoroughbreds at racetracks across the nation, but they had regularly won the Kentucky Derby and other major races; they were frozen out of horseracing early in the twentieth century. Back in 1810 Tom Molineaux, a former American slave, faced a white Englishman for boxing's world heavyweight championship. But Irish-American boxers, who dominated the heavyweight crown in the late nineteenth and early twentieth centuries, refused to fight African Americans. John L. Sullivan, the first of a long line of Irish champions, promised to take on all comers, "except black ones."

This exception continued until 1908 when the Texan Arthur "Jack" Johnson, a lightning-fast boxer with a powerful punch, taunted the world champion Tommy Burns into fighting him in Australia. The masterful Johnson toyed with the smaller Burns before hammering him into submission, and then he meted out the same punishment to several other white boxers (ironically, Johnson avoided matches with other black boxers). Soon the press was searching for "a white hope" to restore the heavyweight crown to its rightful race, or, as Jack London phrased it, "to remove that smile from Johnson's face." White hopes came to rest on the strong shoulders of Jim Jeffries, the former heavyweight champion who had retired undefeated. Emerging from his California alfalfa field in 1910 to fight Johnson in Reno, Nevada, farmer Jeffries assured the white race that he was fit to "defend its athletic superiority." Many boxing analysts predicted Jeffries would win simply because a cerebral white man was bound to beat an emotional, unthinking "darkey." Johnson proved the analysts terribly wrong by easily disposing of Jeffries.

Johnson's victory was a bitter pill for racial chauvinists to swallow, and white America reacted strongly. Racial altercations occurred across the nation as whites attacked and killed at least a dozen blacks brazen enough to celebrate Johnson's triumph. When a young black man entered a grill in Evansville, Indiana, and ordered "a cup of coffee as strong as Jack Johnson and a steak beat up like Jeffries," the white owner promptly shot him five times. Congress took the extraordinary step of banning the showing of films of the Reno match. In the white mind, the brash, high-living Johnson had committed two serious errors for which he had to pay: he beat up white men and he socialized with white women, and even married one. After Johnson defeated Jeffries, the intelligence agencies of the federal government conducted a massive search for incriminating evidence against the black boxer. In 1913 a white jury convicted Johnson of violating of the Mann Act, the federal statute passed by progressives that made it illegal to take women across state lines for immoral purposes.

To whites, Johnson conjured up the image of the savage black brute that set off lynch mobs in the South, and soon this scary image began to show up on the silver screen. At first such films featured the stereotype of the lazy, dumb, and comical African American. The titles of the earliest films about blacks suggest the stereotypical content: *The Pickaninnies Doing a Dance* (1894), *Ballyhoo Cakewalk* (1903), *A Nigger in the Woodpile* (1904), *The Dancing Nig* (1907), *How Rastus Got His Porkchops* (1908), and *Rastus in Zululand* (1910). As the film historian Thomas Cripps proclaimed, the black characters in these films ran the "gamut from A to B." In 1908, however, *The Zulu's*

Heart accentuated "merciless black brutes" who attacked an innocent white family in South Africa, and a year later in *The Girls and Daddy,* a black sexual predator targeted two angelic white girls.

But the damage these early race films did to race relations in America paled in comparison to the carnage of the historic 1915 movie, *The Birth of a Nation.* This movie transformed film technically, for in it the renowned cinematic innovator David Wark Griffith introduced new techniques such as pacing, cut-aways, and fade-outs and showed an unprecedented ability to handle large, epic scenes. A member of a Kentucky family that once held slaves, D. W. Grffith longed to dramatize the white South's version of the Civil War and Reconstruction Eras. Fortunately for him, by 1915 plenty of Yankee-written, racist history existed to help legitimize the director's desire.

Although the first part of Griffith's long movie, covering the Civil War, was reasonably balanced, the second part of *The Birth of a Nation* was a Confederate polemic about Reconstruction. Here the film ridiculed the Republican party's attempt to reform the South and make citizens of blacks. It focused on fraud and corruption and illustrated how Yankee bayonets had cruelly forced black rule upon defenseless white Southerners. *The Birth of a Nation* dwelt on the South Carolina legislature, which Griffith depicted as under the control of bare-footed, whisky-drinking, illiterate blacks who cheered lustily at the announcement of a new law allowing the two races to intermarry. All the major black male characters in the film—all of whom were played by white actors in blackface—wanted one thing: a white woman. The most horrendous scene in the film occurrs when a black soldier tries to rape the young virgin sister of the southern protagonist, a Confederate veteran and leader of the local Ku Klux Klan. The young maiden chooses to leap off a cliff rather than lose her honor to the black beast conjured up by Griffith. At the end of the movie the heroic (though behooded) members of the local KKK ride in triumphantly to save the town and the government from the scurrilous carpetbaggers and uppity Negroes.

The Birth of a Nation was based on the best-selling 1905 novel, *The Clansman,* which was written by a southern Negrophobe and Social Gospel minister, Thomas Dixon, Jr. Dixon, even more so than Griffith, was obsessed with black sexuality and determined to legitimize the southern view of Reconstruction. *The Clansman,* which was made into a popular play that toured the country for years, provided the original name for Griffith's film. However, Griffith changed the name of his project from *The Clansman* to *The Birth of a Nation* to drive home a larger point: that the true birth of the nation occurred only when the North and South became united in the quest for white supremacy. A key scene near the end of the film has two former Union soldiers offering their cabin as a refuge to white Southerners who are being pursued by ruthless black militiamen. The former foes then heroically fight off the black soldiers until the Klan rides in to the rescue.

Both Dixon's novel and Griffith's film succeeded beyond the racebaiters' wildest dreams. The press reported that movie audiences "went wild" with excitement and that *The Birth of a Nation* spread through the imagination of the American public like "a prairie fire in a high wind." Examining some sixty reviews of the film, one historian found that a great majority of the critics praised Griffith's cinematic technique and either supported or took a neutral stance on the grotesquely racist content of the film. *Birth* eclipsed all movies at the box office until *Gone with the Wind* (1939). Moreover, and of much more importance, Griffith's master-race film acted as a midwife for the birth of the second Ku Klux Klan, which reappeared just months after its release.

The white reaction to racially charged events such as *The Clansman,* Johnson's defeat of Jeffries, and *The Birth of a Nation* symbolized the raw racism that engulfed early twentieth-century America. Race relations everywhere mucked up the optimistic progressive model of social harmony and civic improvement. So, despite the great promise of progressivism, African Americans experienced the low point of post-emancipation life in the early twentieth century.

To comprehend the meaning of the nadir, we now must consider how white racism shaped the day-to-day lives of African Americans, especially in the South, where almost nine out of ten blacks lived during the Progressive Era. We also need to explore how southern progressives chose to deal with a large black population that was becoming increasingly frustrated and angry.

CHAPTER THREE

African Americans and Southern Progressivism

Most of the noxious racial trends in the South during the 1890s—disfranchisement, segregation, peonage, economic and educational discrimination, and lynching—continued with little or no abatement in the first two decades of the twentieth century. Some of them even intensified during the consolidation of the Jim Crow system. Disfranchising, segregating, race-baiting, and lynching African Americans went hand-in-hand with the most advanced forms of southern progressivism. A hardening caste system inflicted dire social and economic suffering on southern blacks. By the time the United States entered World War I, blacks had fallen even further behind whites.

This chapter treats two aspects of black-white relations in the Progressive Era. First, it describes and analyzes the dismal social and economic conditions imposed on blacks by the white majority, further explaining how these forced circumstances led to debilitating consequences for African Americans that deepened white racism. Second, it examines the racial attitudes and policies of southern politicians—many of them authentic progressives—and makes clear why the Progressive Era marked the "nadir" of African American life in the postslavery era.

What Racism Wrought:
The Social and Economic Conditions of Blacks

In 1903 in *The Souls of Black Folk,* Du Bois lamented that African Americans always measured themselves "by the tape of a [white] world that looks on in amused contempt and pity." Whites forever measured the social and economic status of blacks, often mockingly, and their assessment deepened their racism and contempt and, in some cases, pity, for the black minority. After pressing African Americans down to the lowest rungs of the socio-economic ladder, whites attributed the lack of black social mobility to racial inferiority, which in turn gave whites more reason to push blacks further down and render them more separate and unequal.

It is important to remember that nearly 90 percent of African Americans lived in the Negrophobic South in 1900. By 1920, despite the increasing black migration to the North and West, about 85 percent of black Americans still resided in the South, typically defined as the eleven former Confederate states plus Kentucky, Maryland, Oklahoma, West Virginia, and the District of Columbia (some studies include Missouri). Of the total American population of 76,094,000 in 1900, 11.5 percent or 8,833,000 were black. While blacks accounted for approximately one-third of the southern population, they comprised a majority of nearly 60 percent in Mississippi and South Carolina at the turn of the century. Moreover, in the states of Alabama, Florida, Georgia, and Louisiana, blacks made up more than 40 percent of the population. In this period blacks had a majority in 108 southern counties, some of them by ratios of 3 to 1 or more.

Most southern blacks labored on the land from sunup to sundown to eke out a living in a system stacked against them. In 1900, 50.4 percent of blacks worked in agriculture. In the so-called Black Belt of the Deep South states of Alabama, Georgia, Louisiana, Mississippi, and South Carolina, the number of blacks engaged in agriculture ranged from 53 to 69 percent. Entrapment in a backward plantation system meant that most blacks lived in deep poverty, and historians show that they had little chance of escaping the system. Many black tenant farmers and sharecroppers never turned a profit and simply fell deeper into debt each year, living off cash advances by the landlord or furnishing merchant and paying outrageous rates of interest from 20 to 35 percent. Droughts, floods, and the infestation of the boll weevil also devastated their crops, and rapacious landlords often cheated the ill-educated croppers out of some or all of their rightful profits. The oppressive system of agriculture made a mockery of the work ethic. In *Trouble in Mind* (1998), a study of the Age of Jim Crow, the historian Leon F. Litwack concluded, "A lifetime of hard work, honesty, diligence, frugality, and punctuality might, in fact, leave them [black farmers] worse off than when they began."

Although one of the greatest desires of blacks was to purchase land, three-fourth of them owned not an acre. Although the number of black landowners increased from 1900 to 1910 (it actually peaked in that year), few blacks ever managed to amass enough capital to buy a sufficient amount of productive land on which to prosper. Although 24 percent of southern blacks owned land in 1910, only 13 percent of them had agricultural acreage in the plantation areas of the Deep South. In the heavily populated, rich-soil, Delta region of Mississippi, the ownership of land by blacks dropped from 7.3 percent in 1900 to 2.9 percent in 1920. Moreover, in 1910 the size of the average black farmer's spread was only 47.3 acres (down from 51.2 acres in 1900), while the average white farm was 141.3 acres. Blacks did somewhat better in the Upper South, with a rate of land ownership there hovering around 40 percent. Most blacks, however, lived in the Deep South.

Not only did the poverty produced by the sharecropping-tenant system militate against black land ownership but whites in the plantation South also conspired to keep blacks landless, poor, and deferential. A large but uncalculated amount of land was wrested from blacks by fraud and intimidation. Generally, African Americans had to pass the test of deference to whites before they could purchase good land from the ruling class. In addition, white farmers formed Klan-like organizations and tried to prevent other whites from selling good farmland to blacks. They also singled out for punishment black landowners who seemed too successful. In parts of the South, especially in Mississippi but also in Georgia and Kentucky, night-riders known as Whitecaps practically declared war on black farmers. In 1903 hundreds of disgruntled, economically depressed white farmers attacked black landowners and sharecroppers in Southwest Mississippi. In this case, bands of Whitecaps repeatedly terrorized black farmers, burning their houses and barns and looting, beating, and killing them. It is estimated that before the end of 1903, nearly one thousand blacks fled Amite County, Mississippi, in the wake of the Whitecaps' rides.

Many debt-ridden black farmers sank into peonage or debt slavery. In 1907 A. J. Hoyt, a seasoned veteran of peonage investigations brought in by the federal government, estimated that as many as one-third of all black farmers in Alabama, Georgia, and Mississippi were being held on and forced to work land involuntarily. Most of the southern states had laws making it a crime for tenant farmers or sharecroppers to leave the land if they owed money to the landowner. Such scandalous cases of peonage came to light in the early twentieth century that in 1911 the Supreme Court struck down a section of an Alabama law that fostered the medieval practice. But peonage did not cease until after World War II. The legislatures of the southern states found ways around federal court rulings, all-white juries generally refused to indict member of their race for peonage, and governors often pardoned those who were convicted of the crime. In short, most white Southerners simply did not consider black peonage immoral or illegal.

And if blacks fared badly in agriculture, they did little better in other occupations. Working in a world of severely constricted economic options, more than 90 percent of blacks working outside agriculture did so as blue-collar laborers. In 1910 fewer than 3 percent of blacks in the nation held skilled jobs. Blacks actually lost ground in skilled jobs after the Civil War. Under slavery, planters trained blacks to work as blacksmiths, carpenters, bricklayers, coopers, and tailors, much to the resentment of their free white competitors. In 1865 black skilled craftsmen in the South outnumbered whites by five to one. By the twentieth century, however, whites had begun to replace blacks in skilled jobs. And in new employment areas such as plumbing and electrical work, blacks barely got a foot in the door. As all-white state boards began to license tradesmen in the Progressive Era, less-educated blacks found it more difficult to get qualified for skilled jobs.

Barbering and railroad work provide examples of how black employment in skilled jobs declined. In the 1890s black barbers far outnumbered white ones; in Georgia the ratio was ten to one. By 1920, though, there were twice as many white barbers as black ones. In the postwar South many black barbers established lucrative businesses catering exclusively to affluent whites. With the rise of Jim Crow, however, all black barbers had to restrict their business to the less-affluent members of their own race. In 1910, 104,000 southern blacks worked for the railroads. But as technology made railroad jobs cleaner and safer, whites began to demand and get more of these jobs. For instance, in 1910, 1,000 black switchmen, brakemen, and firemen worked for the railroads in Mississippi; thirty years later fewer than 100 did.

And, regardless of occupation, no matter how skilled black workers were, they always received lower wages than their white counterparts. Indeed, whites warned that equal pay for blacks would unfairly elevate them above Caucasian workers. As a mill superintendent in South Carolina explained, in a stunning display of self interest:

> The colored man does not expend for his living what the white man does. It costs the white laborer more to live. The result is that if the colored laborer received the same wages as the white man, he would have the advantage of the white man, even in his living.

With job discrimination firmly in place, blacks tended to find employment in the dirtiest and most arduously dangerous jobs, ones so forbidding that few whites cared to take them. And white employers were happy to have cheaper black workers in such southern industries as lumber, turpentine, fertilizer, and shipping. In 1910 blacks occupied 24,647 of the 28,647 jobs in the turpentine industry, considered the worst type of employment imaginable. Turpentine workers toiled in isolated camps for long hours in hot and humid weather near insect-infested swamps and could only spend their meager pay in company stores that charged outrageous prices.

Although southern blacks and whites worked together in steel mills, tobacco factories, coal mines, and southern ports, they seldom labored on equal terms. Blacks composed 39.1 percent of the steelworkers in Birmingham, Alabama, in 1907, but they held the unskilled jobs that paid the least and had the most risks for injury and death. Blacks made up about half the work force in tobacco plants but were assigned the heavy manual labor of hauling tobacco and stemming leaves by hand while whites ran and maintained the machines at higher rates of pay. African Americans received greater opportunities in mining due to interracial unionism and the loathsome and risky nature of the job. In 1900 black coal miners totaled 33.7 percent of all the miners in the South. But even in mining, black employment dropped to 23.3 percent in 1920 and would continue downward to 16 percent in 1940. Moreover, black workers were virtually excluded from jobs in the new and rapidly expanding industries of oil and gas.

The same was true of the textile industry. Proponents of the New South believed that cotton mills would provide work for poor whites and rescue them from degradation and the possibility of sinking below blacks. Blacks therefore had to be excluded from the number-one industry in the South. Though ridiculed as poor white trash and "lintheads," mill families made considerably more money than the ordinary dirt farmer. In *The Politics of Whiteness* (2001), the historian Michelle Brattain revealed that three members of a white family working in a cotton mill—the mills hired women and children for lower wages—could earn about $900 a year, significantly more than a white family of tenants or sharecroppers. During a time when 90 percent of rural inhabitants did not have electricity, telephones, and running water, the paternalistic mill owners provided their employees all of these modern amenities plus indoor plumbing, iceboxes, movie theaters, baseball teams, and laundry service. The "politics of whiteness" helped create a southern working class that allowed a higher living standard for marginal whites and raised them well above most African Americans. Blue-collar whites understood well that their economic trump card lay in color identity and racial solidarity, not in forging interracial, class coalitions.

Black women faced even more limited job options than men, and those who did find employment were subject to sexual exploitation. Roughly 80 to 90 percent of black working women seved as cooks, maids, and laundresses and labored ten to fourteen hours a day, six days a week. Excluded from the traditional female-dominated jobs such as clerical work, black women cleaned, cooked, and washed for white people for $2 to $3 a week. In large northern cities, black women, though but a tiny fraction of the population, made up almost 30 percent of the servants by 1920. At the turn of the century, almost 85 percent of black women in Philadelphia were servants. Although Progressive Era society stigmatized all married women who worked outside the home, in 1910 four-fifths of all the female workers in Mississippi were black, and more than one-third of married black women in New York City held jobs, as compared to 4.2 percent of their white counterparts.

The black maid or Mammy was a prized vestige of Old South culture. Whites coveted good, loyal maids and often grew personally attached to them. Black maids not only managed the households of the white middle and upper classes, they practically raised their employers' children, often to the neglect of their own. Black servants relieved white women of household tasks and freed them up to become southern ladies with time to engage in charitable work or become activists for Prohibition, women's suffrage, or better schools and health. As the historian Grace Elizabeth Hale said of southern ladies during the period, "White womanhood was as much a racial construction as a gendered one."

Since black domestics were always in high demand, they were not always as compliant and docile as whites desired. Sometimes the "colored help" could be cantankerous and sullen, even nasty. Aunt Delia of South Carolina recalled, "How many times I spit in the biscuits and peed in the coffee just to get back at them mean white folks." Delia stressed the tendency of men in a white household to abuse black maids sexually. In 1912 a southern live-in maid complained in the *Independent* not only about the long hours and low pay but also the sexual improprieties of her employers. "I believe," the servant protested, "nearly all whites take, and expect to take, undue liberties with their colored female servants—not only the fathers, but in many cases the sons also."

In the main, northern blacks faced even more economic discrimination than did southern blacks. In 1907 Oswald Garrison Villard, an influential New York publisher, confessed, "It is our northern disgrace that a negro finds it harder to get work here than in the South." In the North, the vast majority of blacks worked as dishwashers, busboys, and ditch diggers. More than 60 percent of black men and more than 80 percent of black women worked in menial jobs in northern cities.

In these places the highest position most blacks could aspire to was a steward on a steamship, a headwaiter in a restaurant, or a sleeping-car porter on a train. Until the manpower shortage in World War I opened up factory jobs to blacks, the industrial revolution in the North essentially bypassed African Americans. In the industrial centers blacks lost out to European immigrants, even the most recent arrivals. In 1910, 33 percent of new immigrants held skilled industrial jobs while only 8 percent of blacks did. In Pittsburgh, Irish, Poles, Italians, and Slavs manned the blast furnaces. After 1900 blacks even began to lose custodial and service jobs to immigrants. In 1906 the swank Plankinton House in Milwaukee hired Greek waiters to replace its African Americans servers. And across the North the rich began to replace their black cooks with French chefs and their dark-complexioned butlers with English ones. Thus, in the relatively prosperous Progressive Era, northern blacks as a group experienced little or no upward social mobility.

African American workers also had to contend with the hostility of white-controlled labor unions. Although Samuel Gompers, the perennial president of the powerful American Federation of Labor, spoke out against the exclusion of blacks from unions in the 1890s, he soon acquiesced in barring them altogether or accepting segregated locals. Adding to the anti-black hostility of unions was the use by callous employers of job-hungry blacks as strikebreakers. To be sure, the liberal use of "nigger scabs" by industrialists incited racial violence and weakened the labor movement.

Railroad unions were among the worst discriminators. All four primary railroad unions restricted membership to whites only, and white railroad workers did everything conceivable to force railroad companies to replace black workers with higher paid white ones. In 1899 a spokesman for the Brotherhood of Railway Trainmen in Little Rock pleaded with the managers of the Arkansas and Choctow Railroad, "We ask nothing out of reason and as citizens and taxpayers, as contributors to the general welfare, we think we are right in asking that we be preferred over cheaper negro labor." When the railroads did not comply with the wishes of white workers, they often went on strike and attacked black workers. In 1911 white railroad men killed ten black firemen who refused to stop working for the Cincinnati,

New Orleans, and Texas Pacific Railroad. During a 1909 railroad strike in Georgia, an arbitration board recommended equal pay for blacks, not out of a sense of equity but because they knew that the railroads would not hire blacks if compensation for both races were identical.

Despite the ingrained racism of most unions, a few accepted African Americans into their ranks and made attempts to forge class solidarity across the color line, most notably the United Mine Workers (UMW) and the Longshoremen's Association. More than half of all black unionists were UMW members, and one-third of all southern miners were black. But interracial unionism proved extremely hard to sustain with the onset of Jim Crow. The UMW constantly had to deny that it was promoting social equality, which it definitely was not. Coal towns were just as segregated as any other southern locales, for the races were separated in schools, churches, saloons, lodges, bands, and athletic teams. White unionist newspapers even played the race card by accusing mining companies of fostering integration and social equality. Of the seven leadership positions in the Alabama locals, four automatically went to whites, despite the fact that 54 percent of miners in the state were black. Nationally, blacks held but a few token offices in the UMW hierarchy. What was true for the UMW largely applied to the Longshoremen's Association, which was about one-third black.

The poor economic opportunities for blacks as a group translated into widespread poverty accompanied by dilapidated housing, poor health, family instability, a high rate of crime, and other forms of social pathology. In the southern countryside, large black families lived in crude, one-room log huts that had no glass or screens in the windows and only dirt for floors. The living space of a typical sharecropper's house was perhaps 200 square feet—about the same as that of a living room in a modest suburban home today. Black farm families lived primarily on a monotonous diet of fatback (pork), corn bread, and molasses that left children deficient in protein and vitamins and therefore subject to chronic anemia and vitamin-deficiency diseases.

The quality of housing urban blacks enjoyed was often no better than it was on the farm, and sometimes it was far worse. By 1900,

27.4 percent of all African Americans lived in cities, and fully one-third of the urban population in the South was African American. Almost every town or city in the South with a sizeable black population had a section the whites called called "Bucktown," "Niggertown," "Black Bottom," "Coon Town," "Smoke Town," "Hog Alley," or some such insulting reference. Not surprisingly the black sections of towns typically lacked paved streets, water and sewage systems, streets lights, and other city services. A 1909 report on Louisville found that 53 percent of blacks lived in dilapidated housing, as opposed to 15 percent of foreign-born whites. A northern minister visiting the South exclaimed that "the wretchedness is pathetic and the poverty colossal." The conditions in which urban blacks lived was a testament to the power of racism and the lack of power by African Americans.

Between 1890 and 1910 some 200,000 blacks, tired of waiting for a better life in the South, migrated to the North and the West. In 1900 Washington, D.C., had the largest black population of any northern city with 86,000; Baltimore, Philadelphia, and New York City followed close behind with more than 50,000 each. By 1920 all of these cities, plus Chicago, had more than 100,000 black residents. As southern migration to northern cities accelerated after 1900, large black ghettos formed. Before 1900 most blacks in northern urban centers lived widely scattered about in predominantly white wards or census tracts. But between 1900 and 1920 residential segregation intensified as a flood of mostly uneducated and rural southern blacks streamed into northern cities. By 1920 blacks were largely concentrated in one or two areas of a given city. For example, two-thirds of all blacks in New York City resided in Harlem by this time.

Urban blacks sank quickly into poverty because of low wages and relatively high rents—the black poet Langston Hughes sarcastically noted that the black ghetto was a place "where a nickel costs a dime." Slum landlords charged higher rent to blacks than whites because housing for African Americans was in short supply and great demand. And since blacks had little choice in housing, landlords had little incentive to maintain rental property. Housing also deteriorated as poor blacks took in boarders (frequently young, single, transient males) to help pay the rent. Only slightly more than one-fifth of African Americans owned homes in 1910, as compared to about one-half of all whites. Even new immigrants in northern cities had a higher percentage of home ownership than did blacks.

And whether in shanty towns, big city slums, or rude and isolated huts in the countryside, blacks generally suffered from poor health. Poverty, poor and often inadequate diets, the lack of social services and medical care, the psychological pressure of being a member of a detested race, and the thoroughly racist justice system gave the average black male a life expectancy of 32.5 years at the turn of the century, 16 years fewer than his white counterpart. In South Carolina, 16 percent of black babies died before reaching the age of one, as compared to 8.6 percent for whites. In Boston and Washington, D.C., 32 percent of black babies never saw their first birthday. In 1915 in Cleveland, the rate of death among blacks from pneumonia was more than double that of whites and more than four times as many blacks died of tuberculosis. Tens of thousands of Southerners of both races fell victim to pellagra and rickets, both of which are caused by the lack of proper nutrition. An equally large number of Southerners fell victim to the debilitating parasite known as hookworm. The black rate of syphilis, a crippling and deadly disease before the use of penicillin, was eight times that of whites. And the paucity of black physicians and nurses made a bad situation worse. Overall, the death rate for blacks nationally was double that of whites.

The dismal social and economic conditions blacks faced inevitably affected family life. Statistics for the Progressive Era show that black families were less stable than white ones or even those of economically depressed and culturally shocked immigrants just off the boat. The high death rate of black males meant that about one-fifth of black women between the ages of 33 and 45 were widows. Single females headed 19.4 percent of black households in Chicago, 23.9 percent in New York City, and 33.7 percent in urban Georgia. With more than 80 percent of all urban black women working outside the home, black children often received little supervision, which resulted in higher rates (as compared to whites) of juvenile delinquency. And the number of black children born out of wedlock was 12.6 percent as opposed to the native white rate of 1.7 percent and an immigrant rate of 5.2 percent. Although the rate of black illegitimacy seems low compared to current rates—or even the 25 percent cited by the urbanologist (and later senator from New York) Daniel Moynihan in his controversial book, *The Negro Family* (1965)—the "black multiple" was the key statistic. In 1910 the number of black births outside wedlock was 7.41 higher than that of native whites and 2.42 higher than that of recent immigrants.

Contemporary black social scientists did not deny the precariousness of the black family. In *Shadow of the Plantation* (1930), the noted sociologist Charles S. Johnson of Fisk University found that no stigma attached to premarital pregnancy in the rural black communities of the Deep South. "There is, in a sense," he said, "no such thing as illegitimacy in this community." In *The Philadelphia Negro* (1899), Du Bois revealed a high rate of promiscuity and illegitimacy among the working class in the Seventh Ward of Philadelphia. "The lax moral habits of the slave regime still show themselves in a large amount of cohabitation without marriage," Du Bois observed. "The great weakness of the Negro family," he continued, "is still the lack of respect for the marriage bond, inconsiderate entrance into it, and bad household economy and family government. Sexual looseness then arises as a secondary consequence, bringing adultery and prostitution in its train." He added that the "unhealthy tone" of social life among proletarian blacks was also disturbingly evident in the black middle class. In conclusion Du Bois attributed family instability and moral laxity to an especially oppressive history and a current bad environment. But for white scholars of the day, these negative findings simply provided more evidence to back their theories of innate black inferiority.

Another aspect of black life universally deplored and feared by whites, and not a few blacks, was crime. White newspapers and magazines concentrated their scanty coverage of African Americans on highly sensationalized stories about black crime, and southern demagogues ranted endlessly about the rising rate of criminality among African Americans. Since the criminal justice system blatantly discriminated against blacks, statistics about black crime in the Progressive Era must be viewed skeptically. Still, whites did not just imagine black crime, nor did they fabricate murder rates for blacks. The homicide rate for blacks in 1920 was about seven times that of whites. As with the subjects of family stability and morality, African American scholars and leaders did not deny the growing problem of black crime. A massive statistical report on the "Negro Population" compiled by three black employees of the Department of Commerce in 1915 revealed that the 2 percent of the northern population that was black committed 26.1 of all the "grave homicides" and that the 33.3 percent of the southern population that was black committed 74.4 percent of the murders.

Du Bois and other African American leaders feared that the high incidence of crime in their communities would retard their efforts to spur black advance in American society. Du Bois denounced the high rates of robbery, burglary, gambling, prostitution, drug use, and violence among city blacks, concluding that the signs of "dissoluteness and crime are more conspicuous than those of poverty." As with the black family, Du Bois attributed the high black crime rate to historical and sociological factors, among them the heritage of slavery, white racism, the pathological surroundings of the slums, the lack of job opportunities, resentment and hopelessness among black communities, and disorganized social life. Other scholars have stressed that blacks had so little respect for the law precisely because the criminal justice system treated them so unfairly. They have explained black-on-black violence as African Americans taking out their bitter anger against whites and society on their own kind. Another factor cited as a cause of black vice and crime was the ubiquitous Red Light district, which was usually located either within or near the boundaries of the black section of town. The overwhelming majority of whites paid no attention to such explanations of black crime and continued to believe that African Americans were inherently violent and criminal.

Some blacks managed to avoid the poverty and squalor that was the lot of most African Americans, but the black middle class was pathetically small. And the black upper class, if measured by wealth, hardly existed. In 1910 no more than 2 to 3 percent of African Americans held white-collar jobs, and most of those positions had resulted from segregation. That is, black teachers and black ministers owed their employment to the creation and maintenance of all-black schools and churches. There were, however, pitifully few black physicians, dentists, lawyers, and other professionals. The only white-collar job in which blacks were proportionately over-represented was the ministry. In 1910 the nation had one black doctor for every 3,194 African Americans, while the figure for whites was one for every 553 people. Eighty-eight counties in Georgia had no black doctors. Moreover, black physicians outnumbered black dentists six to one.

To be certain, the shortage of black lawyers in the nation further lessened the chances of African Americans in securing equal justice. In 1910 there were only 795 black lawyers in the United States, or 0.8 percent of the total number. Racism and segregation made it difficult for black lawyers to practice in the South, and many blacks considered it prudent to have a white lawyer when appearing in a southern court. The percentage of southern black lawyers actually declined between 1910 and 1940. In 1900 there were twenty-four black lawyers in Mississippi, but only five in 1935. In general, black professionals maintained marginal practices because of their economically strapped clientele. As with white doctors and dentists, blacks often assumed that white lawyers had better training and tended to seek them out.

One advantage of segregation was that it created opportunities for black businesspeople. Those entrepreneurs who fulfilled the economic needs of the segregated black community could and did prosper. In her comprehensive, richly researched work, *The History of Black Business* (1998), Judith E. K. Walker argued that the rise of black corporate America in the period between 1900 and the Great Depression represented "a lost page in the African American experience" and in fact constituted "the golden age of black business activity." Despite the extreme racism of the time, some black businesses made substantial progress during this era. The most important advances came from corporate entities that sold stock to raise capital, such as those in insurance, banking, and real estate.

Since white insurance companies either charged African American clients more than their white ones or refused to issue them policies at all, black-owned insurance companies were among the most numerous and successful enterprises. Among the richest black men in America was John Merrick, a former slave, brick mason, and barber who founded the North Carolina Mutual Insurance Company in 1899, the largest concern in this sector of the black economy. At his death in 1927, Merrick was worth $500,000. Second to North Carolina Mutual was the Atlanta Life Insurance, founded by Alonzo Franklin Herndon, who, like Merrick, had been born a slave.

Several national business organizations came into being early in the twentieth century, including the National Bankers Association, the National Association of Negro Insurance Companies, and the National Association of Funeral Directors. In 1912 there were sixty-four black-owned banks in America. Several African Americans gained fortunes in real estate and employed substantial numbers of their race. Founded in 1900, the Metropolitan Mercantile and Reality Company was valued at $400,000 in 1904, and it employed three hundred people. The Memphis businessman Robert Church, the father of the crusading civil rights advocate Mary Church Terrill, accrued a fortune in real estate. Having no competition from whites and providing a necessary service, black morticians usually stood among the economic elite of the black community. Those who catered to the grooming needs of blacks could also prosper. After discovering a hair straightening process around 1905, Madame C. J. Walker, a poor washerwoman who migrated from her birthplace in Louisiana to St. Louis, Missouri, set up shop in Indianapolis and became a near millionaire and perhaps the richest black person in America at her death in 1919.

The National Negro Business League, founded by Booker T. Washington in 1900, encouraged and celebrated black entrepreneurship. Furthermore, Du Bois constantly stressed a strong "racial economy" and exhorted blacks to patronize businesses in their own neighborhood. Both men celebrated commercial development in Atlanta, which in 1911 had two thousand black-owned businesses, including one bank, three insurance companies, twelve drugstores, eighty-three barbershops, and eighty-five groceries. Certain cities provided models of inspired business activity. The business sections of both Durham, North Carolina, and Tulsa, Oklahoma, were proudly known as "the Negro Wall Street."

In the main, though, most businesses owned and run by African Americans were shaky enterprises and notoriously undercapitalized. Du Bois estimated that 78 percent of all black concerns were capitalized at less than $500. Mostly small, mom-and-pop grocery stores and restaurants, 80 percent of black businesses had no paid employees in the Progressive Era. Many black banks were small and wobbly in good times and faltered or folded in bad ones. Even many of the largest and seemingly most secure concerns did not survive a financial panic like that of 1907, or even a short depression such as the one that occurred shortly after World War I. The Great Depression was, of course, devastating for black businesses. As to industrial magnates, no black Carnegies, Rockefellers, and Vanderbilts existed.

While any economic progress blacks made in the face of relentless white racism was remarkable, the economic lot of African Americans was not an abstract matter of the glass being half-full or half-empty. In truth, there was, relatively speaking, hardly a trickle in the black glass in the early twentieth century, all the way up to World War II.

Had politically powerless, economically destitute, and ill-educated African Americans been staunchly unified in purpose, they might have been able to increase their limited chances for upward social mobility. Studies of cities, states, and regions, however, show serious class and color divisions among African Americans. The small black middle class was ambivalent about political activity and segregation, and African American professionals seldom supported black unionists. Established northern blacks railed against the southern "riff-raff" that flooded into northern cities, charging that their crude and criminal behavior only increased racism. T. Thomas Fortune groused in the *New York Age,* "Many of the worthless people of the race are making their way northward."

In addition, color prejudice was rife among African Americans. The black elite, consisting primarily of light-skinned mulattoes, formed exclusive clubs and societies that excluded those with dark skin. Even the church, the most cohesive thread in the black community, divided along class, color, and denominational lines. African Americans could not even agree on what they should be called. Should they be known as *colored, black, Afro-American,* or *Negro*? Du Bois favored the term *Negro* (generally not capitalized during the Progressive Era except by a few racial liberals), but he became a leader of the National Association for the Advancement of Colored People (see Chapter Five).

As anyone can see from the preceding, those who would move African Americans forward in the Progressive Era faced a herculean task. This was particularly true in the South, even though the southern states experienced a genuine Progressive Movement like the rest of the nation.

Southern Progressivism and Race

Southern progressivism in many ways mirrored the reform movement going on in other parts of the United States. But owing to the agricultural nature of the South and the presence there of large numbers of African Americans, southern reform had a unique flavor. As in the North and West, in the South progressives represented a clash of many disparate interest groups that were reacting to the problems of industrialization and urbanization. Yet southern progressivism was somewhat schizoid in that it was an amalgam of two strands of reform. One strand of the movement was led by agrarians or post-Populists who stressed trust busting, the regulation of railroads, banking reform, inflation of the money supply, more democracy, and assistance to poor farmers. The other strand marched to the tune of urban elites, such as lawyers, teachers, ministers, and businesspeople, and they emphasized clean, efficient government, a better system of education, and improvements in health care. As the historian Dewey W. Grantham put it, the educated elite wanted "a more orderly and cohesive community." Historians have differed about which group of progressives dominated, but it is clear that the balance of these two different forces varied significantly from state to state. On the whole, southern progressivism was probably weaker than the northern variety on social justice, support for labor unions, and women's suffrage, but it led the nation in the quest for Prohibition and held its own in calling for the regulation of big business. Both branches of southern progressivism, like the national movement, sought a larger and more active government.

Above all, southern progressives of all kinds emphatically supported white supremacy, and their rule proved detrimental to African Americans on virtually every issue. Furthermore, because southern progressives gained power in Washington in the 1910s, they pursued policies that harmed the other 10 percent of blacks who lived north of the Mason-Dixon line.

Two kinds of white supremacists competed for the leadership of southern progressivism: radicals and moderates. Of the two kinds, the radicals wielded much more power and influence. "Pitchfork" Ben Tillman typified the radical racists in the Progressive Era. As shown earlier, Governor Tillman reconstructed the sturdy edifice of white supremacy in South Carolina in the 1890s. A demagogic, pseudo-reformer, he appeased poor white farmers not with genuine Populistic reforms but by disfranchising blacks, encouraging the lynching of alleged black rapists, and condemning black education as a waste of money.

During his long Senate career from 1895 to 1918, Tillman supported the progressive agrarian William Jennings Bryan and stumped for free silver, railroad regulation, and anti-trust legislation. On the issue of race, though, Senator Tillman was as reactionary as he had been as a governor. Once in Washington he boldly called for the outright repeal of the Fourteenth and Fifteenth Amendments. On the Senate floor he explained how South Carolina disfranchised blacks: "We stuffed ballot boxes. We shot them. We are not ashamed of it. . . . [W]e called a Constitutional Convention, and we eliminated . . . all of the colored people whom we could under the fourteenth and fifteenth amendments." Tillman used every parliamentary trick available to delay presidential appointments of blacks, no matter how minor the post.

Tillman was one of several southern politicians who launched a racial offensive in the North around the turn of the century. He became a well-paid, popular speaker on the Chautauqua lecture circuit where he regularly preached to the North that blacks constituted a savage, uncivilized race that "must remain subordinate or be exterminated." Tillman constantly harped on the threat of interracial marriage, predicting the inevitability of "big buck negroes marrying white women and no law [in the North] to prevent it." He taunted Yankees about their treatment of blacks. "The brotherhood of man exists no longer," he said, "because you shoot negroes in Illinois . . . and we shoot them in South Carolina. You do not love them any better than we do."

White supremacy was expressed and pursued just as flamboyantly by southern politicians who were genuine reformers. James Vardaman provides a good example. Serving as governor of Mississippi from 1904 to 1908, Vardaman favored the election of judges (as opposed to their appointment by governors), primary elections, anti-trust legislation, the regulation of railroads, better roads, the abolition of the convict lease system, and the establishment of a state commission of agriculture. Every bit as colorful and eccentric as Tillman, Vardaman became know as "the White Chief" because he invariably wore immaculate white suits, cowboy boots, and a Stetson hat that adorned the long hair falling down to his shoulders. Although African Americans had been eliminated from Mississippi politics in the 1890s, Vardaman never missed a chance to promise that "white people are going to rule this country and they are not going to let niggers hold office." While he was governor, Mississippi segregated railroads and streetcars and passed a vagrancy law so strict that it consigned many blacks to peonage.

Like Tillman, Vardaman proclaimed that blacks were incapable of higher learning and citizenship. "I am just as much opposed to Booker Washington as a voter, with all his Anglo-Saxon reinforcements," he blared, "as I am to the coconut-headed, chocolate-colored, typical little coon, Andy Dotson, who blacks my shoes every morning. Neither is fit to perform the supreme function of citizenship." In a state with a black majority, Vardaman pitched his campaigns to the fears and hatreds of whites. He saw Mississippi as a place of raw racial struggle where instincts for survival took precedence over law, morality, and common decency. Speaking of the perceived black menace, he said, "We do not stop when we see a wolf to find if it will kill before disposing of it, but assume that it will."

Tillman and Vardaman had a kindred soul in Jeff Davis of Arkansas. Elected governor of Arkansas in 1900, Davis seduced lower-class whites with his theatrical, race-baiting campaigns. He was reelected twice before going to the Senate, where he served from 1907 until his death in 1913. As had Vardaman, Davis took advantage of the new primary system to master Arkansas politics (this system entrusted registered voters to nominate candidates for public office rather than a caucus of scheming politicians in a smoke-filled room, often assisted by the movers and shakers of the business world). Northern reformers saw primaries as a democratic reform to end boss-ridden politics, but primary elections in the South became all-out brawls between competing factions of the Democratic party—by this point, of course, the general elections were no more than formalities because no Republican candidate stood a chance of victory and many Democratic primary winners ran uncontested by a Republican challenger—and the candidate who appeared the most folksy, entertaining, and racist was king. In 1900 Davis won 74 of the 75 county primaries in Arkansas by targeting evil "Yankee trusts" and calling his opponents soft on blacks. On the campaign trail, Davis described blacks as brutal criminals and told whites "that 'nigger' domination will never prevail in this beautiful Southland of yours, as long as shotguns and rifles lie around loose, and we are able to pull the trigger." Davis's melodramatic politics also provided comic relief for isolated and fun-starved Arkansans. Variously called the "Wild Ass of the Ozarks" and the "Karl Marx for Hillbillies," the governor would tell his constituents:

> If you red-necks and hillbillies ever come to Little Rock, be sure and come to see me. . . . If I am not there tell my wife . . . that you are my friend and belong to the sunburned sons of toil. Tell her to give you hog jowls and turnip greens. She may be busy making soap, but that will be all right.

Despite their attempts to pretend kinship with the hard-scrabble sons of toil, Tillman, Vardaman, and Davis came from substantial backgrounds and had good educations.

A parade of radical white supremacists who enacted many progressive reforms followed the path of Tillman, Vardaman, and Davis, usually serving as legislators and governors before moving on to Congress. Cole Blease of South Carolina was, if possible, more anti-black than Tillman, his mentor. Blease was elected governor in 1910 and later served in the Senate. In Mississippi Theodore G. Bilbo, arguably more viciously racist than Vardaman, served as governor of Mississippi from 1910 to 1914 and spread a "Bilbonic plague" over the state before moving to the Senate. Another notable race-baiter was the Alabamian J. Thomas Heflin, who served in House of Representatives from 1904 to 1920 and unleashed some of the most extreme anti-Catholic, anti-Semitic, and anti-black diatribes that Americans heard in this especially bigoted time.

Southern race-baiters relied on a wealth of regional literature to lend pseudo-scholarly support to their harangues, though they also took particular delight in quoting racist Yankee writers. They drew upon many of the numerous "black menace" books that found reputable publishers in the North, such as the novels of Thomas Dixon. On the northern lecture circuit, Vardaman often alluded to *The Color Line: A Brief in Behalf of the Unborn* (1905), an antiblack book authored by William B. Smith, a philosophy and mathematics professor at Tulane University. Other blunt and influential assaults on blacks found useful by race-baiters were Thomas Nelson Page, *The Negro: The Southerner's Problem* (1904); Alfred H. Stone, *Studies in the American Race Problem* (1908); Howard Odum, *Social and Mental Traits of the Negro* (1910); and Thomas Pearce Bailey, *Race Orthodoxy in the South* (1914). Bailey, a professor of psychology at the University of Mississippi, expressed supreme confidence that southern orthodoxy had become the national norm when he asked rhetorically, "Does not the South perceive that all of the fire has gone out of the Northern philanthropic fight for the rights of man?" Tauntingly, Bailey declared, *"The North has surrendered!"*

Although moderate white supremacists represented a minority point of view in the South, they presented such a stark contrast to the fire-eating demagogues that racially cautious northern reformers lionized these more-restrained Southerners to soften the image of the South. The moderates, mostly professionals who earned their living as ministers, professors, and journalists, strongly supported segregation and disfranchisement. They differed from radicals primarily in arguing that blacks were educable and in condemning the justice system and lynching. In contrast to the philippics of the Vardamans and Tillmans, moderates spoke in polite, paternalistic language and supported Booker T. Washington.

Edgar Gardner Murphy, an Episcopal minister and a member of the Social Gospel movement, typified the southern moderate. An Arkansan by birth, Murphy became pastor of the St. John's Episcopal Church in Montgomery, Alabama, in 1898. After ministering in the Upper South and the North, the young minister was shocked by the stark racism of Alabama. Gentle, compassionate, and intellectual, Murphy sought a just and peaceful solution to the race problem. On his arrival in Alabama, he spoke out strongly against the unfair justice system and lynching.

Still, Murphy could not shake his southern upbringing or think outside the parameters of Jim Crow. Murphy not only supported disfranchisement of blacks, but he, like Tillman, favored the repeal of the Fifteenth Amendment. Portraying blacks as "a backward and essentially unassimilable people," he heartily approved legal segregation. Unlike the radicals, though, Murphy stressed the *equal* as well as the separate in Jim Crow. As for interracial unions, he was conventional in cringing at the idea of miscegenation. In 1904 Murphy published his views in *The Present South,* a book wildly acclaimed by northern progressives who fantasized about the "best men" ruling the South.

But they did not. Murphy in fact served as an apologist for the white South and proved to be one of the most effective spokesmen for the Jim Crow system. By reassuring the North that a truly "separate but equal" racial arrangement would eventually prevail, Murphy helped create a national consensus for Jim Crow. He could not see that his brand of paternalistic inequality, when cooked in a neo-Confederate pot, would only brew further exploitation of African Americans. As the historian Bruce Clayton put it, Murphy "demanded the impossible—that the white South, while it kept the Negro ignorant, politically powerless, and socially isolated, be tolerant and humane in its 'dealing with him.'"

Mild-mannered critics like Murphy took pains not to offend the South because the slightest censure of the racial status quo could provoke a furious response from the Jim Crow establishment. For instance, Andrew Sledd, a young Methodist minister from Virginia who had an M.A. in Greek from Harvard and a Ph.D. in Latin from Yale, quickly ran into trouble when he became a professor of Latin at Emory College in Oxford, Georgia. His sojourn in the North and his witnessing of a savage lynching in the South softened his orthodox racial views. In 1902 Sledd published an article in the *Atlantic Monthly* that condemned lynching, defended equal justice, and argued that black Americans had "inalienable rights." The article created an angry uproar, and under pressure Sledd offered his resignation, which the president and the board of Emory eagerly accepted.

A similar event brought grief to the historian John Spencer Bassett of Trinity College (later Duke University). When Bassett published an article in the *South Atlantic Quarterly* in 1903 that questioned the caste system and touted Booker T. Washington as one of the two greatest Southerners of the nineteenth century—the other being Robert E. Lee—whites in North Carolina called for the head of the "nigger lover." The president of Trinity, John C. Kilgo, courageously stood by Bassett and the right of free speech, and the Board of Trustees voted to retain the historian. The board, however, issued a statement saying that Bassett "does not believe in, nor does he teach social equality." Indeed, he did not. Believing devoutly in black inferiority, Bassett described the very thought of black suffrage as "nauseating." But animosity toward Bassett still lingered in North Carolina, and in 1905 he escaped the South by accepting a teaching post at Smith College in Massachusetts.

Bassett was not alone in choosing exile. Several notable southern moderates fled the South, none more esteemed than Walter Hines Page of North Carolina, who served as ambassador to Britain under President Wilson. A mild critic of southern racial practices, Page edited the prestigious *Atlantic Monthly* and the progressive magazine *The World's Work,* and he co-founded the publishing house of Doubleday, Page, and Company. Although he published Washington's *Up From Slavery,* he also eagerly printed the trilogy of luridly racist novels by his fellow North Carolinian Thomas Dixon, as well as several other racist tracts. The longer Page resided in the North, the less he said about race.

Self-serving northern fantasies aside, the "best men" of the South did not decide the fate of blacks. Nor were the best men all that enlightened about black-white relations. Since the views of radical white supremacists reflected majority thought in the South, it was they who determined the shape of race relations. The racist firebrands who constructed the Jim Crow South held five important common ideas that led to the increased oppression of African Americans. What follows is a brief examination of these consequential notions.

1. The New Black Threat:

The racial radicals of the South believed that a dangerous "new Negro" had emerged, threatening white supremacy and racial harmony. They claimed that a new generation of postslavery blacks had shed their deferential and happy demeanor and become dangerously sullen and resentful toward whites. This attitudinal change, they charged, had occasioned a black crime wave. The radicals also argued that the liberal use of alcohol and drugs had emboldened blacks to become bumptious and reckless. On the lecture circuit in the North, Senator Vardaman repeated a speech called "The Impending Crisis" in which he denounced rising black insolence and warned that race relations teetered "on the edge of a volcano." He sounded the alarm about "a restless younger generation of negroes" who traveled southern roads and posed a threat to white womanhood. Senator Tillman said that whites "must hunt these creatures down with the same terrified vigor and perseverance that we would look for tigers and bears" and shoot them "as we would shoot wild beasts."

Although Tillman exhibited severe symptoms of the rape complex, his suspicions about increasing black militancy were not without foundation, for some blacks did resist the new order. They boycotted segregated streetcars and fought disfranchisement. Frederick Douglass and Walter White believed that the increase in lynching stemmed from whites' reaction to blacks' progress and resistance. Blacks increasingly armed themselves and sometimes used their weapons on whites. In 1906 in Wiggins, Mississippi, armed blacks exchanged gunfire with a white mob in an attempt to prevent a lynching. Out of earshot of whites, blacks expressed bitterness and disdain for their oppressors, calling them "rednecks," "peckerwoods," and "crackers." But most blacks learned to conceal their anger and resentment by averting their eyes, shuffling their feet, and feigning humility before whites. Black parents taught their children to be deferential toward whites—as a survival tactic. Many of those who had trouble hiding their true feelings found it prudent to leave the South.

An angry Robert Charles, however, stayed in the South, where he suffered a grisly fate, as did scores of other "uppity" blacks. Charles grew up in Copiah County, Mississippi, where the white fusionist Print Matthews had been gunned down at the polls in 1883. As a young unskilled worker, Charles moved around the state looking for work. He also armed himself with a rifle and a handgun, got in several scrapes with the law, and even had a shootout with a white man over a stolen pistol. One step ahead of the law, Charles moved to New Orleans at the age of thirty-four. There he got a job, became a stylish dresser, and enjoyed the nightlife of the lively, vice-ridden city. Indicative of

his politics, he began to peddle the *Voice of Missions,* the black-na-
tionalist magazine of Bishop Henry Turner. One July evening in 1900
as the nattily dressed Charles waited on the street for his date to ar-
rive, a white policeman needlessly hassled him. When Charles resisted, the policeman fired his pistol at him. Charles pulled out his
own pistol and returned fire, wounding the policeman. During the
subsequent attempts by the police to capture Charles, he barricaded
himself at two different sites and used his personal arsenal to shoot
twenty-seven whites, killing seven, four of them policemen. The aveng-
ing mob finally forced Charles out of the building with fire and brutally killed him. The incident triggered the New Orleans race riot of
1900 in which an enraged mob killed two blacks and wounded fifteen
others. To some in the black community, Charles was a hero, though
one celebrated secretly. The white press described Charles as a deranged "brute," a "bad nigger," and a "bloodthirsty champion of African supremacy."

To be sure, blacks such as Charles scared whites. However, what
frightened them as much, if not more, was the progress that ambi-
tious, law-abiding blacks managed to make in a system designed to
make them fail. Whites thus singled out aggressive, achieving blacks
for humiliation and punishment, as already illustrated by the way the
Whitecaps dealt with successful black farmers in Mississippi and
Georgia. Any black farmer prosperous enough to own a mule or two
might find their animals poisoned by envious poor whites. Because
Anthony P. Crawford was the largest black landowner in the county
surrounding Abbeville, Georgia, and was proud and independent, he
was a marked man. When he reportedly cursed a white merchant for
offering him an inadequate price for his cotton, the businessman attacked him with an ax handle. Although Crawford did not retaliate
against the merchant, he was arrested and placed in jail. An Abbeville
banker said, "Crawford was insolent and he deserved a thrashing."
He got more than that. When Crawford was released from jail, a mob
attacked and seriously beat him. Returned to jail for his protection,
the black farmer was later removed from his cell and lynched. Across
the South, whites assaulted blacks like Crawford or drove them out of
town when they became too successful, as they did in the Wilmington
race riot of 1898.

Whites harassed blacks for exhibiting what would be enviable behavior by Caucasians. Whites grew suspicious of blacks who dressed well and changed jobs or residences in order to better themselves. Benjamin Mays, who later served as president of Morehouse College and become a mentor to Martin Luther King, Jr., remembered how he was attacked in his small-town, South Carolina post office as he waited quietly in line for mail. A local physician suddenly rushed at Mays and struck him, muttering that the clean, dignified, and well-dressed black youth was "trying to look too good anyway." A southern black man found himself in trouble in Houston after being accused of wearing a "Jack Johnson plaid suit" and looking like a "Yankee Nigger." The man apologized profusely to his white tormentors and explained that his job at the circus required him to wear such a suit.

2. The Completion of Disfranchisement

All white supremacists insisted that blacks be removed from politics as a way of dealing with the new black threat. The disfranchisement of blacks that began in Mississippi, South Carolina, and Louisiana in the 1890s went forward in the remaining southern states in the Progressive Era. The states of Alabama, North Carolina, Virginia, Georgia, and the new state of Oklahoma (1907), which was only 10 percent black, amended their constitutions to prevent blacks from voting through the devices of reading and understanding tests and grandfather clauses. Arkansas, Florida, Tennessee, and Texas achieved disfranchisement of most blacks without constitutional changes by the use of poll taxes and secret ballots (another progressive reform that worked against illiterate voters).

Whites sold the disfranchisement of blacks as a progressive measure designed to end voting fraud, bribery, and disorder by cleansing "depraved and ignorant" blacks from the ballot. Although the disfranchising devices could have disfranchised depraved and ignorant whites, politicians had to promise that they would not. When Carter Glass, a future Virginia Senator and the architect of the Federal Reserve Act, was asked how, other than by fraud, all black voters could be eliminated without sacrificing one single white vote, he replied that it "will be discrimination within the letter of the law, and not in violation of the law." Glass further explained: "Discrimination! Why, that is exactly what we propose; that, exactly, is what this Convention was called for . . . to remove every negro voter who can be gotten rid of, legally, without materially impairing the numerical strength of the white electorate."

Disfranchisement campaigns that demonized blacks inevitably led to assaults on them. This fact was illustrated in Georgia in 1906 when black suffrage became the central issue in a long, grueling Democratic primary for the governorship. The election pitted Hoke Smith, a progressive, against Clark Howell, a conservative. Smith, a former supporter of black suffrage, now declared that it had to cease in order "to end the disgraceful spectacle of the wholesale buying and selling of Negro votes. . . ." Howell argued accurately that amending the state constitution to disfranchise blacks was unnecessary because Georgia had already essentially ended black suffrage by other means. Both candidates accused each other of being soft on African Americans, and Smith, who also campaigned for Prohibition, blamed blacks for previous defeats in trying to dry up Atlanta and surrounding areas. Tom Watson, the old Populist black ally, had now become one of the worst race-baiters in Dixie and stirred up whites to vote for Smith and disfranchisement.

Although it was the question of black suffrage that increased racial tensions, it was the issue of rape that led to a bloody race riot in Atlanta. Just before the fall election, a play based on Thomas Dixon's novel, *The Clansman,* inflamed white minds about black sexuality. As in the weeks before the 1898 Wilmington race riot, advocates of disfranchisement in Georgia exaggerated and sensationalized stories about black men raping white women. Prohibitionists linked sexual assaults on white women to black drunkenness. Just before the riot erupted, several newspapers ran extra editions bemoaning the "torrid wave of black lust and fiendishness," and the *Atlanta News* suggested the need for a "war of extermination." On Saturday evening, September 22, a white man held aloft a newspaper that announced the "THIRD ASSAULT" on white women and shouted, "Are white men going to stand for this?" On the edge of the Red Light district near the black section of the city, a gathering white mob responded, "No, Save our Women! Kill the niggers!" Whites then began to roam the streets assaulting any blacks they could find. The riot raged throughout the weekend and into the middle of the next week, resulting in the deaths of about 25 blacks and the wounding or injuring of 150. Blacks resisted when they could and wounded 10 whites.

3. The Rise of Jim Crow Laws

Stripping blacks of political power was not enough for whites; it was only a beginning. Taking away the black vote, of course, made it easier to enact a barrage of segregation laws. Ostensibly, whites demanded legal segregation because they did not want to sit next to unclean, uncouth, and dangerous lower-class blacks. As industrialization and urbanization brought more working-class whites and blacks into competition and conflict, whites called for more segregation to preserve peace and order. But, increasingly, whites also wanted to marginalize successful middle-class blacks socially as well as politically and economically, lest they entertain ideas about social equality. More and more, whites desired to make educated and successful African Americans all but invisible to southern whites. While segregation hardly brought peace and harmony, it did create a rigid caste system that raised the lowest white person above the level of the highest black person. The Jim Crow system helped define "the southern way of life," and by the end of the Progressive Era it was considered immutable.

Once legal segregation began, there seemed to be no logical stopping point. The southern states first concentrated on laws that segregated trains and streetcars. By 1911 ten states had passed laws for that purpose. In 1898 South Carolina segregated trains, then streetcars (1905), train depots and restaurants (1906), textile plants (1915 and 1916), circuses (1917), pool halls (1924), and beaches (1934). As industrialization and urbanization created more public and semipublic places, whites demanded the segregation of streetcars, taxis, golf courses, swimming pools, water fountains, and toilets. Eventually, Oklahoma segregated phone booths, and New Orleans went so far as to separate prostitutes by race. City courts in Atlanta even provided a separate "Jim Crow Bible" for blacks to swear on. As the black urban population increased, cities began to pass laws segregating residential areas. Baltimore led the way in 1910, followed by Richmond and Norfolk in 1911, and Greenville, South Carolina, Winston-Salem,

North Carolina, Louisville, and Atlanta soon after. Clarence H. Poe, editor of the *Progressive Farmer* in North Carolina, tried unsuccessfully to purify the landscape by segregating agricultural land.

The Jim Crow South consisted of a hodgepodge of local, county, and state segregation laws that bred confusion and fear among blacks, especially travelers. In 1891 the Georgia legislature passed a law that required cities to segregate streetcars "as much as possible." Since economics made it impractical to provide separate streetcars for blacks, an unclear, imaginary line was drawn somewhere near the center of each trolley to separate the races, a divide arbitrarily enforced, typically by an ill-educated white conductor. Many such conductors took delight in embarrassing and humiliating African American passengers with their newly granted authority. In 1904, when a black woman from the Upper South took a seat near a white person on a streetcar in Alabama, the conductor scolded her, "Niggers don't sit with white folks down here." Despite the apologies offered by the offending woman, the conductor used the occasion to inform everyone on the trolley that "I'm here . . . to tell niggers their places when they don't know them."

In spite of white demands for comprehensive segregation, there were limits to racial separation. How, for instance, could one effectively segregate a general store, a filling station, an elevator, a theater, a library, or a museum? Since all money was green, white merchants welcomed blacks to the old general store and the new department store as long as they did not expect to be waited on until all whites had been served, as long as they did not intend to try on clothes before buying them, and as long as they did not eat at the lunch counter in the dime stores. Blacks usually had to take the freight elevator. In theaters, African Americans had to sit in the balcony or in a roped-off place in the back. Whites found it impractical to segregate the gas pump, but they could provide blacks with a separate but dirtier toilet.

What laws did not cover, custom did. Custom, for example, dictated that blacks come to the back door with hat in hand when visiting a white home. Owing to this custom, many whites locked only their back doors. Churches, of course, were segregated by the preference of both races soon after the Civil War. A story circulated that a white deacon entered his church to find a black man there. When the deacon asked him why he was in a white church, the black man defensively explained that he was the janitor. Relieved, the deacon said, "Well, that's all right then. But don't let me catch you prayin'."

Custom also created a kind of linguistic Jim Crow to keep blacks in their place. Whites refused to accord even the most educated and sophisticated blacks the titles of "Mr.," "Mrs.," and "Miss." Whites instead addressed blacks by their first names or "boy," "auntie," "uncle," and the like. Telephone operators listened carefully to try to discern the race of the caller lest a black person be accorded a title not fitting for the race.

To be certain, the emergence of the automobile added more complexity to racial mores. Did white motorists always have the right of way at stop signs? Out of prudence, most black drivers deferred to whites at the crossroads, and many feared to pass cars driven by them. A story circulated that a black man who had just purchased an automobile in Atlanta was asked by an incredulous white, "Whose road are you going to drive it on?" In 1917 a Macon, Georgia, newspaper reported an increasingly common incident: whites ordered four blacks to dispose of their automobiles before beating the owners. Early in the automobile age, whites considered any form of transportation above a mule as too good for blacks.

In truth, the "age of segregation" was somewhat of a misnomer, for southern whites simply excluded black from many public places, if not by law, by custom. Typically, libraries, museums, and athletic fields were closed to blacks. The Carnegie Library that opened in Atlanta in 1902 excluded African Americans, but the magnate's money was used to construct a separate library for them in 1921. Many public parks excluded those with dark skins, except on special "Negro days." Some parks placed a sign at their entrances that said, "NEGROES AND DOGS NOT ALLOWED."

Blacks suffered much under the cruel affronts of segregation and exclusion. Some were known to cry out in anguish, " Why does God allow white folk to treat us so bad?" Growing up in Mississippi, young Richard Wright reached the conclusion that God must have cursed the black race. Blacks cooked food for whites, cut their hair, washed their clothes, and even nursed their children, but they were considered too unclean to break bread with whites or sit beside them on a train or in a theater. Every black person who had the privilege of traveling abroad remembered the thrill of escaping segregation. James Weldon Johnson expressed the joy of being abroad in Paris: "I was suddenly free; free from a sense of impending discomfort, insecurity, danger . . . free from special scorn, special tolerance, special condescension, special commiseration; free to be merely a man."

Segregation isolated the best African Americans from contact with white society. Whites mostly interacted with uneducated, menial black workers, which gave them a distorted view of African Americans and strengthened their racism. Jim Crow, Du Bois charged, "narrows opportunities open to Negroes and teaches them to lose self-respect and ambition." He believed that "arbitrary caste proscriptions" were "a potent cause of carelessness, disorder, and crime" among blacks. Worst of all, segregation laws gave legal sanction for racial humiliation and injustice to blacks.

4. Black Education in the South

Segregation also gave African Americans an inferior education. As a poor region of the nation trying to finance a dual school system, the South lagged far behind the North in education for both races. Southern progressives predictably decided to concentrate their limited resources on improving white education. This decision came reflexively as radical white supremacists feared educated blacks anyway. "In educating the negro," Vardaman warned, "we implant in him all manner of aspirations and ambition which we then refuse to allow him to gratify." Fearing black aspirations, Governor and Senator Vardaman did everything he could to limit black education. Other white leaders not only claimed a correlation between black education and civil rights militancy but also associated education with black immorality and criminality. The feminist rabble-rouser Rebecca Felton claimed that black crime rose along with appropriations for black schooling. Congressman Tom Heflin of Alabama anticipated increasing racial clashes because of the new Negro and advised, "I do not believe it is incumbent upon us to lift him up and educate him on an equal footing that he may be armed and equipped when the combat comes." Most whites probably even objected to the industrial education served up by the conservative Booker T. Washington at Tuskegee

Institute. In a 1906 debate in the Alabama legislature over a tax exemption for Tuskegee, a legislator ranted, "I believe Booker Washington and his gang would prove to be the curse of the South and if I had my way I would wipe his institute off the face of the earth."

Facilitating the relative decline of black education was the Southern Education Board (SEB) and the Rockefeller-financed General Education Board (GEB), which were founded, respectively, in 1901 and 1902. Composed of southern moderates such as Edgar Murphy and Walter Hines Page and northern philanthropists such as Robert C. Ogden and William Baldwin, members of these two boards gave white education priority and campaigned for racist demagogues who promised to improve white schools. They reasoned that an educated white would be less racist and ultimately accept the terms of Washington's Atlanta Compromise. Although the SEB hired Washington as one of its "agents," it showed its true colors by not inviting him to its meetings. Between 1901 and 1909 the GEB spent $58 million on southern education, 90 percent of which went to whites. Just as they had supported disfranchisement and segregation, paternalistic moderates embraced white supremacy in education.

Although blacks made some absolute gains in education during the Progressive Era, black education declined compared to that for whites. At the turn of the century the southern states spent approximately twice as much per capita on white students as on black students. By 1915, however, Deep South states such as Mississippi and South Carolina were spending ten to twelve times more per capita on white students. In the more moderate state of North Carolina, black students composed 34 percent of the students in 1900 and received 28 percent of the educational funds. But after the "progressive" reforms of Governor Charles B. Aycock, the black share for educational money fell to 13 percent in 1915. Blacks also had shorter school terms than whites, and in remote areas they often had no schools at all. In 1900 only 22 percent of black children under the age of ten attended school in the southern states. Black urban schools were crowded and had much larger classes than did white institutions. In Atlanta 1,000 black students received no schooling because of a shortage of classrooms. Another 1,000 attended school for only three and a half hours a day due to overcrowding. Across the South, dilapidated shanties, often without indoor plumbing, served as black schools. James Weldon Johnson recalled teaching fifty children in a "shanty of a church" in rural Florida, one "without a blackboard or desks or any other equipment except a rude table."

Public education for black youths usually ended with the sixth or seventh grade. Although public high schools became common in the Progressive Era, exceedingly few existed for southern blacks. Booker T. Washington High School, the first black public institution of its type in Atlanta, opened in 1924. Whatever the level of education, white officials saw to it that black education emphasized industrial training. To make matters worse, African American teachers were poorly trained and badly paid, and only 20 percent of them had obtained more than a grammar school education. In 1915 the average pay of a white elementary teacher in Georgia was $60.25 a month for a man and $45.70 for a woman; for blacks the corresponding figures were $30.14 and $21.69. One thing about the segregated schools was sometimes the same: the textbooks. Black students, for instance, often received old history books—after whites had already used them—that praised slavery and Jim Crow.

As might be expected, a school system established to maintain white supremacy produced abysmal results for most blacks. When Gunnar Myrdal traveled through the South in the late 1930s to conduct research for his celebrated book, *An American Dilemma,* he was astounded to find that black students did not know who the president of the United States was and had no knowledge of the NAACP or the Constitution, though one bright-eyed student volunteered that the "Constitution" was an Atlanta newspaper.

During the Progressive Era northern philanthropists established several funds that aided black elementary and secondary education and kept a pathetic system from getting worse, though much of the funding did not show measurable results until after World War I. Julius Rosenwald, president of Sears, Roebuck, and Company, gave generously from his fortune to build black school buildings. By 1914 the Rosenwald Fund was subsidizing the construction of one hundred school buildings in Alabama alone. By 1932 the Rosenwald Fund had spurred the building of more than five thousand black schools in the South. Similarly, the Anna T. Jeanes Fund, the Phelps-Stokes Foundation, and northern religious denominations funneled money into black education. These philanthropic projects often required matching money, higher taxes for maintenance, and other collective efforts by local blacks. By all accounts, black adults willingly sacrificed time and money to ensure a better education for their children.

Higher education for blacks also lagged behind that of whites. Many black institutions of higher education, including Tuskegee, were unaccredited and were colleges in name only. Of some one hundred black colleges, only thirty-three offered college-level courses. Du Bois's employer, Atlanta University, conferred more high school diplomas than college degrees. A 1917 Phelps-Stokes study concluded that only Fisk and Howard Universities were worthy of being saved. Tougaloo, the best black college in Mississippi, awarded on average only two degrees a year between 1901 and 1930 and did not receive accreditation until 1931. Not only were black degrees of inferior quality, there were also few of them. In 1900 only 156 African Americans out of almost 9 million received B.A. degrees. Although the number of undergraduate degrees awarded to blacks increased to 1,009 in 1920, that number was only slightly more than 2 percent of the almost 50,000 diplomas awarded to whites.

Despite the best efforts of radical racists, blacks still managed to make educational progress. Between 1900 and 1920 the illiteracy rate of southern blacks fell from two-thirds to less than one-half; and literacy rates were far higher for younger blacks. But the southern school system cobbled together by white supremacists during the Progressive Era perpetuated and increased educational inequality and ultimately left blacks even further behind whites.

5. The Southern Justice System

Geared to meet the needs of white supremacy and the prevailing economic interests, the southern justice system was decisively stacked against African Americans. Across the region police forces, juries, lawyers, and judges were almost all white. Poorly paid, lower-class whites dominated the police and sheriff departments and brutalized all classes of African Americans with impunity. White judges handed out sentences to blacks that were wildly disproportionate to their crimes. A South Carolina judge sentenced a black man to three years in jail for stealing a bicycle, but gave a white man three months for the theft of an automobile. During World War I a Texas judge fined a white man $25 for selling alcohol to soldiers but levied a penalty of $225 each on four African Americans convicted of the same offense. Blacks regularly received harsh sentences for such crimes as loitering, walking on the city grass, and spitting on the sidewalk.

Black-on-black crime, however, was often treated lightly, especially if the black defendant enjoyed the respect of influential whites. Often the first thing asked of a black defendant before the court was, "Whose nigger are you?" If a white person swore that a guilty African American was "a good, hard-working darkey," the court most likely would extend mercy to him, as long as the crime in question had been perpetrated against a member of his own race. As a southern police officer said of murder and the law: "If a nigger kills a white man, that's murder. If a white man kills a nigger, that's justifiable homicide. If a nigger kills another nigger, that's one less nigger."

To the great anger of African Americans, white juries almost always found white violence against blacks justifiable. On the other hand, a black assault on a white person for any reason, even self-defense, would bring the full force of the law down on the assailant, provided the defendant was not lynched first. A popular story circulated in the African American community about a black man arrested for kicking a white man. When the judge questioned the defendant about his rash act of interracial violence, the black replied, "Well, Capum, what would you do if someone called you a black son of a bitch?" "That," the judge replied, "would hardly be likely to happen." The accused responded with another question, "Well, capum, spose they call you the kind of a son of a bitch you is?" The lyrics of a blues song captured the cynicism and bitterness of blacks confronting the justice system: "Warden come early that morning for him to be hung / On account of something he hadn't done."

One improvement southern progressives made in the justice system was the termination of the convict lease system. By 1920 all the southern states, except Alabama, had ended the notorious practice of leasing prisoners to private employers. An investigative committee in Alabama reported in 1912, "The convict lease system of Alabama is a relic of barbarism, a species of human slavery, a crime against humanity." Nonetheless, it lingered in Alabama until 1928; adverse publicity and economic factors, more than humanitarian concerns, finally ended the brutal practice.

The southern states replaced convict leasing with the chain gang. While still famous for its brutality, the chain gang had a significantly lower death rate than convict lease. Under the chain gang system, prisoners worked for the state, not for private entrepreneurs. As with convict lease, law enforcement fed the chain gangs with mostly black workers convicted of petty crimes. In Georgia in 1904, 124 men and 25 women worked on the Bibb County chain gang. Of the 149 prison workers for the county, 56 had been convicted for drunkenness, 40 for disorderly conduct, 18 for fighting, 12 for loitering, 4 for reckless driving, 2 for throwing rocks, and 12 for various infractions of minor city ordinances. Most of the prisoners had to work for half a year or more building roads. Since road building was a major progressive objective, the chain gang arguably furthered southern reform.

Although lynching peaked in the 1890s, it continued at a frantic pace in the Progressive Era. More than 1,500 lynchings occurred between 1900 and 1920. The new century opened with 245 lynchings in the first two years, and the first decade of the twentieth century averaged 88.6 mob murders a year. Lynching became more strictly a southern racial phenomenon in the Progressive Era. While 82 percent of the lynchings in the 1890s took place in the South, 92 percent of the mob murders occurred in Dixie in the following decade. Moreover, the proportion of blacks lynched increased from 72 percent in the 1890s to almost 90 percent in the first decade of the new century; and the trend continued throughout the Progressive Era.

Lynching remained as barbaric as ever, unmitigated by the humanitarian impulses of progressive reform. Mobs continued to torture, mutilate, and roast victims in order to make their deaths long and agonizing, for men and women alike. People triumphantly displayed body parts of the victims as souvenirs. Law enforcement personnel seldom resisted lynch mobs. In Georgia 80 percent of the lynching victims were taken from the custody of law enforcement officials. From 1900 to 1920 fewer than a dozen people were convicted for involvement in a southern lynching, and many Deep South states never convicted a single mob participant. As one southern black put it: "They had to have a license to kill anything but a nigger. We was always in season."

And this all-season sport attracted crowds of thousands. The local press often advertised the ritual murders in advance. In 1919 in Jackson, Mississippi, a newspaper reported matter-of-factly: "3,000 WILL BURN NEGRO, JOHN HARTFIELD WILL BE LYNCHED BY ELLISVILLE MOB AT 5 O'CLOCK THIS AFTERNOON." Such events were not seen as lawless happenings but as a semiformal extension of the law. Participants in lynchings did not need to wear masks. Instead they proudly posed for pictures, sometimes making them into postcards to commemorate the new peculiar institution, the "negro barbecue."

Southern legislators, governors, Congressmen, and Senators promised voters that they personally would lead a lynch mob against any black man who raped a white woman. At the same time, whites considered black women so sexually immoral as to be beyond violation. In 1909 Mississippi Senator W. V. Sullivan boasted, "I led the mob which lynched Nelse Patton [a black man accused of rape] and I'm proud of it."

As noted earlier, although by this time whites justified lynching almost exclusively for rape, less than 25 percent of those who were executed by a mob had been accused of sexual assault. Some whites acknowledged that the rationale for lynching went beyond eliminating rapists. They asserted that nothing less than the restraint of terror could keep the postslavery generation of blacks in their place. Whites therefore lynched blacks not just for serious crimes such as rape and murder, but also for breaches of racial etiquette, for showing economic ambition, and for a host of minor offenses. Whites in Georgia lynched an illiterate black man for asking a white girl to read a letter to him. After lynching a black man in Maysville, Kentucky, in 1908, whites ordered seven troublesome blacks to leave town. After the seven had departed, whites presented the black community with a new list of ten names. Eventually, thirty to forty African Americans left the city for their safety. After lynching eleven blacks in four days in 1904 in Saint Charles, Arkansas, a town of five hundred people, members of the drunken mob justified their orgy of murder by saying that they had to crush "the spirit of black resistance." Whites lynched African Americans for a variety of reasons, but as the historian Robert Zangrando wrote in *The NAACP Crusade against Lynching, 1909–1950* (1980): "Primarily . . . lynching was a means to intimidate, degrade, and control black people throughout the southern and border states" up to the middle of the twentieth century.

Progressives, who prized law and order, were torn between their impulses to support white supremacy and their distaste for crude lawlessness. Moderate white supremacists warned that savage white mobs displayed the same characteristics that whites attributed to blacks. They argued that the maintenance of civilization required restraint. Some paternalists argued that it was the duty of the superior race, as an Oklahoma judge put it, "to protect this weaker race from unjustifiable and lawless attacks." These kinds of thoughts, though, did not worry most whites or stop their violent behavior toward African Americans.

It is surprising that under the circumstances so many blacks resisted white outrages. Nevertheless, more than a dozen Georgia sheriffs and town marshals and several policemen died at the hand of black men in the period between 1900 and 1920. Countless black males died protecting their wives and mothers from white assault. And many black women remained quiet about white male advances toward them, lest their men do something foolish.

Yet the brutal enforcement of the caste system forced most blacks to act out a demeaning subordination in order to survive. No black man could expect to die a natural death unless he learned, as Benjamin Mays put it, "to get along with white folks." Black parents thus faced a dilemma in rearing children. If they instilled racial pride and ambition in their children, they might, according to Du Bois, "grow up to despise their own people, hate the white and become embittered with the world." If parents taught children to be long-suffering and deferential, they might grow up to become slavish and cringing. Ultimately, out of the real and immediate concern for their children's safety, most African Americans instructed their children to be humble and deferential before whites. The system, Mays recalled, "put the rabbit" in most blacks. Since black behavior was a matter of life or death,

African Americans had to learn to bow and scrape, grin obsequiously, and tip their hats to whites. As the black poet Paul Lawrence Dunbar summed it up, "We wear the mask that grins and lies."

Blacks shuddered at the realization of how precarious their lives were. They knew what the famous bluesman Robert Johnson meant when he sang of the "hellhound on my trail" or when the jazz artist Billie Holiday sang, "Southern trees bear strange fruit / Blood on the leaves and blood at the root / Black body swinging in the southern breeze / Strange fruit hanging from the poplar tree." The Mississippian Richard Wright said of lynching, "I was compelled to give my entire imagination over to it, an act which blocked the springs of thought and feeling in me." The black novelist Jean Toomer perhaps suggested the ultimate horror of lynching by poetically framing the image of a black body being reduced to white ash, suggesting the ghastly power of marauding whites to render the blackest black person white.

Southern extremists made the South a hellish place for blacks. The minister Edgar Gardner Murphy unwittingly revealed the impotence of southern moderates when he complained in *The Basis of Ascendancy* (1909) that racist demagogues in the South had moved "from an undiscriminating attack upon the Negro's ballot to a like attack upon his school, his labor, his life—from the contention that no Negro shall vote to the contention that no Negro shall learn, that no Negro shall labor, and [by implication] that no Negro shall live."

The worsening plight of blacks, nevertheless, motivated many African American leaders to greater militancy. Black protest, along with the rising concern of white neo-abolitionists, led to the formation of the NAACP in 1909. In the progressive spirit, the NAACP labored to get the race question back into national politics, that volatile and sometimes decisive arena where slavery had been abolished and African Americans had gained citizenship. Would a Republican-controlled federal government be willing once again to contemplate racial reform?

Booker T. Washington, a former slave, led a rags-to-riches life, becoming the most famous and powerful black leader in America until his death in 1915. Photography Collection, Miriam and Ira D. Wallach Division of Art, Prints and Photographs, The New York Public Library, Astor, Lenox, and Tilden Foundations.

Benjamin "Pitchfork" Tillman, the white-supremacist Southern demagogue. Elected governor of South Carolina in 1890, he served in the U.S. Senate from 1895 until 1918, dominating politics in his state for more than twenty years. He offered up African Americans as scapegoats on which the white masses might feast. Box 1 and Folder 20, Benjamin Ryan Tillman Papers, 1767– 1950, Special Collections, Clemson University Libraries, Clemson, South Carolina.

Ida B. Wells, the militant journalist from Memphis, who wrote about racial lynchings. After being forced to flee her hometown in 1892 because of her condemnation of lynching, Wells moved to New York City and then to Chicago (she married a Chicagoan in 1895 and became Wells-Barnett). Photograph ca. 1893–1894, by Cihak and Zima, Chicago, Illinois. Ida B. Wells Papers. Box 10 : 1 : 2 (asas-00055), Special Collections Research Center, University of Chicago Library.

Mary White Ovington, the only white member of the Niagara group, an important force in the formation and survival of the early NAACP. Her interest in the race problem heightened when she heard Washington speak at the Social Reform Club in New York in 1903. She covered the meeting of the Niagara Movement at Harper's Ferry as a journalist. The following year she moved into a black settlement house in New York City to study the conditions of its inhabitants, and then published her muckraking book, Half a Man: The Status of the Negro in New York *(1911). Special Collections and Archives, W. E. B. Du Bois Library, University of Massachusetts, Amherst.*

Theodore Roosevelt, the dynamic reformist president from 1901 to 1909. Although he invited Booker T. Washington to dine at the White House in 1901 and proposed to open a "door of hope" for African Americans, he eventually disappointed many blacks with his words and deeds.. Courtesy of the National Archives. ARC 530950.

Oswald Garrison Villard, the influential journalist who was called to draft a call for a new civil rights organization by Ovington and her allies. Villard, who described himself as "a young radical," was the son of the railroad magnate Henry Villard and the grandson of the famous abolitionist William Lloyd Garrison. Special Collections and Archives, W. E. B. Du Bois Library, University of Massachusetts, Amherst.

William Monroe Trotter, a Harvard graduate and militant civil rights leader from Boston. He bluntly asked President Woodrow Wilson, "Have you a 'new freedom' for white Americans and an new slavery for your Afro-American fellow citizens?" Courtesy Boston Public Library, Print Department.

Woodrow Wilson, a Democratic president from 1913 to 1921 was urged by Oswald Garrison Villard, a founder of the NAACP, to court disaffected black voters in the 1912 election.. Wilson obliged Villard by pledging himself to "absolute fair dealing" with blacks. Wilson further promised that he would "seek to be President of the whole nation and would know no differences of race or creed or section." Once in office, however, Wilson, a Southerner, presided over the segregation of federal agencies in Washington, D.C. and generally turned his back on African Americans. Library of Congress, LC-D416-831 DLC.

W. E. B. Du Bois, black scholar, poet, novelist, and the foremost civil rights leader during the Progressive Era. He searchingly probed the meaning of being black in the United States in his influential book, The Souls of Black Folk *(1903). Here Du Bois is pictured at the Paris Exposition Universelle in the spring of 1900. Special Collections and Archives, W. E. B. Du Bois Library, University of Massachusetts, Amherst.*

The lynching of a black person almost always entailed more than just an unlawful hanging. Although the white victims of lynchings usually got a quick, clean hanging, black victims often suffered prolonged torture and grisly mutilation. Many blacks were burned at the stake, but not before mobs cut off their fingers, ears, noses, and genitals and extracted hunks of flesh with corkscrews. Adults and children alike scrambled, in what sometimes was a carnival-like atmosphere, to retrieve body parts to hail as proud souvenirs.

Above: The lynching of Jesse Washington, a seventeen-year-old mentally deficient boy, Waco, Texas, 1916. The Texas Collections, Baylor University, Waco, Texas.

Above: The lynching of Virgil, Robert, and Thomas Jones, and Joseph Riley, Russellville, Kentucky, 1908. Photo supplied by Logan County Public Library.

Overleaf: The burnt corpse of William Brown, Omaha, Nebraska, 1919. Nebraska State Historical Society, Photograph Collections.

BURNING of BROWN'S BODY   RIOT OF SEPT. 28, 1919

CHAPTER FOUR

National Politics and Race, 1900–1917: The Great Betrayal

Only the intervention of the federal government could have reversed or modified the triumph of white supremacy in the South. Blacks such as Frederick Douglass had felt a keen sense of betrayal during the early 1890s when the Republican majority failed to pass bills that would have policed federal elections and aided black education. But in the first decade of the twentieth century, some blacks found renewed hope as the spirit of righteous reform took hold of the Republican party. Their expectations rose as the party of Lincoln gained solid control of both branches of Congress from 1897 to 1911 and held the presidency until 1913. By increasing its strength in the North and West, the Republican party could now win federal elections without any southern votes.

Furthermore, Theodore Roosevelt, the dynamic, reformist president from 1901 to 1909, proposed to open a "door of hope" for African Americans. During this period of Republican ascendancy, the party continued to call for the enforcement of the Fourteenth and Fifteenth Amendments. Its 1904 platform boldly threatened use of the Fourteenth Amendment to reduce the Congressional representation of the South in areas where suffrage had been "unconstitutionally limited."

In 1908 the Republicans added a lengthy paragraph to their civil rights plank that denounced black disfranchisement as "unfair, un-American and repugnant to the Supreme Law of the Land." In a broader statement, the plank declared, "We demand equal justice for all men without regard to race, creed, or color." It seemed that Republicans once again were about to confront the Jim Crow South. To a new generation of militant blacks, racial change seemed to be a possibility.

The Republican Party and the Race Question

Although the overwhelming majority of blacks remained loyal Republicans, they soon discovered that the ascendancy of their party did not necessarily enhance their freedom and opportunities. William McKinley, the Republican president from 1897 to 1901, took no action after the 1898 Wilmington Massacre, despite passionate pleas from African Americans for federal intervention. McKinley instead led the United States into a war against Spain that gave the nation control of millions of dark-skinned subjects, not citizens. In pondering the acquisition and worth of the Philippine Islands, the president appealed to the largess of the white race toward a dark-skinned people. "If we accept them [the islands] in a spirit worthy of our race and our traditions," he promised, "a great opportunity comes with them." The former Union officer from Ohio made no mention of blacks in his 1901 inaugural address, but he spoke passionately about ending the divisions between northern and southern whites.

When the low-key, conservative McKinley was assassinated in September 1901, the American political scene changed dramatically. To reformers and to many blacks, Theodore Roosevelt's elevation to the presidency seemed providential. The charismatic new president seemed tailor-made to lead a rising America into the modern era. The first president to ride in an automobile, an airplane, and a submarine, Roosevelt was a maverick Republican given to bold and innovative action. An intellectual with a Harvard degree, Roosevelt had broad interests and an unquenchable curiosity. He wrote thirty some books, hundreds of articles and book reviews, and volumes of learned, scintillating letters. A physical fitness buff, a sportsman, and a war hero, the robust president relished the exercise of power and envisioned his office as a "bully pulpit" from which to instill a sense of morality and justice in the American people.

Although Roosevelt was popular with the masses, he had many detractors in his time and thereafter. Some contemporaries described him as a man "drunk with power," a self-aggrandizing politician, a malevolently self-righteous prude, and a radical rabble-rouser. Yet one historian portrayed Roosevelt as a deeply conservative "stabilizer of the status quo." Critics on the left, right, and in the middle agreed on one thing: Roosevelt was a political opportunist. According to one observer, "Roosevelt was always willing, at any time, to contradict himself, by word or deed, if by contradiction he could further his career." In 1901 some blacks waited anxiously to see if this gifted politician would prove to be, like many others, an opportunist on the delicate race issue.

Despite some early, hopeful signs that Roosevelt would be fair and principled toward African Americans, he ultimately proved to be opportunistic on the troublesome race problem. When he bade farewell to his troops in Cuba in 1898, Roosevelt praised the courage of the black soldiers of the Ninth and Tenth Cavalry regiments who had fought beside him, describing them as "an excellent breed of Yankees." A few months later, however, he published slanderous and unfounded remarks suggesting that black soldiers in Cuba had a tendency to flee to the rear. Then during his tenure as governor of New York, Roosevelt signed a bill banning racial discrimination in public places and testified in support of it by announcing that his children happily attended school with African Americans.

Shortly after becoming president in 1901, Roosevelt invited Booker T. Washington to the White House for dinner. Although this presidential gesture pleased African Americans immensely, it set off an orgy of alarm in the South, indicating the mounting racial hysteria of the region. *The Memphis Scimitar* called Roosevelt's action "the most damnable outrage ever perpetrated by any citizen of the United States." On the Senate floor, "Pitchfork" Ben Tillman shouted, "[E]ntertaining that nigger will necessitate our killing a thousand niggers in the South before they will learn their place." Senator Vardaman charged that Roosevelt insulted all whites by taking "this nigger bastard into his home" and entertaining him "on terms of absolute equality." From Roosevelt's allegedly vulgar breach of racial etiquette, the *Richmond Times* deducted that the president favored interracial marriage.

Roosevelt was taken aback by the South's reaction to his having dined with Washington. Afterall, the Democrat Grover Cleveland had invited Frederick Douglass to the White House without creating a furor, and Douglass had a white wife. But Roosevelt stood his ground and defiantly declared, "I shall have him [Washington] to dine just as often as I please. . . ." Seemingly undaunted by southern outrage, in 1903 Roosevelt appointed the black physician William D. Crum as the collector of the port of Charleston, South Carolina. When South Carolina's Senators tried to block the Crum appointment, the president sidestepped Congress with a recess appointment. During the controversy over Crum, Roosevelt declared, "I cannot take the position that the door of hope—the door of opportunity—is to be shut upon any man, no matter how worthy, purely upon the grounds of race or color." A third incident that endeared Roosevelt to blacks in his first term was the squabble over a black postmistress in Indianola, Mississippi. When whites forced the efficient and mild-mannered woman to resign—Benjamin Harrison had appointed her—Roosevelt closed the post office in Indianola in protest. After these incidents, several black leaders began to allude to the "door of hope" that Roosevelt had sensationally opened to blacks.

However, African Americans soon discovered that their confidence in Roosevelt had been misplaced. Although defiant in face of the southern reaction to the Washington dinner, the opportunistic Roosevelt immediately began to regret his action. He complained that the "best whites" of the South had caved into the likes of Tillman and Vardaman. He also groused that he got little, if any, political gain for his pro-black efforts. Roosevelt never again invited Washington to dinner at the White House.

Besides, Roosevelt had invited Washington to the White House strictly to discuss patronage politics, not civil rights or sociology. The historian Louis R. Harlan said of the famous meeting of the two men, "Both were pragmatists willing to sacrifice mere principles for the sake of power. . . . Each spoke and thought of his work in terms of high moral purpose but, when the occasion called for ruthless action, could decide and act in his own interest." Roosevelt was looking ahead to the next election, believing that his primary opponent for the Republican nomination would be Marcus Alonzo Hanna, a critic of Roosevelt and the political boss who had engineered McKinley's rise to the presidency. Hanna controlled the "rotten borough" Republican delegates in the South, who had a disproportionate influence in nominating the party's candidate for president. As late as 1916 more than one-third of the delegates at the Republican national convention came from the South, though the party was practically powerless in the region. On assuming office, Roosevelt appointed black Republicans to displace some of the Hanna appointees. But, all told, Roosevelt appointed fewer blacks to office than McKinley.

After Mark Hanna died unexpectedly in February of 1904, the president turned increasingly to white Southerners instead of Booker T. Washington for political advice on racial matters. After his nomination and election were guaranteed, the president appointed few blacks to positions in the South, supporting mostly white Republicans and the Democratic sons of former Confederates for federal office. In 1904 Roosevelt explained his new strategy to Washington, "The safety for the colored man in Louisiana is to have a white man's party which shall be responsible and honest, in which the colored man . . . shall not be the dominant force." In fairness to Roosevelt, he selected more blacks for northern posts than some of his predecessors and continued to make the usual appointments of African Americans to diplomatic posts in countries such as Haiti. It is clear, however, that Roosevelt's appointments were based on political calculations and not out of a sense of racial justice or a belief in empowering blacks.

It was also Roosevelt's calculation not to speak out against the disfranchisement of blacks. He remained silent on the plank in his party platform that supported the use of the Fourteenth Amendment to reduce southern representation in Congress. Privately, he opposed the suffrage plank and condemned the Fifteenth Amendment as "a mistake." He wrote to Senator Henry Cabot Lodge, "I believe that the great majority of the Negroes in the south are wholly unfit to vote," and he opined that the corrupt black vote "would reduce parts of the south to the level of Haiti." In 1904 the president told the former abolitionist Lyman Abbott, "I have nothing to gain and everything to lose by any agitation of the race question. . . . You will notice that in my speech of acceptance I did not touch upon this matter at all."

Early in Roosevelt's second term, it was clear to a growing number of blacks that Roosevelt had not really opened a door of hope for them. In his Lincoln Day speech in February of 1905, Roosevelt expressed his wish that the "backward race" would conduct its search for freedom in such a way that the "forward race" could "preserve its civilization unharmed." And the president emphatically added, "Race purity must be preserved." In the fall of 1905 Roosevelt toured the South and received a warm welcome by whites. He cleared all his southern speeches with white Democrats so as not to offend the ruling class. He certainly gave no offense by visiting the ancestral home of his southern mother and praising Confederate heroes. But he said nothing directly about disfranchisement or lynching. In a speech at Tuskegee, one pre-approved by its master, the president lauded industrial education, hard work, and sobriety. His effusive praise of industrial education for blacks prompted journalist William Hayes Ward to comment in the *Independent* that the president's racial myopia would not allow him to think of a young black person attending Howard or Fisk, let alone Harvard or Yale. Ward noted that Roosevelt sent his children to liberal arts schools—and he might have added that Washington did too.

On every important issue of civil rights, except peonage, Roosevelt showed he was not ready to disturb the status quo. The ebullient president's sense of justice, however, caused him to draw the line at what he considered the "reintroduction of slavery" in the South. Roosevelt ordered the Justice Department and the federal district attorneys to pursue peonage cases, and by 1908 some eighty such cases were pending. Although some people finally went to jail for peonage under his administration, Roosevelt did not advertise his accomplishments for fear of inciting white Southerners. Moreover, he pardoned two wealthy landowners convicted of peonage.

The president was equally quiet on the subject of lynching, although he was constantly urged by blacks and white liberals to speak out on the issue. On those rare occasions when Roosevelt condemned lynching, he perpetuated the southern myth that the black rape of white women was the primary cause of mob murder. In his annual message to Congress on December 3, 1906, he asserted, "The greatest existing cause of lynching is the perpetration, especially by black men, of the hideous crime of rape." Whenever Roosevelt spoke out against lynching, he also chastised the black community for being soft on black rapists and other criminals. "The respectable colored people must learn not to harbor their criminals," he preached, but must "help the officers of the law in hunting down with all possible earnestness and zeal every such offender." In explaining the "hideous Atlanta [race] riots," he claimed that a major cause of the bloodbath was "the grave and evil fact that the negroes too often band together to shelter their own criminals." It may not have dawned on the president that if ordinary black citizens apprehended criminals of their race—something whites were not expected to do—they might see them taken from jail and murdered by a mob. When it came to African Americans, Roosevelt had a habit of blaming the victims.

By 1906 an increasing number of black leaders had become highly critical of Roosevelt. W. Calvin White of the *Washington Bee* wrote, "President Roosevelt has closed the door of hope and the square deal has gone hunting." Reacting to Roosevelt's annual message to Congress in 1906, the moderate black educator Kelly Miller responded that "the Negro is held up as a race of criminals and rapists, banded together to uphold one another in crime, with only occasional individual exceptions." Forty of fifty blacks interviewed by the *Voice of the Negro,* the mouthpiece of Du Bois's newly formed Niagara Movement, criticized the president. They assailed the lack of backbone Roosevelt had shown and his retrogressive ideas about black education and suffrage. The *Washington Bee* added a new charge in accusing the president of condoning segregation in federal agencies such as Treasury, Interior, and War, a charge historians have since documented.

As blacks became more critical of Roosevelt, white Southerners began to show a new appreciation for the Yankee president. Thomas Nelson Page, the writer of racist, Old-South novels who had once viewed Roosevelt as a neo-abolitionist, now concluded that the president was "more a Democrat than a Republican." William Garrott Brown, an Alabamian who taught at Yale, congratulated the president on "his new attitude on the Southern question."

Of all the racial affronts attributed to Roosevelt, none infuriated blacks as much as the Brownsville affair. On the night of August 13, 1906, a number of black soldiers from the Twenty-fifth Infantry Regiment allegedly shot up the town of Brownsville, Texas, killing one white person and wounding two others. Without waiting for a civilian or military trial, Roosevelt summarily and dishonorably discharged 167 black soldiers from three companies of highly decorated combat veterans, several of whom had won the Medal of Honor. Although a local grand jury could find no evidence to indict the soldiers and none of the soldiers would confess to wrongdoing, the president concluded, "Some of the men were bloody butchers—they ought to be hung." Other soldiers, the president insisted, were covering up the "horrible atrocity." Supremely confident in his judgment, Roosevelt declared, "A blacker [crime] never stained the annals of our army." The president ignored the basic fundamentals of American law in the Brownsville case in challenging the accused soldiers to prove their innocence. As with lynching, Roosevelt thrust collective responsibility upon an entire military unit for the crime committed by the few at Brownsville.

Blacks leaders of all stripes denounced Roosevelt's Brownsville edict. Even the deferential Washington pleaded with the president to reverse his decision, and privately he argued that Roosevelt had "blundered." The *New York Age,* now under the sway of the Tuskegee wizard, called Brownsville an "outrage upon the rights of citizens who are entitled in civil life to a trial by jury and in military life by court martial." The *Washington Bee* characterized Roosevelt's handling of the incident as "vicious and contrary to the spirit of our Constitution."

Much of the northern white press and several northern politicians also pilloried Roosevelt. The *New York World* referred to Brownsville as an "executive lynching." And the *New York Times,* no friend of blacks, argued that a grave injustice had occurred. Even the race-baiting Tillman branded Brownsville a "legal lynching." In the Senate, Joseph B. Foraker, a Republican from Ohio, strongly challenged the methods and findings of the president on Brownsville. Although the Senate Committee on Military Affairs eventually upheld Roosevelt's actions, several northern Senators dissented from the majority report.

Almost all historians have been critical of Roosevelt's handling of the Brownsville case. In his richly researched book, *The Brownsville Raid* (1970), the historian John D. Weaver argues that local whites had framed the soldiers. More than half a century later, in 1972, the U.S. Secretary of the Army granted honorable discharges to all 167 victims of the Brownsville affair, only one of whom was still alive to enjoy his vindication. For whatever reason, Roosevelt did not see fit to mention Brownsville in his autobiography.

Had blacks read Roosevelt's voluminous publications before 1901 and been privy to his vast private correspondence, they never would have considered him a potential supporter of black rights. Roosevelt, of course, had grandly been exposed to "scientific racism" at Harvard. Nonetheless, Roosevelt was more flexible in his racial beliefs than most American thinkers. Rejecting the popular idea that racial characteristics were fixed, he embraced the now-discredited idea of Lamarckianism. This theory, espoused by the French naturalist-philosopher Jean Baptiste Lamarck, held that the acquired characteristics of human beings could be inherited by their offspring, a theory that at least offered some hope for the "backward races."

Although Roosevelt ranked races hierarchically, he eventually softened his Anglo-Saxonism with a dash of environmentalism. And he eventually abandoned the idea of Anglo-Saxon superiority altogether, arguing that a new American race or "English-speaking" race had been created in the struggle to tame the western frontier. In the *Winning of the West* (1882), Roosevelt argued that human strains from all over Europe had come together in the Darwinian struggle against the barbaric Indians to create a superior human stock. He condemned American Indians as savage and lazy and lambasted Indian reformers as naive sentimentalists. He even judged the massacre of hundreds of Indian women and children at Sand Creek, Colorado, in 1864 "as righteous and beneficial a deed as ever took place on the frontier." In his mind, such atrocities were just the unfortunate collateral damage that accompanied the vital race formation that was destined to propel America to world leadership.

Roosevelt probably thought and wrote more about race than any other American president. The historian Thomas G. Dyer argued in

Theodore Roosevelt and the Idea of Race (1980) that his ideas about race permeated all of his notions about human organization and history. "Race provided him a window on the past," Dyer wrote, "through which he could examine the grand principles of historical development." The historian Gary Gerstle neatly summed up the president's preoccupation with race: "If for Karl Marx history was the history of class conflict, for Roosevelt it was the history of race conflict." An inveterate imperialist, Roosevelt believed "racial expansion" drove historical progress. To him, American history was "race history."

Oddly enough, Roosevelt believed that superior whites were committing "race suicide." While he lamented the rapid proliferation of inferior races, he accused superior whites of "willful sterility" and said that well-bred white women who avoided marriage and family were traitors to their race. Roosevelt favored tax breaks to encourage white women to become heroic breeders. In 1913 he wrote Charles Davenport, his friend and an esteemed eugenicist: "Some day we will realize that the prime duty, the inescapable duty, of the *good* citizen of the right type is to leave his or her blood behind him in the world; and that we have no business to permit the perpetuation of citizens of the wrong type."

As for blacks, Roosevelt placed them at the bottom of the racial hierarchy. He believed that African Americans, burdened by bad genes and a sordid history, could not be assimilated into American society any more than could Asians or American Indians. In brooding over the race question in the *North American Review* in 1895, the future president stated "that a perfectly stupid race can never rise to a very high plane." He asserted that the black man "has been kept down as much by lack of intellectual development as by anything else." In a 1906 letter to his friend Owen Wister, Roosevelt prefaced his criticism of the novelist's rigid southern views on the Civil War and blacks with this concession: "Now as to the negroes! I entirely agree with you that as a race they . . . are altogether inferior to whites."

Like many progressives who were confident about solving the problems facing the United States, Roosevelt admitted that he had no answer to the race problem. In 1901 he wrote to the former abolitionist Albion Tourgée, "I have not been able to think out any solution of the terrible problem offered by the presence of the negro on this continent. . . ." Roosevelt only knew "that inasmuch as he is here and can neither be killed nor driven away," whites had to treat him in an honorable and Christian way. In a 1904 letter to the southern politician Hilary A. Hebert, he confessed: "I am at my wit's end to know what to do about the negro in the South." He vowed nonetheless to "approach the subject with the utmost caution and care and with the most earnest and conscientious desire to do nothing but what is for the good of the white people of the South—my mother's people, and therefore mine." In short, African Americans could expect little from the Roosevelt White House. As Frederick Douglass had said of Lincoln, Theodore Roosevelt was preeminently a white man's president.

As Roosevelt's second term drew to a close, he handpicked William Howard Taft, his secretary of war, to succeed him. Before becoming president, Taft had alarmed blacks with some of his remarks. At Tuskegee in 1906 he said that blacks were "a people not fit to enjoy or maintain higher education." Washington and his aides at Tuskegee found the Republican nominee so obtuse on the race question that they rewrote his acceptance speech to make it more palatable to blacks. Archie Butt, a friend of Taft, wrote in his diary that the rotund Ohioan "dislikes" blacks "and his highest ambition is to eliminate them from politics."

In the 1908 presidential election between Taft and the populist Democrat William Jennings Bryan, Du Bois and William Monroe Trotter, a militant civil rights leader from Boston, supported the latter. Du Bois argued that Taft, "a false friend," was worse than Bryan, "an avowed enemy." Bryan was a staunch supporter of white supremacy and openly advocated segregation and the disfranchisement of blacks. A close political friend of Senator Vardaman of Mississippi, Bryan opposed the customary appointment of an African American as minister to Haiti when he served as Wilson's secretary of state. He was in fact flabbergasted to learn that "niggers" spoke French in that Caribbean island. Unfortunately for blacks, The Taft-Bryan contest of 1908 represented the kind of empty choices that they faced in the Progressive Era.

After being elected in 1908, Taft, like McKinley and Roosevelt, took a tour of the South. In one of his speeches entitled "The Winning of the South," he repeated the now popular Republican myth that "the best friend of the Negro was the Southern white man." He character-ized disfranchisement as something that gave the South "political safety from . . . an ignorant electorate. . . ." Looking ahead, Taft told blacks that they were destined for "agricultural and kindred pursuits" alone. In a word, Taft told African Americans to hitch their wagons not to a star but a mule.

President Taft never invited Washington or any other black lead-ers to the White House. Determined not to offend southern whites, Taft appointed no blacks to office in the South and worked on build-ing a lily-white Republican party in Dixie. Under Taft, more segrega-tion crept into the federal bureaucracy. The single course of action that marred his negative civil rights record was the prosecution of peonage cases initiated under Roosevelt. As Taft neared the end of his presidency, eighteen bishops, fifty-seven ministers, and several edu-cators—all of them black—issued the following statement, "At no time, since the Negro has been a citizen, has he been so thoroughly ignored as a part and parcel of this great government, as he has since William Howard Taft has been President of the United States."

The Watershed Election of 1912: The Democratic Triumph

The rising American Socialist party, the left wing of progressivism, would seem a logical alternative to the Republican party for African Americans. By 1912 the Socialist party reached its zenith and had elected about 1,200 local officials, including 79 mayors in 24 states. Eugene V. Debs, a perennial candidate for president on the Socialist ticket in the Progressive Era, was personally sympathetic to blacks, but his party subsumed the race problem under the class struggle. The American Socialist party and its more rigidly Marxist cousin, the So-cial Labor party, preached that the fall of capitalism would magically solve the race problem. "We have nothing special to offer the Negro," Debs declared, "and we cannot make separate appeals to all races." The National Committee of the Socialist party voted down a resolu-tion to condemn publicly Roosevelt's high-handed actions in the Brownsville affair by a count of 28 to 4, with 25 abstentions.

And unlike Debs, several leading Socialists were outright racists. In 1902 Victor Berger stated in the Socialist *Democratic Herald,* "There can be no doubt that the negroes and mulattoes constitute a lower race—that the Caucasian and indeed even the Mongolian have the start on them in civilization by many thousand years." Socialist novelists such as Jack London and Upton Sinclair similarly characterized African Americans as a hopeless people. Given the record of the Socialist party on race, it is not surprising that few African Americans supported Debs in 1912.

During the exciting four-way presidential race of 1912, the Socialist party was not alone in trying to evade the race question. The Republican party, which had recently embellished its long-standing civil rights plank in 1908, now removed it entirely. In the raucous fight between Taft and Roosevelt for the Republican nomination in 1912, the incumbent president emerged victorious. Rejected by his lifelong party, an embittered Roosevelt quickly formed the Progressive party, popularly known as the Bull Moose party. The Progressive platform supported an advanced program of social and economic reform that would not be surpassed until the New Deal of the 1930s. Some Progressives hoped Roosevelt's new party would be as advanced on the race question as on other issues. Some racial liberals in fact called upon Du Bois to draft a civil rights plank for the new party. The Du Bois plank stated that the party "recognizes that distinctions of race or class in political life have no place in a democracy," and it demanded "the repeal of unfair discriminatory laws and the right to vote on the same terms on which other citizens vote."

But Roosevelt was having none of Du Bois's reformism. He was intent on breaking the Democratic stranglehold on the South. "Really, if I could carry one of the eleven ex-Confederate states," Roosevelt wrote to a prominent southern Progressive, "I feel as though I could die happy." And the former president hoped to break the Solid South by secretly building a lily-white Bull Moose party in the South, a plan that jibed perfectly with the desires of white southern party members. This plan faltered nonetheless when four southern states sent dual delegations to the national convention, one black and one white. Forced to make a choice, Roosevelt essentially read southern blacks out of the party. In a long, public letter, Roosevelt recounted how southern politics had been corrupted by the contest for black votes. To end this corruption he asked southern blacks to place their interests in the hands of the "wisest and justest white men" of the South. Not surprisingly, the convention seated none of the black delegations. As David Lewis, the biographer of Du Bois concluded, "The 'New Nationalism' had no place for New Negroes."

It was not unexpected that white Southerners demanded a "white man's party" at the Progressive convention, but the almost enthusiastic acquiescence of northern progressives spoke volumes about the emerging national consensus on blacks. Holding views typical of the delegates to the Progressive party convention was Medill McCormick, a well-connected journalist from Chicago—his father was a diplomat and his mother was the daugher of the publisher of the *Chicago Tribune,* Joseph Medill. Like the white Southerners in his party, McCormick, who was elected to the Congress in 1912 and to the Senate in 1918, agreed that the Bull Moose party should exclude African Americans. Committeemen from Michigan, Wisconsin, and California agreed. E. C. Carrington, Jr., of Maryland warned that if the black delegates were seated, the party would lose his state. The most outspoken Northerner on the issue was Matthew Hale of Massachusetts, a prosperous businessman and a Phi Beta Kappa at Harvard. Hale confessed to Southerners that his forebears had been misguided on the race issue. "Your attitude on the negro problem is right," Hale said, "and ours is wrong." He asked only that his southern colleagues show the retreating northern Progressives the same courtesy that Grant gave Lee at Appomattox. He pleaded with the southern delegates to be more tactful about the party's racial exclusion so as not to hurt Roosevelt's chances with the northern black vote. The major difference between the southern and northern progressives was that one wanted to strip blacks of their rights in broad daylight and the other wanted to relieve them of their civic baggage under the cover of darkness. The *Independent* indignantly wrote, "A bull is an unwelcome apparition in a china shop, and the Progressive party convention gave no kindlier welcome to the Negro question."

Rebuffed by the Progressive and Republican parties, some black leaders were willing to see what the New Freedom of the Democrat

Woodrow Wilson had to offer. Oswald Garrison Villard, a founder of
the NAACP and a strong supporter of Wilson, urged the Democratic
standard bearer to court disaffected black voters. In a letter to the
black Bishop Alexander Walters, Wilson obliged Villard by pledging
himself to "absolute fair dealing" with blacks. "My earnest wish is to
see justice done them in every matter," Wilson told Walters, "and not
merely grudging justice, but justice executed with liberality and cor-
dial good feeling." Before a delegation of blacks, Wilson promised
that he would "seek to be President of the whole nation and would
know no differences of race or creed or section, but to act in good
conscience and in Christian spirit through it all." The future president
also indicated he would speak out against lynching, and he delighted
Villard with assurances that he would appoint a National Race Commission to study the race problem if Congress permitted.

Such promises garnered for Wilson the votes of black militants
such as Walters, Du Bois, and Trotter. Wilson, a Ph.D. and former
president of Princeton University, impressed Du Bois, who reasoned
that it was time to "prove once and for all if the Democratic party
dares to be Democratic when it comes to the black man." Sensing a
close race, the Democrats expended considerable effort and money in
courting the black vote, spending $52,255 for this purpose. While the
Democrats probably got less than 10 percent of the black vote, the
1912 election still marked a singular defection by blacks from the
Republican party.

Moreover, the split in the Republican party between the Taft and
Roosevelt factions enabled the Democrats to win the election of 1912.
With Democrats in firm control of Congress, Wilson proved to be an
effective reformer. In the first two years of his presidency, he began to
put his New Freedom proposals into law by enacting an antitrust bill,
banking reform, a reduction of import taxes, and income-tax legislation. In 1914 Wilson moved beyond the New Freedom and enacted
much of Roosevelt's more advanced New Nationalism, including a
maximum eight-hour workday for railroad workers, federal loans to
farmers, and federal aid to state education and highway building.

Wilson's administration also dramatically changed the atmosphere
in the nation's capital, much as Roosevelt had done in 1901. The first
southern president since the Civil War, Wilson put five Southerners in

his cabinet and picked as his closest advisor, Edward M. "Colonel" House, a Texan. Southerners also dominated the powerful committees in Congress, in which an Alabamian became Senate majority leader and a Virginian led the House. Presiding over the Supreme Court was Chief Justice Edward D. White of Louisiana. Ambassadorships went to Thomas Nelson Page of Virginia and Walter Hines Page of North Carolina. The historian C. Vann Woodward described the change in Wilsonian Washington as "a revolution in the geographical distribution of power." After more than a decade of Republican rule, the change in the national government was as though southern generals had suddenly taken command of the Union Army.

Like those of Roosevelt, Wilson's pre-presidential racial views hardly suggested that he would, once the chief executive, be a friend to blacks. Born in 1856 in Virginia and raised in Georgia, Wilson held racial views typical of a white Southerner reared during the Civil War and Reconstruction Eras. His father, a prominent Presbyterian minister, believed that the Bible sanctioned slavery. Wilson's personal views on race had been widely circulated in scholarly and popular publications, massive writings on American history and government laced with assertions of the superiority of Anglo-Saxons. Wilson demonized the abolitionists and characterized slavery as a civilizing process for "a host of dusky children untimely put out of school." He cherished southern values and said the South was the "only place in the country . . . where nothing had to be explained to me." In step with the Dunning School of historians, Wilson declared in his five-volume work, *A History of the American People* (1902), that Reconstruction constituted "the veritable overthrow of civilization in the South." While president of Princeton University, Wilson kept the elite institution lily-white. In July 1913, the president spoke at the fiftieth anniversary commemoration of the Battle of Gettysburg, which more than 50,000 veterans and a host of dignitaries attended. On the hallowed ground where Lincoln spoke of a "government of the people, by the people, and for the people," Wilson rejoiced that sectional strife had ended and Americans had become "as brothers and comrades" with all quarrels forgotten. The Gettysburg celebration was a love fest of Yankees and Confederates that boded ill for African Americans. As the historian David W. Blight described the occasion, "all sectional strife was gone" and "all racial strife ignored."

One day after Wilson spoke at Gettysburg, the Post Office began to segregate its employees by race. A week later the Treasury Department directed whites and blacks to use separate toilets. Although some segregation of the federal bureaucracy had occurred under Roosevelt and Taft, Wilson essentially southernized the racial practices of the capital city. The members of the Wilson administration most closely associated with the segregation of Washington, D.C., were Secretary of the Treasury William Gibbs McAdoo of Georgia and the Postmaster General Albert Sidney Burleson of Texas, but many others deserve blame for assaulting the federal fortress of dignified employment for blacks. McAdoo vowed, "I shall not be a party to the enforced and unwelcome juxtaposition of white and negro employees. . . ." Burleson complained that it was "almost impossible to have different drinking vessels and different towels or places to wash" when blacks and whites were working in the same postal vehicles. Josephus Daniels, the North Carolina journalist who had helped instigate the 1898 Wilmington race riot, set out as secretary of the navy to segregate the races in his department for "health and safety" reasons.

Other government bureaus and federal cafeterias gradually fell to segregation as emboldened white federal workers registered protests against working and eating with blacks. Outsiders bombarded Wilson and his cabinet with complaints about the specter of social equality in Washington. The badly misnamed National Democratic Fair Play Association protested to the postmaster general that a southern woman, the daughter of a Confederate officer, could not tolerate working beside a "dark-skinned, wooly-headed negro." Another white woman in the office of the Recorder of Deeds swore in an affidavit that she contracted a vaginal infection from using the same toilet as diseased blacks. Thomas Dixon of *Clansman* fame wrote to his friend Wilson in July 1913, "I am heartsick over the announcement that you have appointed a negro to boss white girls at Register of the Treasury." Before the segregationist makeover of the federal bureaucracy, the president's southern wife, Ellen Axson Wilson, expressed shock at the sight of blacks and whites working and eating together in the nation's capital.

Though not a radical white supremacist, Wilson capitulated to the demands of the extremists. He had no desire to humiliate or be cruel to blacks, but he believed segregation was necessary to eliminate "the friction or rather the discontent and uneasiness which has prevailed in many departments." The president assured Dixon in 1913 that he was proceeding with a plan that "will put them [blacks] all together and will not in any one bureau mix the two races." He told Villard that segregation did not entail "humiliation" for blacks but was "distinctly to the advantage of the colored people themselves." No official directive went out to segregate the machinery of government, but secret letters, word-of-mouth, and the steely resolve of southern appointees to extend the ways of Jim Crow to the capital did the job. In his research on Wilson's racial policies for *Separate and Unequal: Black Americans and the US Federal Government* (1995), the political scientist Desmond King found that the president's belief that segregation would benefit blacks amounted to self-deception. Not only were blacks humiliated, they were treated unfairly. Under segregation, blacks held the lowest jobs and seldom advanced beyond the lowest ranks as federal employees.

Indeed, under Wilson the government hired significantly fewer blacks, and the president cut back drastically on black appointments. Whites took diplomatic posts in the Dominican Republic and Haiti, jobs that had traditionally gone to blacks, even under the Democrat Grover Cleveland. But even had Wilson been generous with his black appointments, the Democratic Congress would have rejected them. Wilson's nominee for the Register of the Treasury, a black Democrat from Oklahoma, went down to defeat in the Senate. During the length of his presidency, Wilson appointed only two black persons to significant posts and retained only six from previous administrations, far poorer than Taft's record of seventeen black appointments and fourteen retentions. To make things worse, in 1914 the U.S. Civil Service Commission made a person's photograph a mandatory component of all job applications; one needs little imagination to guess how this affected black employment in a government substantially controlled by white Southerners. The number of black civil servants in the federal government fell from 6 percent in 1910 to 4.9 percent in 1918.

Two events that occurred during Wilson's first term banished any doubts about his racial sentiments. The first event involved his reaction to a special White House screening of the incendiary film, *The Birth of a Nation*. His friend Thomas Dixon arranged the showing of the film, which was roughly based on his novel, *The Clansman*. Dixon had campaigned strenuously for Wilson in 1912, and now he was eager to show the president a film that he believed uniquely ordained to expose the dangerous threat that blacks posed and explain the necessity for the formation of the Ku Klux Klan. Dixon told the president that the movie would "revolutionize every man . . . into a good Democrat." After seeing the film, Wilson seemed to agree. "It is like writing history with lightning," the president exclaimed, "and my only regret is that it is all so terribly true."

The second event that brought out his true racial feelings was a clash he had with William Monroe Trotter, a Harvard-educated black militant. Villard arranged for Wilson to meet in 1914 with a delegation of disgruntled blacks that included Trotter. Several of the blacks in the group politely questioned Wilson's segregationist policies, asking the president if he thought a person could work with any self-respect if he were set off behind a screen because of his color. But Trotter, as always, was more blunt when he asked the president, "Have you a 'new freedom' for white Americans and a new slavery for your Afro-American fellow citizens?" Disturbed by Trotter's manner and tone, Wilson grew flushed and abruptly dismissed the black delegation. Apparently, Woodrow Wilson could not tolerate an uppity black man.

Wilson's policies aroused great bitterness among blacks, especially those who had voted for him. The National Negro Press Association denounced Wilson's policies as "unjust and un-American." Du Bois lambasted the president for breaking his promise to speak out against lynching. Even Booker T. Washington, who had no clout whatsoever with the Democratic president, expressed his discontent in a letter to Villard, who relayed it to Wilson. "I have recently spent several days in Washington," the Tuskegee educator told Villard, "and I have never seen the colored people so discouraged and bitter as they are at the present time." After Wilson sent Americans abroad on a crusade to make the world safe for democracy (the U.S. entry into World War I), blacks parodied the president's racially suspect idealism. As one black writer said of Wilson, "He believed in democracy for humanity but not for Mississippi." The poet and novelist Claude McKay had one of his characters say, "For according to my eyesight, and Ise one sure-seeing nigger, the wul' safe for democracy is a wul' safe for crackerdom."

In 1914 the *New Republic* editorialized: "The President used fair words in 1912 in his appeal to the Negroes for votes. We know now that those words meant nothing." Like Roosevelt, Wilson was defeatist on the race issue. When Villard hounded Wilson about setting up a race commission as he had promised, the president confessed to Villard that he was quite distressed by the race problem. "I say it with shame and humiliation," he lamented, "but I have thought about this thing for twenty years and I see no way out. It will take a very big man to solve this thing." In short, neither Roosevelt nor Wilson had a solution to the race problem—except to keep blacks in permanent subordination and hope that they would gracefully accept their assigned place.

During Wilson's first term the Democratic Congress of 1913–15 initiated a surge of bills designed to discriminiate against African Americans. Led by radical racists such as Tillman, Vardaman, Heflin, Furnifold Simmons of North Carolina, Martin Dies of Texas (later of the House Un-American Activities Committee fame), and "Cotton" Ed Smith of South Carolina, legislators introduced a stack of anti-black bills, though none passed. Several bills called for segregated streetcars and the banning of interracial marriages in the District of Columbia. Others would have prohibited the immigration of any non-white persons, excluded blacks from the military, and repealed the Fourteenth and Fifteenth Amendments.

Few northern progressives effectively answered the radical white supremacists in Congress. With relatively few blacks in their con-stituencies, many northern legislators were largely indifferent to the race issue, though virtually all of them were white supremacists. Even Congressman Edgar D. Crumpacker, who tried repeatedly to use the Fourteenth Amendment to reduce southern representation in Congress, said, "No one questions the superiority of the white race. . . ." At best, northern progressives went along with southern moderates and occa-sionally denounced southern radicals for their intemperance and de-cried atrocities such as lynching. Virtually all embraced Booker T. Washington's gradualism. Senator Robert "Fighting Bob" La Follette of Wisconsin, one of the most outspoken northern politicians on the race question, supported the federal voting rights act of 1890 and ve-hemently protested Wilson's segregation policies. Yet even La Follette did not gravitate toward Du Bois and the NAACP.

The Supreme Court and Jim Crow

If the successive presidents and Congresses proved hostile to black rights, could the aggrieved minority find hope in the Supreme Court? Hardly. In 1896 the Supreme Court had opened the floodgates of Jim Crow legislation with *Plessy* v. *Ferguson*. Subsequently, the highest court in the land continued to affirm segregation and the disfranchisement of African Americans. It displayed little interest in reviewing civil rights cases brought to it under the Fourteenth Amendment. According to one study, the court considered 528 cases under the Reconstruction amendment between 1890 and 1910, only 19 of which dealt with race. The court also closed loopholes in basic law that threatened segregated edu-cation and transportation. In *Cummings* v. *Richmond County Board* (1899), the court allowed a Georgia county to close the black high school while keeping the white one open, arguing that it would be better to spend money on black elementary education. In *Berea College* v. *Kentucky* (1908), the court upheld a state law that required the segregation of private schools. Incidentally, by 1900 Berea College, once an aboli-tionist stronghold of higher education with a majority of black students, enrolled only a few black students. In addition, the formerly integrated college now segregated its dorms, cafeterias, and athletic teams and banned interracial dating.

After upholding Mississippi's legal disfranchisement of blacks in 1898, the Supreme Court did the same for Alabama in *Giles* v. *Harris* (1903). The court also put its imprimatur on America's rule over foreign colored people in *Downes* v. *Bidwell* (1901), a case con-cerning the Philippine Islands in which the justices ruled that the rights in the United States Constitution did not "follow the flag" to far-flung places. In other words, the court saw no need for constitutional pro-tection of Filipino subjects, saying that the "Anglo-Saxon character" of the American officials overseeing the country would ensure justice for its brown-skinned inhabitants.

On the question of race, the Supreme Court essentially operated a minimalist court. It dodged issues on procedural grounds or issued narrow rulings that did not halt the assault on the civil rights of blacks. As already noted, even though the court struck a blow against peonage in *Bailey* v. *Alabama* (1911), widespread peonage continued in the South. In *Bailey* the court ruled on narrow, formalistic grounds, indicating that it was more interested in upholding the honor of the court than in stopping peonage. Even the most celebrated victories of the NAACP before the Supreme Court rang hollow. Although the court, in *Guinn* v. *United States* (1915), struck down the grandfather clause, its opinion did not deter black disfranchisement in the least. Nor did the court's ruling in *Buchanan* v. *Warley* (1917), which ostensibly prohibited de jure residential segregation, deter the separation of the races in the cities North or South. And *Buchanan* was decided not on the grounds of human rights, but on those of white property rights. In the few civil rights cases the court chose to consider, it, at best, upheld, as the legal scholar Michael Klarman put it, "formal compliance with the Constitution" while simultaneously maintaining segregation and white supremacy. At worst, the Supreme Court confirmed the racist attitudes that infused American law, and it did nothing to arrest the deteriorating status of African Americans.

Ironically, Justice John Marshall Harlan, the Southerner who had dissented passionately in *Plessy* and served on the Supreme Court until 1911, remained the most liberal member of the court in regard to civil rights. More typical of the court's makeup in the Progressive Era were Oliver Wendell Holmes, Jr., and Chief Justice White. Holmes, a Boston jurist appointed by Roosevelt, seemed completely immune to the abolitionist heritage of his native state. A strict constructionist who believed that the law should be left to the "felt necessities of the time" as determined by legislators, Holmes was disinclined to intervene judicially to support civil rights for blacks. Chief Justice White of Louisiana, who served on the court from 1894 to 1910, had fought for the Confederacy and had been a member of the Ku Klux Klan. Like Wilson, he received a special screening of *The Birth of a Nation* at the behest of Dixon. After seeing the movie in the Supreme Court Building, White declared that it had captured "for the first time" the true story of the Klan. The Chief Justice proudly told Dixon: "I was a member of the Klan, sir. Through many a dark night, I walked my sentinel's beat through the ugliest streets of New Orleans with a rifle on my shoulder. . . . You've told the true story of that uprising of outraged manhood." The Supreme Court would not mount any real challenge to racial inequality until the 1930s and 1940s.

Black-White Relations in the North: Slouching toward the Nadir

The early years of the twentieth century saw increasing hostility toward blacks in the North as well as the South. More and more, blacks faced segregation in or exclusion from northern restaurants, hotels, and theaters. As already noted, housing in northern cities became progressively more segregated after 1900. In the Gilded Age, blacks had been elected to state legislatures and city councils in the North, but by the turn of the century blacks began to disappear from elective office. Mary Church Terrell, a founder of the NAACP, attended an integrated Oberlin College in the 1880s, but a quarter of a century later her children endured segregation at the Ohio school. After discovering that three blacks had gained admission into the American Bar Association in 1912, the organization revoked their memberships and banned black lawyers from entrance. In the late nineteenth century, blacks played professional baseball with whites, while black jockeys rode at major as well as minor tracks, but that had changed by the twentieth century. Even "racial advances" reminded African Americans of how far they had sunk in public esteem. In 1915 the New York legislature banned "Hit the Nigger" games, popular contests at carnivals and amusement parks in which whites hurled baseballs at grotesque images of black persons.

Jack Johnson's victories over white boxers, the eugenics movement, and the general atmosphere in the nation's capital, all acted as catalysts for the introduction of numerous laws against interracial marriage in the North. These proposed laws gave the ultimate sanction to racial caste. All the southern states, of course, had antimiscegenation laws, but between 1880 and 1920 thirteen western states also passed such statutes. In 1920 a total of thirty states forbade interracial marriage. During the Progressive Era, legislators introduced bills against interracial unions in fourteen northern states, including Ohio, Illinois, Michigan, New York, Pennsylvania, and Wisconsin. Although none of the bills passed, they received serious consideration and were sometimes defeated by narrow margins.

More ominous, the first two decades of the twentieth century also witnessed the eruption of race riots in northern cities that matched the intensity of those in New Orleans and Atlanta. The following cities suffered major racial disturbances: New York (1900), Evansville, Indiana (1903), Springfield, Ohio (1904), Greensburg, Indiana (1906), and Springfield, Illinois (1908). Moreover, between 1917 and 1921, some twenty-five race riots broke out across the nation. These riots closely correlated with the increased migration of blacks to northern cities. Although the overall percentage of the black population in the North remained small, about three-fourths of the southern migrants concentrated in the larger cities and created a critical mass for race conflict. The rapid influx of blacks into the North also led to the formation of miserable slums in which disease, vice, and crime flourished—and for which whites held African Americans solely responsible.

Harassment of blacks by urban police forces, often composed largely of black-hating immigrants, led to chronic racial confrontations in northern cities. The New York City race riot of 1900 began after a black man killed a plainclothes police officer who had assaulted him. The death of the white policeman caused white mobs to randomly attack blacks throughout the city. And the police did little or nothing to stop the mayhem. But big cities such as New York were not unique in this regard. In northen cities big and small, anytime black migrants approached 10 percent of the population, whites began to consider them a threat to white supremacy. In the rough Ohio River town of Evansville, Indiana, the black population had grown to 13 percent by 1900, and soon thereafter whites began to blame the recent arrivals for escalating vice, crime, and disorder. Racial tensions soared in 1903 when a black man of unsavory reputation killed a white policeman. A race riot erupted after law enforcement officials prevented the lynching of the accused murderer—he was spirited away to another city. Only the intervention of the police and the state militia prevented an outright race war. Intimidated by events, 400 to 500 blacks fled Evansville for good.

In 1908 a highly symbolic and much bloodier race riot occurred in Springfield, Illinois, the hometown of Lincoln. As in Atlanta two years earlier, the white press in Springfield played up reports of crime committed by blacks before the riot, especially the offense of rape. The *Illinois State Journal* and the *Illinois State Register* ran headlines such as, "NEGRO'S HEINOUS CRIME" and "DRAGGED FROM HER BED AND OUTRAGED BY A NEGRO." The spark that set off the riot was a white woman's accusation of rape against a black man, a false charge that she later recanted. When police prevented whites from lynching the alleged rapist and protected another black man accused of killing a police officer, an enraged mob attacked the entire black community, particularly singling out successful blacks. The mob looted, burned, assaulted, and killed eight blacks. In the shadow of Lincoln's tomb, members of the mob yelled, "Curse the day that Lincoln freed the nigger." Only swift action by the governor, the mayor, the sheriff, and the militia prevented more casualties.

In the wake of the violence, thousands of blacks fled Springfield in terror. Finding refuge in surrounding areas, however, proved difficult, for many Illinois towns had laws and customs warning blacks not to let the sun set on them. Although the identity of many of the mob leaders was known and 190 whites were indicted for participating in the Springfield riot—four policemen were indicted for not carrying out their duty to stop the rioters—most witnesses refused to testify against the vigilantes. In the end, only two whites were convicted of any crime.

William English Walling, a leftist journalist who happened to be in Chicago when the riot broke out, went down to the state capital to cover the event and published his findings in the New York *Independent*. Walling discovered that whites of all classes were unrepentant and shameless about the riot, telling him, "Why the niggers came to think they were as good as we are." On the lecture circuit, southern Senators taunted Northerners about the riots. Tillman gloated that the North was just as racist as the South, and Vardaman crowed that southern lynch mobs were more careful to punish the guilty parties than northern mobs, which, he charged, plundered and killed indiscriminately.

Even as the United States of America prepared to make the world safe for democracy in 1917, everything at home seemed to militate against making democracy safe for African Americans. The white South, the president, the Congress, the Supreme Court, the two major political parties plus the Socialists, organized labor, science, and religion—all supported a system and a mindset that held blacks down and denied them the basic rights of citizenship. On the eve of the United States' entrance into World War I, blacks found themselves more powerless, more reviled, more segregated, and more discriminated against than at anytime since the days of slavery.

By the beginning of World War I, sectionalism on the issue of race was eroding in favor of a national consensus. A 1903 editorial in the *New York Times* had reported that "practically the whole country had acquiesced in the South's answer to the race question." Ten years later the *Charlotte Observer* gave credence to that view when it boasted that "the country has fairly come to be of one mind upon the so-called negro problem." Whereas Tillman had been seen as a southern ogre at the turn of the century, by the end of the Progressive Era northern newspapers complimented him on his intellectual growth while in Washington. In 1918 the *New York World* likened the bombastic racist to a cocoanut, "rough, hard, [and] shaggy" on the outside but full of the "milk of human kindness" inside. Tillman had not changed, the North had.

The night is sometimes darkest before the dawn. The Springfield riot aroused an unusual amount of anger and alarm in liberal quarters. The racial situation prodded Du Bois and his growing number of followers into action, and it stirred a small band of white neo-abolitionists to organize the NAACP to fight for black rights. The Progressive Era may have been the nadir for blacks, but it was also the dawning of the modern civil rights movement.

CHAPTER FIVE

The Washington–Du Bois Feud, the "New Negro," and the Rise of the NAACP

At the dawn of the twentieth century, Booker T. Washington bestrode America like a black colossus. His acquiescence in the disfranchisement and segregation of blacks in his electrifying Atlanta address of 1895 won the immediate acceptance of the great majority of northern and southern whites and eventually a large number of blacks. But as conditions of African Americans worsened under Washington's leadership, black protest leaders such as William Monroe Trotter revolted against the Tuskegeean. In 1903 W.E.B. Du Bois reluctantly joined the battle against Washington in his classic work, *The Souls of Black Folk*. Angered by Washington's ruthless use of the "Tuskegee Machine," Du Bois invited other anti-Washington militants to form the Niagara Movement in 1905. The "New Negroes" of the movement demanded equal access to higher education, equal treatment in the marketplace, and all rights promised to them in the Constitution.

Although the Niagara Movement faced overwhelming opposition and faded quickly, the increasing racial tension and violence in the early twentieth century galvanized a small group of northern white racial liberals or neo-abolitionists to form the National Association for the Advancement of Colored People in 1909. Popularly known as the NAACP, the new organization absorbed the spirit of the Niagara Movement and gained the protest genius of Du Bois as well. By the time of Washington's death in 1915, his influence had waned considerably, and the trend toward increasing black militancy had hardened. Though largely ignored by mainstream reformers, African Americans created their own Progressive Movement and in so doing established a vital beachhead for the twentieth-century civil rights movement.

Booker T. Washington and the Strategy of Compromise and Gradualism

After Washington delivered his Atlanta speech, powerful whites used their influence and wealth to make him the most powerful black man in America. As mentioned earlier, in 1901 President Roosevelt confirmed Washington's primacy by inviting him to the White House to discuss political patronage—and incidentally to have dinner. White leaders embraced Washington's speech, which became known as the Atlanta Compromise, and praised his recipe for black advance: industrial education over liberal learning, duties over rights, hard work at menial jobs, and strict moral behavior. Washington believed that whites would grant blacks better treatment once the latter cleaned themselves up and adopted proper Victorian standards of behavior. By any standard, Washington's philosophy and program were astoundingly conservative for the leader of a downtrodden and despised race. When Prince Peter Kropotkin, a Russian anarchist, heard that African Americans had a conservative leader, he chortled, "What on earth do they have to conserve?" To understand better Washington's program of accommodation and gradualism, we must briefly examine his early life and consider the historical context in which his ideas and personality evolved.

Washington was born a slave in Virginia in 1856, the son of an unknown white man. He grew up in a rude, one-room shack with a dirt floor that also served as his bed. Young Booker wore no shoes until the age of eight, and his clothing consisted of a rough, scratchy shirt of flax. He and his half-brother John ate sporadically, living on leftover scraps from the plantation on which his mother, Jane, worked as a cook. He received no schooling during his nine years of slavery.

Washington's family moved to Malden, West Virginia, after the Civil War and lived in a house that was little better than the slave hut it had left in Virginia. At Malden, Washington's stepfather first got the young boy a job at a salt furnace and later in the coal mines. At the age of ten Washington became a houseboy for Viola Ruffner, an affluent woman of the town. Her husband, Lewis Ruffner, was a former slaveholder and Union general whose family had been large landholders and mine operators in the Malden area since the eighteenth century. Mrs. Ruffner, a native of New England, demanded near-perfection from her employees. She taught Washington the values of efficiency, punctuality, and cleanliness. She instilled proper manners in him and encouraged his interest in education. This stern and demanding lady sparked an ambition in Washington to rise above his mean beginnings.

While working in the mines, Washington heard about the Hampton Normal and Agricultural Institute, a black school on the Virginia coast that he was determined to attend. In his autobiographical writings and speeches, Washington made the long trek to Hampton legendary. He took the train part of the way, begged rides on stagecoaches, and walked the remainder of the way. Dirty, hungry, and in need of a haircut, Washington, only sixteen, arrived penniless at Hampton on October 5, 1872, shortly after the fall term had begun.

Washington persuaded Hampton to accept him, in spite of his appearance and destitution. Established by the American Missionary Association in 1868, Hampton was decisively shaped by its first principal, Samuel Chapman Armstrong. During the Civil War, Armstrong fought courageously for the Union and achieved the rank of brigadier general. He also served with the Ninth U.S. Colored Troops and developed a concern for the fate of African Americans. After the war he worked for the government's primary agency for black welfare, the Freedmen's Bureau.

Armstrong established a unique type of education at Hampton. A devout Christian and the son of missionaries to Hawaii, the paternalistic general had a sense of noblesse oblige toward "backward races" in the "early stages of civilization." Like his parents, he viewed Hawaiians as "children of the tropics" and "a savage people." And he did not have a high regard for the intelligence of African Americans. The black race, he declared, "will act up to its light, but its best light is dim." As for black suffrage, Armstrong advised the freedmen to abandon political activity. He in fact believed that most blacks were incapable of higher education and needed to be trained for menial jobs in the South. Overeducated blacks, he held, would become troublesome rebels. While Hampton blacks received some instruction in English, math, science, political economy, and history, it was at a very low level. Most students never went beyond the fourth grade.

Despite the many problems facing blacks, Armstrong thought that their main problem was not so much their incapacity for government or intellectual pursuits as their lack of "the right instincts" about "morals and hard work." What blacks needed most, he insisted, was the discipline of hard work and strong moral training. To keep black students out of trouble and avoid scandal, Armstrong kept his charges busy during every wakeful hour. From dawn to bedtime, he closely supervised the students, and the slightest infraction of Victorian morality constituted grounds for expulsion. Hampton virtually turned educational practice on its head. Here students used spare time for study, and they invested normal school hours in manual work and moral training. The harsh regimen at the institute caused about one-fifth of the students to leave there in the first three weeks. About an equal amount managed to graduate and get a rudimentary education. In 1875 the black *Virginia Star* likened Hampton to a "Reform School," while the black nationalist Henry M. Turner bristled at the pictures of Andrew Johnson and Robert E. Lee hanging on its walls.

Black critics charged that Hampton teachers trained the protest out of students and prepared them for life in a white-controlled society. The faculty taught African Americans that their position in society stemmed not from racial discrimination but from the arrested stage of black development. Hampton students also learned that labor unions conspired against the natural laws of economics. Ironically, the school produced few skilled craftsmen. Instead of receiving training as carpenters, Hampton students complained that they had been made to labor in sawmills as menial workers. Despite the emphasis on industrial education, Hampton operated as a normal school with 90 percent of its graduates becoming enthusiastic, if undereducated, teachers who dutifully spread the "Hampton idea" far and wide.

During his time at Hampton, Washington adopted wholesale the conservative ideas of Armstrong, who became the father the black student never had. Armstrong reinforced Washington's ideas about hard work, thrift, politeness, and cleanliness that he had learned from the Ruffners. For three years Washington thrived in the highly regimented atmosphere of Hampton, working his way through school as a janitor, always eager to impress his white overseer. In 1875 Washington completed the requirements for an elementary school teacher, an occupation he considered essential for helping his people.

After three years of teaching and engaging in multiple endeavors of community uplift in Malden, Washington returned, on Armstrong's invitation, to teach at Hampton. Washington was thrilled to work for his old boss, whom he called "a great man—the noblest, rarest human being that it has ever been my privilege to meet." Armstrong, too, held Washington in high esteem, saying his prize pupil was "no ordinary darkey." In performing his duties as supervisor of the Indian dormitory at Hampton—in Armstrong's mind American Indians constituted another backward race he might civilize—Washington impressed his white mentor with his leadership and his faithful allegiance to the Hampton idea.

In May of 1881, the state commissioners of education for Alabama asked Armstrong to recommend someone to head a normal school for blacks in Tuskegee. Armstrong replied, "The only man I can suggest is one Mr. Booker Washington . . . a very competent capable mulatto . . . the best man we ever had here." The commissioners told Armstrong to send Washington immediately. But when he arrived in Tuskegee in June of 1881, Washington was dismayed to find that no school existed. Nor would there be any state funds for buying land and constructing buildings until October. Still, in July Washington found a way to conduct in a black church Tuskegee's first class of thirty-seven students. That summer he also spotted a farm with several buildings that he thought might make a suitable educational site, and he borrowed money from Armstrong to purchase the property.

Before Washington rocketed to national fame in 1895, he slowly built up Tuskegee and gained the respect of whites as he faithfully applied the Hampton idea in the new school under his direction. Although Tuskegee primarily trained teachers, Washington also stressed industrial education and manual labor. Under Washington and staff, students worked a forty-hour week for one dollar, and they literally constructed the buildings on campus with their own hands. When the school needed benches, boys learned enough carpentry to build them. When students needed more clothes, girls learned how to sew and then made them. As at Hampton, far more students dropped out than ever graduated from Tuskegee. The institute was at best a glorified high school with a strange amalgam of vocational and academic training. Louis Harlan, the major biographer of Washington, found that Tuskegee graduates "murdered the King's English." The institute never gained accreditation during Washington's lifetime.

Washington ran his fiefdom with an iron hand. He overworked and underpaid the teachers under him. He hectored, threatened, and dismissed independent-minded teachers without due process. As one faculty member complained, "Mr. Washington's scheme is to have such control over his teachers that they will tremble at his approach." Washington dismissed students for trivial offenses, such as drinking on the eve of graduation. Like a zealous overseer, he strode the campus, paying attention to every detail and scolding students and staff for dirty kitchens, unkempt clothes, faulty gates, squeaking pumps, and missing buttons. Both faculty and students rejoiced whenever Washington left campus on one of his fund-raising, promotional tours.

Under Washington's guidance, Tuskegee grew rapidly and flourished financially. From the poor, makeshift school of the early 1880s, the Alabama institute was transformed into a showplace of black education. After Washington's Atlanta speech, the publication of his autobiography, and his invitation to the White House—all by 1901— money flowed to Tuskegee in torrents. Industrial moguls adored Washington's pro-capital and anti-labor philosophy, his program of industrial education, and his glorification of the white elite. After reading *Up From Slavery,* George Eastman of Eastman Kodak sent a $5,000 check to Washington and gave him $10,000 annually from 1910 to 1915. On Washington's death, he contributed $250,000 to Tuskegee. After hearing Washington speak, Andrew Carnegie handed him ten $1,000 bills. In 1903 the steel baron donated $600,000 to the Alabama school, earmarking one-fourth of it for the personal use of the man he called "the modern Moses." Not only were plutocrats kind to

Washington, but Congress granted 250,000 acres of federal land to Tuskegee in 1899. Between 1895 and 1900 thirteen new building arose on campus, many of them inscribed with the names of his rich white benefactors.

With rich resources and influential friends in high places, Washington constructed what Du Bois famously labeled the "Tuskegee Machine." The Tuskegee educator ruthlessly used his power to diminish and defame his opponents. Washington performed like an urban political boss, but his web of power and influence was national in scope. "The man who disparaged the importance of political power for his race," C. Vann Woodward observed, "came to exercise political power such as few if any Southern white men of his time ever enjoyed." In the Republican era of Roosevelt and Taft, Washington controlled black appointments to federal positions, not just in the South, but across the nation. Many among the black elite who did not agree with Washington's conservative philosophy nonetheless danced to his tune because he decided who got what in the black educational and political world.

Washington also tried to control the black press. The white press was so overwhelmingly pro-Washington that it posed no problem. Washington gained sway over the National Negro Press Bureau and employed a staff of ghostwriters to flood the bureau with articles proclaiming the sanctity of the Tuskegee idea and his leadership. Washington subsidized black newspapers that agreed to help undermine his opponents. He tried to intimidate opposing editors by suing them for slander if they criticized him too strongly. Notably, Washington used his resources to gain control of the influential *New York Age* and seduce its once-militant editor, T. Thomas Fortune, to his strategy. Nothing affecting blacks seemed to be beyond Washington's grasp. The management of the Yazoo and Mississippi Railroad consulted Washington to inquire whether he thought it should write "Negro" or "Colored" above the doors of its segregated waiting rooms.

Defenders of Washington have argued that he was a sincere and authentic leader with a realistic program that fit the perilous times. During the dark and violent days after Reconstruction, they argued, it would have been suicidal for southern blacks to advocate suffrage and integration. Furthermore, the black strategy of self-help, self-segregation, and withdrawal from politics had begun before Washington came to Tuskegee. And despite Washington's conservative methods, his defenders emphasized, his ultimate goal was racial equality. Historical research has revealed that the Tuskegeean secretly fought Jim Crow laws and restrictions on the ballot. Washington also appealed to race pride and group solidarity, an orientation that appealed to the rising black middle class, which included Du Bois. The very fact that so many powerful whites lionized Washington and made him an international celebrity bolstered black pride and helped ease an oppressed race through the nadir of its existence.

As for education, Washington's defenders maintained that at the turn of the twentieth century the question was not what kind of schooling blacks would receive, but whether they would get any at all. Washington's industrial education was more palatable to hostile whites, many of whom opposed any kind of schooling for blacks. Although Tuskegee offered outdated industrial education, Washington's supporters argued that it produced teachers that the black community sorely needed. Washington also tapped into various educational funds from the North and spread substantial amounts of money throughout the beleaguered South. The black educator was not opposed to liberal arts education in principle, but he believed that industrial education was best for most blacks, given their current state of social development.

Even so, much of Washington's approach to race relations proved to be wrong. Holding anachronistic ideas about industrial education, he looked back to an age of independent artisans, small business proprietors, and yeoman farmers rather than forward to the machine age of the twentieth century. And while Tuskegee did produce needed teachers, why, critics asked, did Washington set such low academic standards? Poorly trained teachers only perpetuated second-rate black education. In *The Education of Blacks in the South, 1860–1935* (1988), The historian James D. Anderson quipped, "Washington and Tuskegee were Armstrong and Hampton in blackface." Giving up suffrage and acquiescing in segregation for the promise of more economic opportunity, critics argued, turned out to be a bad bargain. How, Washington's detractors asked, could a people advance economically by performing only menial work and having no rights or political power?

The principal flaw in Washington's scheme was that it hinged on the promise that whites would treat blacks better once they conformed to the middle-class standards taught at Tuskegee. In this case, Washington was clearly naive. In his Atlanta address, he told his people to stay in the South because white Southerners were their friends and would "administer absolute justice" and create material prosperity that would "bring into our beloved South a new heaven and a new earth." He placed hope in almost any white person who did not wear a sheet. In 1895 he wrote the following to the vicious race-baiter Senator Tillman: "I was born a slave; you a freeman. I am but a humble member of an unfortunate race; you a member of the greatest legislative body on earth, and of the great, intelligent Caucasian race." Washington went on to say to Tillman that he was sure that the "great and magnanimous" Senator from South Carolina would not inflict any harm on blacks as he represented "the chivalry of the South, which has claimed no higher praise than that of protectors of the defenseless." No one could outdo the wizard of Tuskegee in flattering southern whites.

Washington seemed to lack the capacity for righteous indignation against racial injustice. He seldom spoke out against the scourge of lynching. And when he did, he did so meekly and, like Roosevelt, always attached the caveat that blacks invited mob violence by their excessive criminality. He never explained, as Du Bois did, the sociological reasons that underlay crime. Lacking passion, Washington never inspired great zeal or intense dedication among his followers. His clout came from his patronage for blacks and his prestige among whites. He had no realistic program to combat white racism and black poverty. The most powerful black man in America could not even shape the policies of his northern benefactors; he could only acquiesce in them.

Although Washington's ultimate goal may have been racial equality, he routinely led whites to believe that blacks would settle for much less, inferring that industrial education meant menial jobs for blacks. His humble and deferential manner around whites seemed to signal that he accepted the inferiority and subordination of his race. And he helped perpetuate black stereotypes by telling "darkey stories" to white audiences, his jokes underscoring black ignorance and the alleged propensity of his kind for stealing chickens—or having, as he put it, in their possession feathered creatures "gathered from miscellaneous sources." In 1900 Washington declared that "the white man is three thousand years ahead of us, and this fact we might as well face now. . . ." Just how long, critics wondered, did Washington suggest it would be before blacks were worthy of equal rights?

Washington's uncritical view of industrial capitalism, his anti-union stance, and his acceptance of the Horatio-Alger myth all went against the grain of progressivism. Washington flailed against the tide of history by advising blacks to stay on the farm. His program was predicated on rule by *moderate* whites, but the sad fact was that *radical* white supremacists ruled the South. Furthermore, his pronounced contempt for black intellectuals was petty and myopic. Not a few scholars have argued persuasively that Washington was as much concerned about his own fame and power as the fate of his race.

One of the worst errors Washington made was in never wavering from his compromising strategy in the face of worsening race relations. His extravagant optimism throughout a malignant and tragic era of race relations was inexcusably obtuse. He never seemed to realize, let alone acknowledge, that by the 1890s southern leaders did not just want to keep blacks down, but they wanted to humiliate and degrade them. As the historian Joel Williamson observed, "Under Washington . . . black resistance began from a kneeling position to face an onrushing, powerful, and fanatical foe bent upon nothing less than rendering black people prostrate."

W. E. B. Du Bois and the Strategy of Protest

William Edward Burghardt Du Bois (pronounced "Due Boys") was born free in Great Barrington, Massachusetts, in 1868, the son of Alfred and Mary Du Bois. His mother descended from Tom Burghardt, an African slave who gained his freedom by fighting in the American Revolution. Several generations of Burghardts became respectable, church-going small farmers in the vicinity of Great Barrington, a town of about five thousand people. As agriculture in the area languished after the Civil War, many of the Burghardts left the land to become waiters, cooks, housemaids, barbers, and common laborers in the city. Du Bois's father was born in Haiti, the grandson of a wealthy French planter and one of his slaves. A charming, romantic, indolent drifter, Alfred Du Bois fought in the Civil War before he happened into Great Barrington and married Mary Burghardt. Evidence suggests that Alfred had deserted a previous wife before coming to town. Young Du Bois, known as "Will," never knew his father, for Alfred deserted the family two or three years after his marriage and was never heard from again.

Later in life Du Bois tended to romanticize his father, ignoring the man's obvious character flaws. He speculated that the darker complexioned Burghardts had intimidated his father and driven him away because he was "too good looking, too white." Ever sensitive to skin tones, Du Bois depicted his father as "just tinted with the sun" and his mother as "brown" compared to the darker Burghardts. The only tangible contact Du Bois had with the paternal side of the family occurred when as a teenager he visited his grandfather, Alexander Du Bois, in New Bedford, Massachusetts. Du Bois was impressed with his grandfather, who had a good education and a hint of aristocracy. His proud grandfather gave Du Bois a sense of having significant origins. Of his diverse ancestry, Du Bois later said that he was born "with a flood of Negro blood, a strain of French, a bit of Dutch, but thank God! no 'Anglo-Saxon.'"

Life was not easy for the female-headed Du Bois family. Mary worked as a housemaid, and Will and his half-brother, Adelbert, worked at a variety of odd jobs to help support the family. The family also took in a boarder to help meet expenses. Hard times, however, seemed to strengthen family ties, and Du Bois and his mother enjoyed a close and loving relationship. Although Du Bois hardly realized it at the time, his family's economic situation was precarious.

Yet Du Bois had fond memories of his youth in Great Barrington, which was located in the scenic Berkshire Mountains in western Massachusetts. He recalled that he was born by "a golden river in the shadow of two great hills." There he frolicked in the woods, climbed mountains, and swam and fished. He warmly recalled church gatherings, strawberry festivals, and public debates. Showing an intellectual bent even as a child, he read voraciously and served as a local reporter for T. Thomas Fortune's *New York Globe*. Frank Hosmer, the principal of Great Barrington High School, encouraged Du Bois to take college preparatory classes and arranged for the purchase of his textbooks. Excelling in school, Du Bois graduated first in his class of 1884, the lone African American among his senior classmates.

Du Bois later recalled that there was little racial discrimination against him in Great Barrington. But he did write about a defining moment in his childhood when the students in his elementary class exchanged "gorgeous visiting cards." All was "merry," Du Bois recollected, until the new girl in town refused his calling card because he was black. Suddenly, it occurred to him that he was different. After the card incident, Du Bois was more sensitive to racial slights and did not push himself on whites. Instead he became combative toward them. "The sky was bluest," he recalled, "when I could beat my [white] mates at examination-time, or beat them at a foot-race, or even beat their stringy heads."

As he neared graduation in Great Barrington, Du Bois set his sights on attending Harvard University. However, the townspeople who raised money for Du Bois's college education decided that he should study among his "own people" at Fisk University in Nashville, Tennessee. Du Bois was deeply disappointed at not being able to attend America's premier university, but his rerouting to Fisk proved fortunate in many ways. Fisk was one of the best black liberal arts colleges, and it attracted some of the best black scholars, all of whom had a missionary zeal to uplift their race. Du Bois stood out academically at Fisk, but perhaps more significantly it was there that he embraced blacks, in his words, as "my people," where he first professed pride in "the black blood" that coursed through his veins. No longer just a man, Du Bois now proclaimed he was "a Negro," adding, "and I glory in the name!" Moreover, while at Fisk he taught in rural elementary schools in Tennessee for two summers. This eye-opening experience made him aware of the poverty and backwardness of southern blacks and revealed to him how the people furthest down the socioeconomic scale suffered materially, socially, and spiritually under an oppressive Jim Crow system that he considered a new form of slavery.

After getting his degree at Fisk, Du Bois achieved his dream of attending Harvard. He entered the prestigious university in 1888 on a scholarship, although he had to repeat his junior and senior years because authorities at Cambridge considered the validity of some of Fisk's courses suspect. During his time at Harvard he had virtually no social interaction with white students, though he enjoyed an active social life among African Americans in Boston. Du Bois excelled in his philosophy major and impressed several famous professors, among them the esteemed philosophers William James and George Santayana and the noted historian Albert B. Hart. James, whose Pragmatism had a lasting impact on Du Bois, advised him to abandon philosophy and take up the more practical field of sociology, which he thought could be applied more effectively to the race problem. Since Harvard did not yet offer a major in sociology, Du Bois earned a master's degree in history in 1891 under the direction of Professor Hart, a hard-nosed empiricist.

After entering graduate school, Du Bois began to plan to get a doctorate in Europe. In 1892 he won a scholarship from the Slater Fund to study in Germany. He studied for two years at the University of Berlin and traveled around Europe as a gentleman-scholar. Dropping his usual reserve toward whites, Du Bois ate, drank, and sang with Germans, conversing fluently with them in their language. He fell in love with a German woman and had an affair with his landlady's daughter. A devotee of German high culture, he took on elitist mannerisms, growing a goatee and wearing fancy clothes. One of the many paradoxes surrounding Du Bois is how Eurocentric this fiery race man became in his formative years.

In Germany Du Bois studied under some of the most respected scholars in Europe. He did much of his advanced research under the guidance of Gustav von Schmoller, a specialist in historical economics. Although his research was deemed sufficient for a doctoral dissertation, he found he could not earn a Ph.D. unless he stayed in Berlin another year to satisfy the residency requirements. Lacking money to accomplish this, Du Bois returned to the United States to complete his doctorate at Harvard. His time in Germany, though, strengthened his belief that empirical inquiry could solve social problems, marking him as a rather elitist and conservative thinker.

But he was hardly conservative when he envisioned his role in the world. Indeed, in Berlin he came to see himself as a man of destiny. Celebrating his twenty-fifth birthday there, he declared in his diary that his goal was "to make a name in [social?] science, to make a name in literature and thus to raise my race." Before returning to his homeland, Du Bois solemnly dedicated his life to engaging in scientific scholarship that would assist "the rise of the Negro people, taking for granted that their best development is now one and the same with the best development of the world." Thinking of his future as a race leader, he ruled out marriage to a German woman he loved, and in Boston he avoided matrimony with some strikingly attractive "black" women because they could pass for white. As a future leader of black America, he felt he had to marry someone who could at least pass for black.

Du Bois returned to the United States in 1894 and accepted a teaching position at Wilberforce University, a black school in Ohio. Meanwhile, he worked on his dissertation, which was an extended version of his master's thesis on the trans-Atlantic slave trade. Working again under Professor Hart, Du Bois completed his dissertation and received his Ph.D. in 1895, the first black person to earn a doctorate at Harvard. The following year his dissertation, titled *The Suppression of the African Slave Trade to the United States of America, 1638–1870,* was published by Harvard. In this book, which became the standard work on the topic for decades, Du Bois analyzed one of the darkest pages in Western history in conservative, dispassionate language.

In 1897 at the first meeting of the American Negro Academy in Washington, D.C., Du Bois delivered a fifteen-page paper titled "The Conservation of the Races." The black academy was the idea of the aging Reverend Alexander Crummell, the longtime black nationalist and intellectual who, like Du Bois, hoped to advance blacks in America and Africa through unflinching, objective scholarship. On this historic occasion, Du Bois argued emphatically, like Theodore Roosevelt and many "scientific" racists of the time, that race was central in explaining history. He claimed that the white, black, and yellow races made up the three "great families of human beings," which could be subdivided into eight regional races: Slavs, Teutons, English, Romance nations, Negroes, Semites, Hindus, and Mongolians. Race was not just an odious social construct to Du Bois, but something to nourish and conserve. Race went beyond mere physical qualities, he said, and entailed "spiritual and psychic differences." He declared that "the history of the world is the history, not of individuals, but of groups, not of nations, but of races, and he who ignores or seeks to override the race idea in human history ignores and overrides the central thought of all history."

Du Bois further explained that each race had a certain genius and something important to contribute to the world. In 1903 in *The Souls of Black Folk* he singled out the black "gifts" of music, humor, and religion, describing the Negro as a "religious animal." In a 1904 article he defined black genius as "the sweetness of its soul, and its strength in that meekness which shall yet inherit this turbulent earth." He emphasized the ability of blacks to endure pain and sufferings with dignity and forgiveness.

Like most thinkers of his time, Du Bois hopelessly confused race, nationality, and culture. He was also unclear about whether race was biological or cultural in nature. For the most part, he rejected the biological determinism of his time and stressed the historical and environmental factors in the formation of race. Yet at times he seemed to accept inherent racial differences and conflate biological and sociohistorical factors. He, for example, linked race with "common blood" and "physical peculiarities." Du Bois's idea of race drew upon the thinking of his Berlin teacher, Heinrich von Treitschke, and other German thinkers such as Johann Gottfried von Herder and Johann Gottlieb Fichte, all of whom lauded the contributions of different races to civilization. In 1897 Du Bois could be described as a romantic racialist, a description that, as we have seen, fit many white abolitionists. Not surprisingly, ascribing different gifts to different races could easily play into the hands of virulent white racists whose stock and trade was to play up racial differences to the crippling disadvantage of blacks. To say that blacks brought song, dance, humor, and meekness to the modern world, at the same time Anglo-Saxon chauvinists boasted that their race had contributed republican government, modern science, technology, and virtually everything prized by white Americans, was a racial trap for African Americans. Although Du Bois never abandoned his romantic racialism entirely, he later realized that his early emphasis on racial gifts and differences was not an

effective strategy for securing the civil rights (individual and constitutional) of blacks.

In his academy address, Du Bois also raised searching questions
about black identity and assimilation into American society. He asked,
"[W]hat after all, am I? Am I an American or am I a Negro? Can I
be both?" These troubling questions about identity derived from
Du Bois's—and every other black person's—daily confrontation with
race prejudice. Nonetheless, Du Bois stated his belief that blacks would
eventually be accepted as Americans. Because blacks and whites had
"substantial agreement in law, language and religion," he concluded
that it was "entirely feasible and practicable for two races . . . to develop side by side in peace and mutual happiness. . . ." For all his high
hopes about racial harmony, Du Bois did not insist on integration but
instead called for separate black development. "For the development
of black genius, of Negro literature and art, of Negro spirit," he advised, "only Negroes bound and wedded together, Negroes inspired
by one vast ideal, can work out in its fullness the great message we
have for humanity."

In keeping with his call for blacks to "unflinchingly and bravely
face the truth" about themselves, he argued before the academy "that
the first and greatest step toward the settlement of the present friction
between the races lies in the correction of the immorality, crime and
laziness among Negroes. . . ." He warned, "[U]*nless we conquer our
present vices they will conquer us* [emphasis in original]." In addition
to the vices of "loafing, gambling, and crime," he judged that "an
alarmingly large percentage of our men and women are sexually im-
pure." Given the shortcomings of his race, Du Bois conceded that
demands for "social equality" were unworkable at the time.

As Du Bois delivered his paper on race, he was already working
on his next scientific treatise on blacks. In 1896 his reputation for
objective scholarship brought him an offer from the University of
Pennsylvania to undertake a sociological study of the black community in Philadelphia. For almost two years Du Bois and his wife Nina
lived in the black section of Philadelphia's Seventh Ward, a decaying
slum where the black scholar carried out a block-by-block sociological inquiry that led to the publication of *The Philadelphia Negro* in
1899. Again, Du Bois was brutally frank about black vices and crime,

describing a "class of criminals, prostitutes and loafers." He depicted Philadelphia blacks as "willing tools" of a corrupt Republican political machine and called the northern influx of southern blacks a "migration of barbarians." He concluded that the subjects of his study were, "as a rule, careless, unreliable and unsteady." Sounding a lot like Washington, Du Bois advised, "Negroes must cultivate a spirit of calm, patient persistence in their attitude."

Du Bois's haughty moralizing about lower-class blacks has annoyed some historians. Du Bois's preeminent biographer, David Lewis, chastised the black leader's "prim sententiousness about bottom-class manners and institutions." Du Bois, no doubt, tried to render his book as unthreatening to whites as possible so that his underlying, though somewhat veiled, thesis blaming white racism for the pitiful condition of blacks in the City of Brotherly Love would not be summarily rejected. Because of this hedging, *The Philadelphia Negro* was, Lewis said, a "great, schizoid monograph." At the time, however, many white journals praised Du Bois for his honesty about black Philadelphians. Lyman Abbott's *Outlook* noted that Du Bois did not try "to bend the facts so as to plead for his race." And the *American Historical Review* lauded Du Bois for being "perfectly frank, laying all necessary stress on the weakness of his people."

Du Bois's similarities to Washington in the 1890s were unmistakable. Du Bois opposed the Federal Elections Bill of 1890, commenting in the *New York Age,* "When you have the right sort of black voters you will need no election laws." Reacting to Washington's 1895 Atlanta address, he deemed it "a word fitly spoken" and "a good general statement." He further speculated that "here might be the basis of a real settlement between white and blacks in the South, if the South opened to the Negroes the doors of economic opportunity and the Negroes co-operated with the white South in political sympathy." After Washington's famous speech, Du Bois even applied for a job at Tuskegee.

Over the years, historians and biographers of Du Bois have puzzled over the many changes in his ideas in the course of his long life—he died in Africa as a Communist in 1963. Du Bois was a creative and eclectic thinker who modified his philosophy and tactics as the racial situation changed. He zigged and zagged between accom-

modation and protest, idealism and pragmatism, integration and separation, Eurocentrism and Afrocentrism, scientific scholarship and pro-
pagandistic agitation, and pacifism and support for war. As will be
seen in the further discussion of *The Souls of Black Folk* below, his
very being was nearly torn asunder by the clashing ideas and feelings
in his mind. The fact that Du Bois left massive correspondence, published hundreds of articles and editorials, and wrote sixteen nonfiction books and five novels over a period of nearly seventy years gave
historians much grist for the mill. The concept that best lends some
consistency and continuity to his changing ideas is pluralism. He was
an early cultural pluralist who rejected the Melting Pot model and
steered a middle course between integrationists like Frederick Douglass
and black nationalists like Marcus Garvey, the back-to-Africa leader
who was prominent after World War I. Du Bois's mutability was not
atypical of black leaders who lived in a flamboyantly hostile and rapidly changing society, facing daily a kind of sociology of the absurd.
As Gunnar Myrdal observed about blacks prior to the 1940s, *"Negroes seem to be held in a state of eternal preparedness for a great
number of contradictory opinions*—ready to accept one type or another depending on how they are driven by pressures or where they
see an opportunity."

However much Du Bois seemed to agree with Washington in the
1890s, one difference between him and the Tuskegee boss was profound. Unlike Washington, Du Bois always charged that white racism
lay at the heart of the race problem. And after Du Bois took a position
at Atlanta University in 1898, the philosophical gap between Washington and him soon widened. Living in the Deep South, Du Bois
modified his view that objective scholarship could change the minds
of whites about blacks. After the bloody Wilmington race riot and the
heinous murders of postmaster Fraser Baker and members of his family in South Carolina in 1898 and the especially brutal lynching of
Sam Hose near Atlanta the following year, Du Bois declared, "One
could not be a calm, cool, and detached scientist while Negroes were
lynched, murdered and starved."

In spite of his hardening views, Du Bois was not eager to alienate
the most powerful black man in America. In 1899 Du Bois and Wash-

ington in fact collaborated in an effort to defeat a disfranchisement law in Georgia and contest the lack of first-class railroad cars for blacks. Du Bois was impressed that Washington fought against peonage and the exclusion of blacks from juries, even if all such endeavors were done in secret. In 1899 Du Bois also helped squelch an effort to censure Washington at a meeting of the National Afro-American Council in Chicago. Moreover, in that same year Washington offered Du Bois a position at Tuskegee and gave him a grand tour of the campus. Although Du Bois declined to take the job, in 1901 he accepted Washington's invitation to go camping and fishing in West Virginia, and in 1903 Du Bois taught summer school at Tuskegee.

Nevertheless, by 1900 Du Bois was already drifting toward the anti-Washington camp. Du Bois suspected that Washington's influence prevented him from getting two jobs that he applied for in Washington, D.C., one as superintendent of public schools and the other as a professor at Howard University. He also grew tired of Washington's apologies for the accumulating white atrocities against blacks and resented the way Washington directed large amounts of northern money to vocational schools at the expense of liberal arts colleges, such as his own Atlanta University. Reviewing *Up From Slavery* in 1901, Du Bois voiced in a mild way some of his growing resentment toward Washington. It was the publication of *The Souls of Black Folk* in 1903, however, that halted the uneasy cooperation of the two leaders.

Souls presented a prolonged reflection, in Du Bois's words, on "the strange meaning of being black" in a society that looked on African Americans "with amused contempt and pity." It was a deep meditation on racism, politics, economics, and the development of black culture before and after slavery. In this classic, Du Bois abandoned his usual scholarly reserve and bared his suffering and angry soul to the world, powerfully conveying how it felt to be an exquisitely educated and highly sensitive black man at the turn of the twentieth century, and doing it all with majesty and a stunning lyricism. The book was actually a collection of fourteen essays, nine of which had been published in magazines and journals between 1897 and 1903. Yet the collection of these essays in one accessible place gave them new force, and Du Bois's personal touch and his urgent and often fiery tone gave the book a unique power. Du Bois wore all his professional hats in the book, skillfully displaying his talents as a historian, social scientist, philosopher, poet, and racial prophet.

The riveting first chapter of *Souls,* "Of Our Spiritual Strivings," posed the melancholy questions: "How does it feel to be a problem?" and "Why did God make me an outcast and a stranger in mine own house?" Here he also posited his theory about "double-consciousness," which, he argued, compelled black Americans always to look at themselves through the eyes of unfriendly whites. In doing so, he said:

> One ever feels his two-ness,—an American, a Negro; two souls, two thoughts, two unreconciled strivings; two warring ideals in one dark body, whose dogged strength alone keeps it from being torn asunder.

Although Du Bois laid down a fighting manifesto for African Americans in *Souls,* in it he advocated neither integration nor separation. He left the question of where in society blacks belonged shrouded in ambiguity and clearly tried to assure whites at the outset, just as he had in the "Conservation of the Races," that recognizing the humanity of African Americans would not result in social equality:

> He [the Negro] would not Africanize America, for America has too much to teach the world and Africa. He would not bleach his Negro soul in a flood of white Americanism, for he knows that Negro blood has a message for the world. He simply wishes to make it possible for a man to be both a Negro and an American, without being cursed and spit upon by his fellow, without having the doors of Opportunity closed roughly in his face.

As previously, Du Bois did not romanticize ordinary blacks or give them artificial agency. He referred to uneducated black farmers as "lewd," "vicious," and given to "sexual immoriality" because of the heritage of slavery. Still, he squarely placed primary blame for the condition of blacks on white racism, which he metaphorically referred to as "the veil." He, for example, declared that the "red stain of bastardy" attributed to blacks came from "two centuries of systematic defilement of Negro women" by white men.

In the opening sentence of the second chapter, "Of the Dawn of Freedom," Du Bois repeated the projection he had made at the Pan-African Congress in Paris in 1900, "The problem of the twentieth century is the problem of the color line. . . ." Acting as a revisionist historian, Du Bois argued against the negative view of Reconstruction and praised federal efforts to empower blacks. He lauded the much-damned Freedmen's Bureau as "on the whole successful beyond the dreams of thoughtful men." He suggested that a permanent Freedmen's Bureau could have prepared former slaves for citizenship and might have made strides toward solving the race problem, an interpretation more in line with historical thinking today.

The third chapter of *Souls,* "Of Mr. Booker T. Washington and Others," had the strongest and most immediate impact. In a tone that was civil and respectful, Du Bois first outlined Washington's philosophy and program without being judgmental. He said that the Tuskegee leader was "certainly the most distinguished Southerner since Jefferson Davis," and he applauded Washington for his emphasis on "Thrift, Patience, and Industrial Training for the masses." He also charged that some of the black opposition to Washington stemmed from envy of his success and power.

But, in the end, Du Bois's criticism of Washington turned scathing. He claimed that whites had made Washington the black leader, and he attacked the Tuskegee Machine by charging that "the hushing of the criticism of honest opposition was a dangerous thing." He claimed that Washington "practically accepts the alleged inferiority of the Negro race" and insisted, as never before, that blacks needed all their constitutional rights, including the right to vote and higher education for talented blacks. In a later chapter, Du Bois further explained the necessity of higher education to develop the black elite or the "Talented Tenth," whose leadership, he argued, was vital to gain the respect of the world and raise the race. Du Bois reminded readers that African Americans had lost many of their rights and had been subjected to increasing violence under Washington's leadership. "Is it possible, and probable," Du Bois asked, "that nine millions of men can make effective progress in economic lines if they are deprived of political rights, made a servile caste, and allowed only the most meagre chance for developing their exceptional men?" The answer, he exclaimed, was an "emphatic *No.*" Washington's program, he fumed, would lead to "industrial slavery" and "civic death."

In its highly varied chapters, *Souls* gravitated between despair and hope, gradualism and radicalism, bitterness and forgiveness, and elitism and egalitarianism. Reviewers of *Souls* thus came to widely different conclusions about the book. Du Bois's philosopher friend, William James, thought there was too much anger and despair in the tract, to which Du Bois replied that he was "tuned to the most aggressive and unquenchable hopefulness." Most of the white South ignored the book—as did the Tuskegee-controlled black press—although the *Houston Chronicle* accused Du Bois of "inciting rape." The antiblack *New York Times* was predictably hostile. Encouraging though was the fact that the *New York Evening Post* and the *Nation,* which the pro-Washington and influential Oswald Garrison Villard owned, carried highly favorable reviews of the book.

And Du Bois's book left its mark on the world. It sold well and went through several printings in the first five years. It quickly achieved national and international acclaim and was published abroad. James Weldon Johnson, a black leader whose multiple talents rivaled those of Du Bois, believed that the book's influence was "greater upon and within the Negro race than any other single book published in this country since *Uncle Tom's Cabin.*" After reading the book, the black poet Paul Lawrence Dunbar said, "Du Bois is our great man." He assured his friends that Du Bois "has passion and eloquence and he is going to express us." William H. Ferris, a black critic of Washington, declared *Souls* to be "the Bible of the Negro race."

The Niagara Movement and the Revolt against Washington

Oddly enough, Du Bois did not think his attack on Washington in *The Souls of Black Folk* would cause an irrevocable break between him and the imperious wizard of Tuskegee. When Professor Du Bois left Tuskegee after teaching summer school there to travel to Boston in the summer of 1903, he had no intention of joining an anti-Washington coalition. But that was before the so-called "Boston riot" that erupted on July 30.

Ever since Washington's Atlanta Compromise speech, several blacks had stridently attacked Washington's leadership. But one man stood out by pursuing Washington with almost manic ardor: William Monroe Trotter, the owner of the *Boston Guardian.* Trotter was a light-skinned African American who had grown up in comfort in Hyde Park, a white area in Boston. Like Du Bois, he graduated at the top of his class in a mostly white high school. Unlike Du Bois, he mixed freely and easily with Caucasians and had many white friends. Entering Harvard in 1891, the dapper and energetic Trotter played sports, made Phi Beta Kappa, and graduated *magna cum laude.*

Not only did Trotter have a Harvard degree, he also had an inheritance. In 1892 his father died of tuberculosis and left him $20,000, the equivalent of a small fortune in that time. Intensely political, Trotter helped organize the Boston Literary and Historical Association in 1901, which became a forum for racial militancy. More important, in November of that year he and his partner George W. Forbes put out the first issue of the *Boston Guardian.* Financially independent, Trotter could not be cowed by the Tuskegee Machine. In fact, Washington's attempts to intimidate him only incited him to greater militancy, as agitation and rage seemed inherent in his personality. Du Bois liked Trotter personally but kept him at a distance because of his lack of restraint. While they both agreed in substance on the weaknesses of Washington's program, Du Bois cringed when Trotter publicly called Washington, among other things, a "self-seeker," a "skulking coward," "Pope Washington," and "the Benedict Arnold of the Negro race."

Trotter and kindred militants tried to perform a coup d'état against Washington at the Louisville meeting of the Afro-American Council in early 1903, but the plot failed. Undaunted, the Boston editor and his radical allies—among them William Ferris, a Yale prodigy with a master's degree from Harvard; Archibald W. Grimké, a lawyer with a Harvard degree; and Clement Morgan, a brilliant Harvard classmate of Du Bois—planned to confront Washington at a meeting of the National Negro Business League in Boston on July 30. When Washington began to speak in a hot and crowded church, Trotter and his allies interrupted the Southerner and peppered him with rude questions, such as, "Is the rope and the torch all the race is to get under your leadership?" Soon a melee broke out between the opposing factions and policemen arrived to restore order. Trotter was arrested and later fined $50 and sentenced to thirty days in jail.

Although Du Bois did not attend the Boston meeting and had no knowledge of Trotter's plans, the event helped turn him against Washington. Du Bois deplored the way the Tuskegee Machine tried to ruin Trotter and his fellow conspirators and link Du Bois to the plot. First, pro-Washington men pressed charges against Trotter and secured his jail sentence for allegedly starting the riot. Then Washington bribed a black student at Yale to sue Trotter for libel, which forced the Boston editor to make a costly out-of-court settlement. Bookerites also tried to remove Trotter's co-editor Forbes from his job at the West End Library. The Tuskegee Machine in fact did everything it could to bankrupt the *Guardian*. The neutral Kelly Miller described the intraracial feud as a "war to the knife and the knife to the hilt."

In April of 1905, Du Bois told Professor Hart of Harvard that Washington had "done the race infinite harm & I'm working against [him] with all my might." Two months later Du Bois issued a "Call" for black leaders to meet in July in Buffalo, New York, for the purpose of organizing an aggressive campaign for black equality. Fifty-nine men representing the vanguard of the Talented Tenth signed the call, and twenty-nine of them converged on Niagara, Canada, on July 11 for a three-day meeting—they met on the Canadian side of the river because hotels in Buffalo refused service to the black delegation. The delegates drew up a "Declaration of Principles" that called for determined action to achieve for blacks all constitutional rights, the full range of education, and equal economic opportunity. The declaration of principles urged Congress to enact the "appropriate legislation for securing the proper enforcement of those articles of freedom" that are enshrined in "the thirteenth, fourteenth and fifteenth amendments of the Constitution." Here were no mystical ruminations on racial gifts, blackness, or separate development. At Niagara Du Bois invoked the individual rights written into the United States Constitution by abolitionists in the 1860s and 1870s.

At the second annual meeting of the Niagara Movement at Harper's Ferry in August of 1906, many of the roughly 150 delegates, which now included women, walked bare-footed and silently over the hallowed trail trod by John Brown. At Harper's Ferry Du Bois now demanded something he had conceded earlier: social equality, insisting on "the right to walk, talk, and be with them that wish to be with us." He no longer apologized for black crime, declaring instead, "We are not more lawless than the white race, we are more often arrested, convicted and mobbed." On the final day of the conference, Du Bois's "Address to the Country" moved the delegates with these words: "We claim for ourselves every single right that belongs to a freeborn American, political, civil and social; and until we get those rights we will never cease to protest and to assail the ears of America." The civil rights movement of the twentieth century had begun in eloquence and earnest.

Although the ranks of the Niagara Movement eventually grew to about four hundred, the organization became moribund within five years. One reason for the decline was that Washington's Tuskegee Machine turned all of its guns on the new organization. The machine employed Melvin J. Chisum to spy on the first Niagara meeting, but Chisum missed the convention because he arrived late and did not know the meeting had moved from Buffalo to Niagara. It also persuaded much of the black press to either blot out coverage of the new organization or condemn it as subversive. Washington's influence also kept rich whites from financing the militants, and he used his clout to scare off all five of the black southern members of the movement with carrots and sticks. He informed the president of Atlanta University that he could expect to receive no further donations from white philanthropists as long as Du Bois was on the faculty there. For his strong support of Du Bois, J. Max Barber lost his journal, the *Voice of the Negro,* as well as his teaching job at a black school. David Wallace wrote Du Bois that he could not continue in the organization without harm to his career but would ever remain a "secret comrade."

And after 1905 Washington relentlessly tried to destroy the personal reputation of Du Bois. Knowing of Du Bois's amorous tendencies, Washington hired investigators to look for sexual improprieties by the Niagara leader. His ghostwriters informed the public that the great proponent of suffrage did not vote—Du Bois refused to pay the poll tax on principle. After the Atlanta race riot, Washington's machine circulated an untrue story that Du Bois had acted in a cowardly manner by remaining in Alabama—where he was doing research—

until the riot had ended. Du Bois later conceded that the Tuskegee Machine did more harm to the movement than he ever imagined.

Still, the Niagara Movement failed for a number of other reasons. It never raised enough money to be an effective civil rights organization, and it lacked an official mouthpiece for publicity. Du Bois and others started two unofficial journals, the *Moon* and *Horizon,* both of which failed in short order. Almost all of the white press ignored the organization or characterized it as radical. Finally, the aloof and haughty Du Bois was not a natural leader. Many wondered why he did not "warm up" to people. "I could not slap people on the back and make friends of strangers," Du Bois said. "I could not easily break down an inherited reserve."

But even as the Niagara Movement waned, a stronger and more enduring civil rights organization took its place: the NAACP. The mounting injustices against blacks had finally galvanized a group of white neo-abolitionists who, along with Du Bois and his allies, re-energized the quest for racial equality in 1909.

The Rise of the NAACP

The immediate event that led to the formation of the NAACP was the murderous race riot in Springfield, Illinois, in August 1908, which, as mentioned earlier, the radical journalist William English Walling had rushed down from Chicago to cover for the *Independent*. Walling reported that the rioters showed no remorse or shame for the barbaric bloodletting and property destruction that they had inflicted on blacks in Lincoln's hometown. He furthermore discovered a contagion of racism sweeping across the Midwest with whites of all classes conducting "permanent warfare with the negro race." Sounding like an old abolitionist, Walling warned the nation, "Either the spirit of Lincoln and Lovejoy [a martyred abolitionist] must be revived and we must come to treat the negro on a plane of absolute political and social equality or Vardaman and Tillman will soon have transferred the race war to the North." "What large and powerful body of citizens," Walling asked, was ready to come to the rescue of endangered blacks?

By the time of the tragic event in Springfield, a small group of racially liberal progressives or "new abolitionists" had already begun to tune out Washington and listen to the voices of Du Bois and Trotter. One of the important new abolitionists was John Milholland, a rich Republican businessman from New York. Once a supporter of Washington, Milholland broke with Tuskegee and founded the Constitution League in New York City in 1906. The intensely religious Milholland explained his motivation in his diary, "I feel that my time has come at last—to lead . . . this Crusade for the Negro's Political & Civil Rights . . . the Supreme Moral Issue of the Hour and this Republic." The Constitution League campaigned against disfranchisement, peonage, and mob violence and won the support of black activists such as Du Bois, Trotter, Archibald Grimké, Bishop Walters, and Mary Terrell. Milholland's league constituted an important link between white and black liberals and provided a base for the NAACP.

No one was more important for the formation and survival of the early NAACP than Mary White Ovington. A descendant of abolitionists, Ovington grew up in an affluent family in Brooklyn, New York, and attended Radcliffe College in the early 1890s. Ovington's interest in the race problem heightened when she heard Washington speak at the Social Reform Club in New York in 1903, but she was more impressed with Du Bois, whom she met the following year. Persuaded that Du Bois was on the right path, she covered the meeting of the Niagara Movement at Harper's Ferry as a journalist. In 1907, at Du Bois's invitation, she became the only white member of the Niagara group. The following year she moved into a black settlement house in New York City to study the conditions of its inhabitants, an experience that led to the publication of her muckraking book, *Half a Man: The Status of the Negro in New York* (1911). Although Ovington, like Walling, was a Socialist, she hid her political orientation so as not to endanger the cause of racial equality.

Ovington became obsessed with Walling's call to action at Springfield and committed herself to forming an effective organization to work for racial change. In the first week of 1909, Ovington met in New York City with Walling, Charles Russell, and Henry Moskowitz— all radical reformers like herself. They decided to enlist the influential journalist Oswald Garrison Villard to draft a call for a new civil rights organization, which they planned to release on the centenary of Lincoln's birth on February 12.

Ovington and her allies could not have picked a better person to sound the battle cry of racial reform. Villard, who described himself as "a young radical . . . ready to believe truths which shocked were sometimes called for," was the son of the railroad magnate Henry Villard and the grandson of the famous abolitionist William Lloyd Garrison. It was his love of the unvarnished truth that had soured him on the meek and platitudinous rhetoric of Washington.

When the "Call" was indeed released on Lincoln's birthday, sixty-nine prestigious progressives had attached their names to it, including Jane Addams, Clarence Darrow, William Dean Howells, Lincoln Steffens, and William Hayes Ward. Powerfully worded, Villard's call asked what Lincoln would think if he miraculously returned to America in 1909 and found that blacks and whites could not mingle in a common market place, ride trains together, or watch a play in the same area of a theater. "This government cannot exist half slave and half free any better today than it could in 1861," Villard declared. He concluded with the following invitation, "We call upon all believers in democracy to join in a national conference for the discussion of present evils, the voicing of protests, and the renewal of the struggle for civil and political liberty."

Meeting from May 31 through June 1, 1909, some three hundred men and women—Booker T. Washington was not among them—gathered to establish what would become the NAACP. William Ward, the longtime supporter of civil rights and the editor of the *Independent,* said in the keynote address that it was time to proclaim the "absolute divergence of view between the ruling majority in the South" and northern reformers. Color-blind justice had long been extinguished in the South, he continued, and it was retreating rapidly in the North. On the last day of the meeting, the conference organizers nominated an interim governing body known as the Committee of Forty, which had the power to decide the administrative shape of the new organization and pick its board of directors.

Despite the enthusiasm at the interracial conference, the last day of meetings revealed signs of racial discord. Ida Wells-Barnett and Monroe Trotter argued heatedly with more-conservative whites about the strategy and goals of the organization. How, they asked, could there be "too much racial agitation"? Wells-Barnett and Trotter then complained that whites were trying to dominate the proceedings and set goals for blacks. More acrimony ensued when these two outspoken blacks were excluded from the Committee of Forty, with Du Bois's acquiescence. Villard, who still hoped the NAACP might work with Washington and his followers, omitted Wells-Barnett and Trotter from the all-important committee because he thought they spoke with "a nasty spirit" that would make cooperation with Tuskegee impossible.

Predictably, the Tuskegee Machine sprang into action and tried to nip the new agency in the bud. Though usually reluctant to attack white people, this time Washington used the power at his disposal to try to tarnish all the leaders of the NAACP. Washington's men particularly targeted the white women of the NAACP and planted slanderous articles full of sexual innuendo in the press about white women dining with black men at the Cosmopolitan Club and in private homes. The attractive Mary Ovington received so many obscene letters that she had to have male relatives screen her mail for her. Washington asked the businessman William Baldwin to get his wife to start a conservative organization in New York to compete with the NAACP, a request that helped lead to the formation of the National Urban League in 1911. Washington's ability to limit the flow of white money to the NAACP probably damaged the organization more than anything else, for lack of funds was a constant and pressing problem the organization faced in its early years.

Publicity posed another problem. Officials of the NAACP constantly complained that it could not get the mainstream press to publicize its activities. The *New York Times* gave only the barest mention of Villard's call in 1909, while Washington's attendance at the annual Lincoln Dinner in the Waldorf-Astoria made headlines. The nation's most prestigious newspaper described Washington as a man of "penetrating intelligence" and "lofty ideals." February 12, 1909, was also the one hundredth anniversary of the birth of Charles Darwin, and in close proximity to its praise of Washington, the *Times* lauded the theorist whose views had unwittingly facilitated the entrapment of Americans in a web of scientific racism.

Without doubt, the most brilliant act of the newborn NAACP was the selection of Du Bois as the Director of Publicity and Research in 1910. The only full-time black employee of the NAACP for many years, Du Bois was taking a chance on a job guaranteed him for only a year. He took the risk because he believed the NAACP offered a golden chance for blacks and whites to work together as equals. He also thought the agency would give him the opportunity to fulfill his self-avowed destiny as the leader of his race. In 1910 Du Bois finally stepped out of his "ivory tower of statistics and investigation" and became a full-time agitator for black equality. The black Brahmin had crossed the Rubicon.

Du Bois's great weapon for racial agitation was *The Crisis,* the official magazine of the NAACP. For more than twenty years the editor of *The Crisis* powerfully articulated the aims of the civil rights organization. In a flamboyant style laced with vituperation and sarcasm, Du Bois condemned race prejudice, forced segregation, disfranchisement, lynching, and the denial of equal education and economic opportunity for blacks. His trademark was ennobled grievance. Du Bois asked God never to forgive him if "I ever weakly admit . . . that wrong is not wrong, that insult is not insult, or that color discrimination is anything but an inhuman and damnable shame." In the first issues of *The Crisis*, Du Bois assaulted every racial taboo known to Americans, including social equality. He thundered that blacks who did not have the courage to demand social equality should keep a dignified silence. On the subject of lynching, he was at his fulminating best. When a black man was burned alive in 1911 before a large crowd in Coatesville, Pennsylvania, Du Bois described the atrocity with searing eloquence:

> The flames beat and curled against the moonlit sky. The church bells chimed. The scorched and crooked thing, self-wounded and chained to his cot, crawled to the edge of the ash with a stifled groan, but the brave and sturdy farmers pricked him back with the bloody pitchforks until the deed was done.
>   Let the eagle scream!
>   Civilization is again safe.

Du Bois encouraged blacks to resist such outrages, crying out, "If we must die, in God's name let us perish like men and not like bales of hay."

Nor did Du Bois spare African Americans from his barbs. He lambasted compromising black editors, preachers, and educators. He charged that the black press was anti-intellectual and often ungrammatical. In response to some of Du Bois's diatribes, Moorfield Storey, a noted white lawyer and the first president of the NAACP, complained to Villard that Du Bois must be deranged from his long subjection to racism.

The Crisis nonetheless struck a chord in African Americans; and it prospered. In the first year the circulation of the magazine reached 10,000 a month, which by the end of the second year had climbed to 20,000. By 1919 *The Crisis* enjoyed a readership of 100,000 a month, about 80 percent of it being African American. By the time the United States entered World War I, *The Crisis* had helped forge an new measure of black pride and unity in the nation.

While *The Crisis* brought more unity and self-identity to blacks, it sorely divided officials at the NAACP. Du Bois was quickly at odds with Villard, the chairman of the board. Paternalistic and condescending toward assertive blacks, Villard objected strongly to Du Bois's vitriolic attacks on Washington and his blanket indictment of whites. He also insisted that the board of directors had ultimate power in the NAACP and could censor *The Crisis*. Du Bois, on the other hand, considered the magazine his "soul-child" and treated it as a separate entity from the NAACP. He wanted a magazine with independence, personality, and focus, something no large board could create. Since *The Crisis* was self-supporting, Du Bois had bargaining power and knew in fact that he was indispensable, a reality that made him even less amenable to compromise.

Unfortunately, Du Bois had a tendency to assume that all whites were racists, and he was programmed to expect insults from them. To be sure, Du Bois had reason to believe that the condescending Villard had not been fully cleansed of racism, a view reinforced by the fact that the journalist's southern wife would not allow him to entertain blacks in their home. Even so, Du Bois was too quick to discern racism even in the most well-intentioned whites. Although Du Bois had warned blacks against undue race pride and blind hatred of all whites, he often lashed out angrily and judged all whites as debauched. He almost seemed to enjoy adversity with whites, as he apparently had

back in Great Barrington, when he longed "to beat their stringy heads."
During the Atlanta race riot, Du Bois sat on his porch with a newly
purchased double-barreled shotgun and buckshot and anxiously
awaited the arrival of white vigilantes. With some bravado, he recalled, "I would without hesitation have sprayed their guts over the
grass." His poem about the riot, "A Litany at Atlanta," curtly lectured
the Deity:

> Sit no longer blind, Lord God, deaf to our prayer and dumb to our
>   dumb suffering
> Surely, Thou, too, art not white. O Lord, a pale, bloodless, heartless
>   thing!

About mere white mortals, he later versisfied:

> I hate them, Oh!
> I hate them well,
> I hate them Christ!
> As I hate hell!
> If I were God,
> I'd sound their knell
> This day!

Du Bois's race pride also grew year by year. In 1907 in "The Song of
Smoke," Du Bois beat his light-skinned breast and chanted "I am the
smoke king / I am black."

If not all black leaders exhibited Du Bois's intense suspicion of
whites, they largely shared his romantic racialism and attraction to
the black mystique—Washington and Trotter were noted exceptions.
African American leaders of all stripes simultaneously attacked white
racism and celebrated the superior gifts of the black race. William
Ferris wrote that blacks had "poetic imagination" and "a loveable
nature, a spiritual earnestness and a musical genius." The Reverend
Reverdy Ransom spoke of "the deep emotional nature" of blacks that
made them innately religious. James Weldon Johnson characterized
blacks as being "warmed by the poetic blood of Africa," giving them
"extreme rhythm, color, warmth, abandon, and movement." To him,
the black woman with "her rich coloring, her gaiety, her laughter and

song" was more alluring than her "sallow, songless, lipless, hipless, tired-looking, tired moving white sister." Kelly Miller wrote, "The Negro possesses patience, meekness, [and] forgiveness and spirit which surpasses that yet manifested by other races." The belief in the saving grace of blackness led many blacks to the messianic conviction that African Americans had a mission to save America and the world from aggressive and grasping whites. Blacks understandably needed an escape valve for the steady diet of white racism that they were subjected to, but racial chauvinism was, like Washington's timid accommodation, a problematic way for black leaders to advance the cause of racial equality, especially in an interracial setting. In any case, Du Bois's racial chauvinism made it impossible for him to work harmoniously with Villard and many other whites of the NAACP.

Du Bois's suspicions about Villard's bigotry, however, constituted only a fraction of the rancor between the two men. For example, Villard had written an unfair and scathing review of Du Bois's 1909 biography of John Brown, just before he brought out his own biography of the martyred abolitionist. Furthermore, *The Crisis* was published in the offices of Villard's *New York Evening Post,* where the veteran journalist cast a critical eye on what he considered Du Bois's sloppy administrative practices. The friction grew so intense that Villard resigned from the NAACP in 1913 and threatened to take his rich white friends with him.

Fortunately, Du Bois found two whites at the NAACP whom he could admire and trust. Foremost was Joel Spingarn, who replaced Villard as chairman of the board. Spingarn was an affluent Jew and a Renaissance man. A professor of comparative literature at Columbia University, a poet, a horticulturalist, a soldier, and a pluralist like Du Bois, he did not seem to have a racist bone in his body. It was the NAACP's good luck that Spingarn lost his job at Columbia in 1911 over a dispute with the president of the university. At the age of thirty-six this talented man was free to devote much of his time to the NAACP. Du Bois confided in his correspondence and autobiography that Spingarn had more influence on him than any other white man.

The other white person at the NAACP that Du Bois liked and trusted was Mary Ovington. Walter White called her the "Fighting Saint" of the movement. For more than thirty years Ovington devoted her life to the work of the NAACP. She sat on the first executive committee of the board and served without pay as acting chair and chair of the board from 1917 to 1932 and as treasurer from 1937 to 1941. Ovington and Spingarn generally defended Du Bois against attacks in board meetings, but privately they also criticized him for his obstinacy and for needlessly offending whites (actually, Du Bois argued with everyone, including blacks at the NAACP). As chairman, Spingarn, like Villard, explained to Du Bois that *The Crisis* could not be autonomous. In the end, Spingarn and Ovington worked out a fuzzy compromise with Du Bois and the board that designated *The Crisis* as the official organ of the NAACP but stated that its editorials would be considered the views of the editor alone. The board further elicited a promise from Du Bois that he would keep his editorials free from pettiness, insult, and vulgarity—a promise he only partially kept.

Although the NAACP grew and wielded increasing influence in the Progressive Era, it never became a mass movement. Top-heavy and ruled by a self-perpetuating board in New York, the NAACP had but 6,000 members and 50 branches in 1914. At the end of World War I, however, it had more than 90,000 members and 310 branches. The 1915 controversy over the cinematic bombshell, *The Birth of a Nation,* attracted new members as NAACP chapters demanded that the notoriously racist movie be banned. Even Booker T. Washington waged war against the film. Another factor boosting membership in the NAACP was the appointment of James Weldon Johnson as field organizer in 1916. A lawyer, novelist, poet, songwriter of Broadway hits, and a diplomat for the State Department, Johnson organized many new branches of the NAACP in the South and on the West Coast between 1916 and 1919. In 1920 he became the first black executive secretary of the NAACP.

The NAACP had some notable successes in its first decade. Its crusade against lynching persuaded many whites of the necessity of a federal antilynching bill. The Dyer antilynching bill pushed by the NAACP passed the House in the early 1920s but died in the Senate. The NAACP's investigation of lynching also led to the publication of the important document, *Thirty Years of Lynching, 1889–1918* (1919). *The Crisis* exposed the horror of the race riots that plagued the nation during and after the war. In 1917 Du Bois and Johnson lead a silent march down Fifth Avenue to protest the race riot in East St. Louis, Illinois. With the help of Moorfield Storey, former president of the American Bar Association, the NAACP won victories before the Supreme Court in *Guinn* v. *United States* (1915) and *Buchanan* v. *Warley* (1917), which, respectively, outlawed the grandfather clause and statutes requiring residential segregation. As stated earlier, these victories were rather hollow and did not end the disfranchisement of blacks or urban segregation.

Meanwhile, as the NAACP rose in visibility and significance, the decline of Washington's influence, which had begun with his support of Roosevelt's high-handed discharge of black soldiers at Brownsville and his acceptance of the lily-white policies of Taft, fell to its low point under President Wilson. Washington lost his remaining political patronage when the Democrats captured the federal government in 1913. Wilson's segregation of the federal city and deteriorating race relations even pushed Washington to the left. After a visit to the capital in 1913, he confessed that he had never seen blacks "so discouraged and bitter." In an article of his published in the *New Republic* shortly after his death, Washington condemned segregation as "not only unnecessary, but, in most cases, unjust."

The death of Washington in 1915 ground to a halt the Tuskegee Machine and eased tensions between the Bookerites and the anti-Bookerites. In 1916 Du Bois proposed a meeting of reconciliation between the black factions, and Spingarn offered to host the conference at his magnificent estate in Amenia, New York. Invitations went out to radical and conservative black leaders, and to those in the middle. More than fifty African Americans attended the Amenia Conference in August, including James Weldon Johnson. Inviting Johnson was a masterstroke. No longer a member of the diplomatic corps, he emerged from the conference as the consensus choice as the NAACP's national organizer. Although Johnson had been closely tied to Booker Washington in the past, he was an easy-going, gracious man who had no trouble getting along with the irascible Du Bois. In any case, Johnson's views, like those of many other blacks, had been moving closer to that of Du Bois since Wilson's victory in 1912.

The placid, beautiful setting at Amenia seemed to have the right effect on the delegates. The conferees unanimously agreed on an agenda that stressed support for black suffrage, education of all kinds, and full rights under the Constitution. As a concession to southern blacks, the agreement made allowances for those who had to temper their militancy in the Jim-Crow South. The Amenia Conference marked a shift in the position of black leaders toward Du Bois's position. As America mobilized to make the world safe for democracy, African Americans were more determined to make America safe and equal for blacks than at anytime since Reconstruction.

Other Voices and Other Paths to Racial Uplift

The feud between Washington and Du Bois left its mark on African Americans at all levels of society, and it shaped the debate about how to improve the lot of blacks in the Progressive Era. But not all blacks chose sides in the debate, or at least not decisively; and many of them changed sides as circumstances changed. In their own locales, many blacks, especially those in the South, melded the strategies of accommodation and protest in a quest for "racial uplift" that took on the general qualities of white progressivism. Many worked through the church to advance the race. Others mounted bold protests over local grievances, and increasing numbers of blacks even defended themselves against white violence. Some still advocated migration out of the United States as a path to a better life, but after the 1890s few African Americans left the country; thousands more migrated out of the American South to western and northern cities. Space limitations do not permit a full discussion of all the other important voices of dissent and hope, but what follows does discuss some of the talented and worthy, if less known, black leaders and organizations that have often been obscured by the focus on Washington and Du Bois, and to some extent, Trotter.

Several important black leaders chose sides early in the Washington–Du Bois feud and remained fairly steadfast in their loyalty. T. Thomas Fortune, Emmett Scott, Charles Anderson, Robert Terrell, and almost anyone who held a federal post or education position subject to the power of the Tuskegee Machine supported Washington. Many who supported Washington were more liberal than he, but they stayed in his camp for economic and political reasons. On the other

side, Wells-Barnett, Trotter, Reverdy Ransom, J. Max Barber, Bishop
Walters, Harry C. Smith, publisher of the *Cleveland Gazette,* Mary
Terrell, and Dr. William L. Bulkley, the only black high school princi-
pal in New York City, stood solidly with Du Bois and the NAACP.

Many blacks, however, changed their positions over time. S. Laing
Williams of Chicago and John Quincy Adams of St. Paul, at one time
two of Washington's strongest supporters, became officials in their
local NAACP chapters. John Mitchell, Jr., the longtime editor of the
Richmond Planet, fought disfranchisement, attacked lynching with
Ida Wells, and led a boycott of segregated streetcars in Richmond in
1904. But after he got involved in real estate and banking, he grew
much more conservative and gravitated toward Washington. William
H. Lewis, a brilliant Harvard student and football star, delivered a
strong anti-Washington speech in Boston in 1898 but later fell into
the Tuskegee camp in order to secure an appointment as an assistant
U.S. attorney. Sutton Griggs, who wrote a series of militant black-
nationalist novels between 1899 and 1908, joined the Niagara Movement in 1905. But by 1908 Griggs had became a Bookerite or worse,
branding blacks "a crude and undeveloped race" that was innately
submissive. The eccentric William Ferris, who had degrees from Yale
and Harvard and was an ordained minister in the African Methodist
Episcopal church, moved from the Washington faction in 1905 into
the Niagara Movement, but after World War I he became a follower of
Du Bois's arch-rival, the flamboyant black nationalist, Marcus Garvey.
And even T. Thomas Fortune, who began as a radical in the 1880s and
then followed Washington for over two decades, fell into the Garvey
camp late in his life in the 1920s.

Kelly Miller perhaps best typified black leaders who straddled
the political fence between the Washington and Du Bois camps for
most of his adult life. Born on a tenant farm in South Carolina in
1863, Miller graduated from Howard University in 1886 and did advanced study in mathematics at Johns Hopkins. He returned to Howard
in 1890 as a professor of mathematics and later became the dean of
arts and sciences. Like Du Bois, Miller was a founding member of the
American Negro Academy in 1897. At first he generally supported
Washington's program, refusing Du Bois's personal plea to join the
Niagara Movement. But eventually Miller became an active member

of the NAACP and fought President Wilson's segregationist policies. Yet Miller also served on the board of the National Urban League, which was considered a conservative alternative to the NAACP. Miller's thinking represented that of many blacks who had grown up in the South, experienced the full force of southern racism, and later left the region to become part of the Talented Tenth. Miller saw merit in the approaches of both Washington and Du Bois and worked conscientiously to unify the African American community for more effective action.

Two southern migrants who took a more militant path than Miller were the brothers Archibald and Francis J. Grimké, the sons of a distinguished white South Carolina planter, Henry Grimké, and one of his slaves. They were also the nephews of the renowned white abolitionist sisters, Sarah and Angelina Grimké. After the Civil War, Archibald and Francis traveled north to attend Lincoln University in Pennsylvania, a school formed in 1856 to train Christian leaders "for missionary and colonization work in Africa." After his study at Lincoln, Archibald got his undergraduate degree at Harvard and received a law degree from Howard University. A first-rate intellectual, he was, after Du Bois, the president of the American Negro Academy and wrote weighty papers for it. Disillusioned with the Republicans, Archibald supported New England Democrats, grew close to Trotter, feuded with Du Bois, and became the highly active leader of the Washington branch of the NAACP.

Francis became a Presbyterian minister after he graduated from the Princeton Seminary. The minister of the fashionable Fifteenth Street Presbyterian Church in Washington, D.C., for many years, Francis supported Washington in the 1890s but allied himself with Du Bois after reading *The Souls of Black Folk*. Francis became a supporter of the NAACP and effectively used his pulpit as a civil rights platform in the Progressive Era.

Charles W. Chestnutt, the noted author of short stories and novels, remained friendly with both Washington and Du Bois during their open feud. Born the son of free blacks in Cleveland in 1858, Chestnutt became a lawyer and a prosperous businessman before gaining fame as a writer. He corresponded regularly with Washington and supported much of his program, but he also upbraided the Tuskegeean for not standing up for the rights of blacks and for apologizing for white racism. The Brownsville Affair and the Atlanta race riot drove Chestnutt squarely into the militants' camp. He attended the annual meeting of the Niagara Movement in 1908 and later supported the NAACP.

The black press, which Gunnar Myrdal called "the single greatest power" in the black community, traipsed back and forth between accommodation and militancy. Black newspapers and journals increased from about 25 in 1880 to 150 in the early 1900s. A large part of the black press was clearly under the influence of the Tuskegee Machine, including Fortune's subsidized *New York Age.* The editors of the *Boston Guardian,* the *Cleveland Gazette,* and the *Washington Bee,* however, agitated for black rights and skewered Washington. But the position of much of the black press lay somewhere in the middle and made forays into both camps. Many black editors, particularly those in the South, fought racism indirectly by trying to build black self-esteem and foster self-help, though others spoke out forcefully against segregation and disfranchisement. The militant *Chicago Defender,* established in 1905 by Robert S. Abbott, essentially became a national newspaper during World War I, with editions going to all parts of the nation. The *Defender* was prized in the South as a black face that did not wear the mask. As one black editor put it, "negroes grab the *Defender* like a hungry mule grabs fodder." Thousands of southern blacks took the *Defender*'s impassioned advice to migrate to the North.

One of the principal agencies established to ease the process of urbanization for poor, uneducated black migrants was the National Urban League. Founded, as mentioned, in 1911, the Urban League offered social services and help in job procurement, the same type of assistance that European immigrants might get at the settlement houses. The first executive director of the Urban League was George E. Haynes, a sociologist and the first black to earn a Ph.D. at Columbia University. The interracial Urban League successfully solicited donations from white philanthropists who shied away from the NAACP. Since the board of the Urban League was composed primarily of Washington followers, the organization stressed for blacks—in addition to job placement and acculturation to urban living—personal hygiene, good manners, proper speech, and hard work. After Washington's death, the NAACP and the Urban League developed a friendly understanding that the older organization would address civil rights issues and the newer agency would deal with economic and social concerns. By 1918 the Urban League had twenty-seven affiliates, mostly in large northern cities.

Another agency that assisted blacks in adapting to city life was the Young Men's Christian Association. The YMCA came from Britain to Boston in 1852 and spread throughout the United States in the 1870s and 1880s. The "Y" sought to help young men lead healthy and moral lives. It blended in with the Social Gospel movement and the Progressive Movement by focusing on the human problems of the rising industrial city. Some of the black elite in northern cities fought for integrated YMCAs, but by the early twentieth century most blacks had acquiesced in separate organizations, which were more successful in attracting money from whites. Separate YMCAs also schooled blacks in valuable leadership and organizational skills. They also performed many settlement house functions and cooperated with black churches on social work. Both Washington and Du Bois applauded the work of the Y. The history and work of the Young Women's Christian Association (YWCA) paralleled that of the YMCA and was often led by women who were crucial to the leadership of the black women's club movement.

And it should be noted that black women played a major role in social and political work, a function now much more visible owing to a number of recent books and articles on black female activists. As noted earlier, black clubwomen, who were, by and large, excluded from the white clubwomen's movement, founded the National Association of Colored Women (NACW) in 1896. Although led by middle-class women who believed in the "cult of domesticity" and wanted to improve the reputation of black women, they eventually took on the essence of progressivism and broadened their attack to include an assault on the "structures of oppression" that affected all blacks. By 1916 the national association had many state and local affiliates and more than 100,000 members. Following the organization's slogan, "Lifting as We Climb," the clubwomen fought for suffrage, public health, day care for working women, prison reform, juvenile courts, better schools, playgrounds in black neighborhoods, higher pay for black teachers, better working conditions, and an end to the convict lease system and lynching. Across the nation, black women founded Mothers' Clubs, Phyllis Wheatley Clubs, and Sojourner Truth Clubs. While continuing her crusade against lynching, Ida Wells-Barnett established the Negro Fellowship League in Chicago in 1908, for which she became known as "the black Jane Addams."

Lugenia Burns Hope, the talented and well-educated wife of the president of Atlanta Baptist College, John Hope, founded the Neighborhood Union in 1908. As her biographer Jacqueline Anne Rouse has shown, Hope used the Neighborhood Union to coordinate social work in Atlanta for "moral, social, intellectual and religious uplift," particularly aspiring to "make the world safe for babies and children." The Neighborhood Union of Atlanta stressed improved health and set up an antituberculosis clinic. It also established day-care centers, kindergartens, playgrounds, outreach program for girls, and organized assistance for the sick and aged. Hope also waged a long war against overcrowded black public schools in Atlanta and joined white reformers in trying to close saloons, dives, and houses of prostitution on notorious Decatur Street, where the Atlanta race riot began. Many of Hope's projects were reasonably successful and the Neighborhood Union became a model for organizing black communities.

Many black women activists believed that females had special insight into racial problems because they were instinctual nurturers who suffered from both racism and sexism. Some did Du Bois one better by claiming that black women suffered from a triple consciousness of being female, black, and American. Perhaps the eminent educator and clubwoman Anna Julia Cooper best expressed the idea of black women's manifest destiny when she said in an 1892 speech,

> When and where I enter in the quiet, undisputed dignity of my womanhood without violence and without suing or special patronage, then and there the whole Negro race enters with me.

The bond between women helped unite people at different ends of the political spectrum. Mary Terrell, a founder of the NAACP, and Margaret Murray Washington, Booker Washington's third wife, worked together amicably and effectively in the NACW. Although some white women were willing to work with black women as equals, the women's movement remained largely a segregated affair.

Critics of racial uplift have characterized the black elites as prissy, moralistic control freaks. A pointed example of this view can be found in Kevin K. Gaines, *Uplifting the Race* (1996). Gaines charged that the racial uplifters acted as "ventriloquists for stereotypes of Negro depravity," and he hurled at them the now-familiar charge of blaming the victims. But it was white racism and oppression that widened class differences among African Americans and denied jobs and education to poor blacks at the bottom, not the black elite. Who else but the elite, paternalistic or not, could lead blacks out of the Jim Crow wilderness?

A scant number of blacks took the path of Socialism. One who did was the Reverend George Washington Woodbey. He became a Socialist firebrand after reading Edward Bellamy's utopian novel, *Looking Backward* (1888). Woodbey, a Baptist minister and native of Tennessee, migrated to San Diego in 1902 and spent the next twenty years in a revolving door that saw him in and out of jail for expressing his radical beliefs. As a delegate to several Socialist conventions, he delivered animated speeches that mixed the Bible with the writings of Karl Marx. He also authored a pamphlet titled *Why the Negro Should Vote the Socialist Ticket* and in 1914 ran unsuccessfully for treasurer of California on the Socialist ticket.

Many of the black elite believed that the dissemination of black literature and black history would enhance race pride and help advance the quest for equality. Black southern clubwomen wrote their version of African American history to refute the myths of the Lost Cause, and they read the works of Paul Lawrence Dunbar, Chestnutt, and Du Bois at their literary sessions. In 1911 John Edward Bruce and Arthur A. Schomburg formed the Negro Society for Historical Research in New York City. Two years later Benjamin Brawley, an English professor at Howard with degrees from the University of Chicago and Harvard, published *A Short History of the American Negro*. In 1915 Carter G. Woodson founded the Association for the Study of Negro Life and History and began the publication of the *Journal of Negro History* one year later. Bruce, Schomburg, Brawley, and

Woodson were all determined to reveal the positive achievements of blacks and get them into the textbooks.

The black church also played an important role in social work in the black community. The church was the center of black society, and about half of all African Americans had membership in some denomination, making the rate of church membership higher among blacks than whites. Slightly more than half of all blacks were Baptists, and around one-third belonged to the various Methodist churches. A small minority attended the Presbyterian, Episcopal, Congregational, Catholic, and other churches. Both Washington and Du Bois criticized some of the black churches for the emotional excesses of their services and their uneducated and corrupt clergy. Still, Du Bois recognized the potential of the black clergy in *The Souls of Black Folk* when he wrote, "The preacher is the most unique personality developed by the Negro on American soil. A leader, a politician, an orator, a boss, an intriguer, and idealist—all this he is. . . ." And, in truth, some of the most charismatic, educated, and able blacks served in the ministry. Preachers such as Reverdy Ransom, Francis Grimké, and Bishop Alexander Walters served as leading figures in the Social Gospel movement *and* were active members of the NAACP.

The black Baptist church provided a microcosm of African American society, as it comprised mostly working-class adherents. It was also representative of all black churches in that it caught the progressive spirit and entered heavily in social and educational work after the formation of the National Baptist Convention in 1895. Organized in 1900, the Women's Convention (WC) of the Baptist Church centralized the charitable and social work of the denomination. The dynamic Nannie Helen Burroughs headed the WC and enlisted into her organization a far higher number of working-class women than did black clubwomen. Burroughs in fact sought to improve the occupation that employed most black women: domestic work. Burroughs wanted to professionalize and give respectability to domestic work by encouraging housemaids, cooks, and laundresses to do ordinary things extraordinarily well. Under Burroughs, the WC established the National Training School for Girls and Women in Washington, D.C., in 1909. The school stressed "the Bible, the bath, [and] the broom." The WC always made race pride an essential ingredient in its programs. The black dolls manufactured by the Negro Doll Company got the hearty endorsement of the WC in 1914.

The Baptist Women's Convention and Burroughs, like the NACW, did not ignore civil rights. Influenced greatly by *The Souls of Black Folk,* Burroughs inserted on the 1907 agenda of the WC such topics as "Some Essential Racial Reforms, "Lessons on the Race Problem from Magazines and Daily Papers," and "The Labor Question and the Negro's Relation to It." She further called for suffrage for all blacks, equal rights in the courts, equal if separate schools, and an end to lynching and convict lease. By 1902 the Baptist Church supported eighty black schools and published more than forty newspapers. More than a place of worship, the Baptist Church, like most black churches, was also a school, a lodge, and a political caucus for racial change. As Europe prepared to plunge into war, Burroughs told the 1914 National Baptist Convention, "A New day is dawning for us." In typical progressive discourse, the magnetic Burroughs explained her optimism, "The most hopeful sign is the awakening within to fundamental needs and a setting in motion of a new force to beat back fanatic race prejudice." Burroughs, like Du Bois and Trotter, represented the New Negro who was filled with "righteous discontent" and setting in motion forces that would one day ameliorate the racial scandal in American democracy.

For black adults the African American fraternal orders and lodges came in second only to the church as a social institution. While the main purpose of fraternal orders was to provide fellowship and entertainment, they also increased the welfare and security of African Americans. The lodges gave blacks a feeling of belonging in a hostile world. Tens of thousands of black men joined the Odd Fellows, the Prince Hall Masons, the Knights of Pythias, and the Elks. By 1900 the Odd Fellows, the largest of these orders, had 2,000 chapters and 155,000 members. In New York City in 1909, 35 percent of black families had membership in a lodge. One of the main activities of the orders was to sell burial insurance to poor blacks for pennies a week so that even the poorest person might hope to have a respectable funeral; more than 90 percent of black families in Chicago had such insurance. The orders established homes for orphans, indigents, and the aged, and they strongly supported black business and the National

Negro Business League. The Grand Lodge of Texas founded a bank in 1911 capitalized at $100,000. In addition, many of the orders tried to counter minstrel stereotypes of blacks by teaching their members the virtues of sobriety, honesty, reliability, and hard work.

The varied activities of blacks illustrated that although whites largely excluded them from the Progressive Movement, African Americans did not exclude themselves from progressive reform. In addition to the black leaders and organizations discussed above, countless individuals and local groups stood up to white racism in myriad ways. Already mentioned were the numerous boycotts against segregated streetcars in the South around the turn of the century. Noah Walter Parden, a courageous, smart black lawyer from Chattanooga, took a case to the Supreme Court that stayed the execution of a black man falsely accused of rape and established an important legal precedent for fair trials in *U.S.* v. *Shipp* (1909).

The demeaning subordination of blacks during the Progressive Era propelled many African Americans—and some whites—into the civil rights arena. The idea of the New Negro, a phenomenon often associated with the 1920s, became prominent during the Progressive Era. The black press used the term as early as 1895 and, ironically, Booker T. Washington employed it when he recommended Robert Terrell to President Roosevelt for a federal position. By the time the United States entered World War I, a New Negro, a new racial consciousness, and an acute sense of grievance had arisen among blacks. Most blacks, of course, had to accommodate the racist power structure in order to survive. But across the nation, even in the Deep South, African Americans now anticipated a day when it would not be counterproductive or lethal to voice their growing grievances and resentments. The seeds of far-reaching racial change had been planted.

World War I and Beyond

Although President Wilson enlisted America in a crusade to make the world "safe for democracy" in 1917, he made little effort to make the nation safe for African Americans. Indeed, forces unleashed by World War I provoked a tremendous white backlash and ushered in a period of escalating racial tension and violence. The "liberal possibilities" of the war envisioned by black leaders and many white progressives did not materialize in regard to the color line. The war instead caused deep bitterness and resentment among blacks, which in turn provoked white fears and generated more race prejudice. After the war, whites resorted to even more repressive measures to put the New Negroes back in their old place of mean subordination.

Most of the African American elite and the black press, however, believed in the reform potential of the war as did many white progressives and argued that blacks should support America's call to arms. After all, African Americans had fought in all the wars waged by the United States; and they had even made tangible gains from some of them. The war against Great Britain that led to the formation of the United States of America, for instance, resulted in the abolition of slavery in the northern states. As already mentioned, the Civil War, in which 200,000 blacks participated, struck down slavery in the Southern and Border States and led to the establishment of citizenship for African Americans. And with all the Wilsonian rhetoric about spreading democracy during World War I, most blacks naturally saw a glimmer of hope that the international conflict might just be a catalyst for beneficial racial change. Even the ever-skeptical Du Bois expressed faith that the war could advance the cause of civil rights for blacks. In 1917, he predicted, "Out of this war will rise . . . an American Negro with a right to vote and a right to work and a right to live without insult." In his "Close Ranks" editorial in *The Crisis* of July 1918, Du Bois advised, "Let us, while this war lasts, forget our special grievances and close our ranks shoulder to shoulder with our white citizens and the allied nations that are fighting for democracy." Given the earlier betrayal of blacks by President Wilson, many African Americans wondered why Du Bois was so optimistic about the racial outcome of the war.

Several blacks in fact expressed dismay at Du Bois's unconditional backing of the war. Monroe Trotter called Du Bois an Uncle Tom and "a rank quitter." Byron Gunner, Du Bois's old friend in the Niagara Movement, argued, "Now is the most opportune time for us to push and keep our special grievances to the fore." Several black leaders cynically linked Du Bois's support of the war to his effort to secure a commission as a captain in the U.S. Army. A. Philip Randolph, a Socialist who opposed the war, sarcastically referred to Du Bois as "Der Kapitan." Ordinary blacks showed even less enthusiasm for the war than the elite. Southern blacks feared the "Huns" in Alabama and Mississippi more than those in France. One black worker proclaimed, "The Germans ain't done nothin' to me, and if they have, I forgive 'em."

In one way, though, the war proved beneficial to African Americans. The European conflict stimulated American industry and created a great many new jobs. Blacks who had been virtually shut out of industrial jobs in the North now found better paying jobs open to them because of the acute shortage of labor created by the war. With opportunity beckoning, between 700,000 to 1,000,000 blacks migrated to northern and western cities during the war period. This black exodus was, as one historian observed, "a tremendous feat of initiative, planning, courage, and perseverance," not by the Talented Tenth, but by thousands of "perfectly average southern Negroes."

For those blacks hoping to find acceptance and security in the North, however, life would bring grave disappointments. The influx of poor, uneducated sharecroppers and tenant farmers caused the black population of several northern cities to double almost overnight. Even under the best of circumstances, the surge of southern immigrants would have strained the resources and social cohesion of any city.

The flood of migrants into industrial East St. Louis in 1916 and 1917 blew apart the social fabric of the city like dynamite. White workers were soon up in arms, fearful that black migrants would drive down wages and take their jobs. Then the Aluminum Ore Company added to white hostility by hiring black strikebreakers ("scabs") to replace white unionists who had walked off the job. After a rumor spread that blacks had killed a white man, a white mob of 3,000 stormed the streets of East St. Louis on July 2, 1917, randomly beating, knifing, hanging, and shooting blacks. A sobbing black boy of ten looking frantically for his mother was shot and thrown into a burning house the mob had torched. Whites shot a black mother trying to protect her baby and threw both of them into the flames. A black woman had her throat slashed by a white woman. City police officers sympathized with the white rioters, and when Illinois National Guardsmen arrived to restore order, they shot blacks without provocation but killed no whites. All told, at least thirty-nine blacks and eight whites died in the riot. But in this event, as the white death toll indicated, blacks fought back. A carload of blacks brazenly invaded a white neighborhood and killed two people, further escalating the riot.

Blacks across the nation expressed outrage over East St. Louis. After the riot, the *Norfolk Journal and Guide* thundered that "the United States government should renounce its purposes for entering the world war and stand convicted among the nations of the earth as the greatest hypocrites of all times." On July 28, 1917, 10,000 African Americans participated in a silent protest march on Fifth Avenue in New York City. Marchers carried signs, some of which read:

> Mother, Do Lynchers Go To Heaven?
> Treat Us So That We May Love Our Country.
> Mr. President, Why Not Make America Safe For Democracy?

Racial tensions mounted dangerously in American cities during the war, and in 1919 some twenty-five major race riots broke out. The largest race riot of that bloody year occurred in Chicago, a city in which the black population increased from 44,103 to 109,594 between 1910 and 1920. Recent European immigrants largely manned the police and the labor unions in the Midwest metropolis, and ethnic gangs regularly harassed blacks. As ghetto-imprisoned blacks sought better housing in white areas, whites formed neighborhood associations that vowed to keep the undesirables out. In the twenty months preceding the riot, whites set off more than fifty bombs and destroyed twenty-seven black dwellings, killing at least three blacks, including a six-year-old girl.

A tinderbox of racial unrest, Chicago needed only a spark in the hot summer of 1919 to ignite a race riot. That spark came on July 27, when bathers on a Lake Michigan beach customarily used by whites cursed and stoned five black boys who floated into the area on a home-made raft, drowning one of the youths. A false rumor quickly spread around the city that an Irish policeman had kept expert swimmers from saving the injured boy. For almost two weeks after the drowning incident, disorder, looting, assault, and murder plagued Chicago. When a howling white mob cornered a black veteran, he cried out, "[T]his is a fine reception to give a man just home from the war." Unmoved, the mob beat the veteran to death. Thirty-eight people died in the riot, fifteen whites and twenty-three blacks. Additionally, 517 people were injured and more than 1,000 families, mostly black, were left homeless. As in East St. Louis, blacks fought back. The typical black immigrant in Chicago was a young, unattached male between the ages of twenty and forty-four, some of whom were disaffected veterans from a Jim Crow army. These New Negroes were inclined to defend themselves and even participate in retaliatory violence, as they did in Chicago.

The racial explosions of 1919 were more like race wars than earlier race riots such as Wilmington in 1898. Deadly and destructive clashes broke out in Washington, D.C., Knoxville, Omaha, Longview, Texas, and Elaine, Arkansas. The latter disturbance engulfed much of Phillips County, a rural area along the Mississippi River that was 74 percent black. When poor black farmers tried to unionize to fight for higher cotton prices, armed whites rose up en masse against what they viewed as a black-supremacist conspiracy. A call went out to whites across eastern Arkansas to come to Phillips County to suppress an insurrection, and about one thousand responded. Ultimately, five hundred U.S. Army troops armed with machine guns hurried in from Camp Pike to join the mob. Together civilians and soldiers slaughtered dozens of blacks, with casualty estimates ranging from 100 to 800.

The number of lynchings also remained high during World War I and rose in 1918 and 1919. Sixty-four people died at the hands of lynchers in 1918—sixty-two of them black. In 1919, eighty-three lynchings took place, the highest number since 1903. Especially callous was the fact that black soldiers newly returned home from the war became favorite targets of lynch mobs. Whites lynched at least ten black veterans, several of them in uniform. In Little Rock, Arkansas, a white mob tied a black veteran to a tree and riddled his body with bullets for refusing to get off the sidewalk to let a white woman pass. Whites in Georgia killed a black officer because they felt he wore his uniform too long after the war.

Evidently, the sight of thousands of uniformed and armed black men aroused passionate fear among southern whites. A noted southern sociologist observed, "There is something about the Negro in uniform which gives the more ignorant Southerner a first-class case of jitters and spawns the most absurd fantasies." Senator Vardaman of Mississippi predicted that millions of "arrogant, strutting" black soldiers would incite race riots.

Unfortunately, Vardaman's prophecy proved true. When a hardened battalion of army regulars from the Twenty-fourth Infantry was transferred from the far West to Camp Logan near Houston in 1917, blacks soldiers immediately encountered the humiliation of Jim Crow and constant harassment by local citizens and police. On August 23, a black soldier tried to stop a white policeman from assaulting a black woman. The policeman then clubbed the soldier and sent him to jail. Later a corporal came to the scene to investigate what had happened, and he, too, was beaten and jailed. Hearing about the beatings, angry troops from Camp Logan then marched on Houston and mounted a two-hour attack on the police station, killing five policemen and eleven other white and Hispanic residents. Four black soldiers and two black civilians also lay dead after the shootout.

The Army charged sixty-three soldiers with mutiny, and within three months thirteen of them had been hanged. Six more black soldiers were executed in the following year. More than fifty soldiers received life sentences. Unlike in Brownsville, the soldiers were undeniably guilty, but the swiftness of the military trials and the speed of the executions smacked of Jim Crow justice to blacks.

In short, African Americans soon discovered that they could expect no more opportunity or justice in the military than in civilian life. The U.S. Army, the one branch of the military that accepted large numbers of blacks (though not in the new Army Air Corps), segregated blacks and blatantly exploited and discriminated against them. The U.S. Navy, which historically had accorded the fairest treatment of all the services to blacks, now largely restricted African Americans to duty as mess attendants or "sea-going bellhops." The Marines accepted no blacks, nor did the Armed Forces Nurse Corps. The Army also rejected all black physicians and dentists who applied for commissions. Although a segregated officers' school was established for blacks in Des Moines in 1917, the nearly one thousand officers it produced were kept in the lower ranks as lieutenants and captains. So frightened was the Army at the specter of black officers giving orders to whites that it forcefully retired from service the West Point graduate Lieutenant Colonel Charles Young on false charges of ill health.

Although some of the armed services banned blacks, the all-white draft boards in the South were eager to induct them into the Army. The civilian boards allowed fewer exemptions for black men and drafted African Americans who had dependents, were in poor health, or even illiterate. Blacks in Georgia thus supplied more than half the draftees from that state, though they only made up 40 percent of its population. Nationally, 34 percent of black registrants were drafted as compared to 24 percent of whites. While 9.6 percent of those eligible for the draft were black, 13 percents of the draftees in the Army were African American. All told, about 380,000 blacks served in the Great War.

Yet the military had no intention of using black soldiers in combat. The Army deliberately kept four regular black regiments of distinguished veterans of the Indian wars and the Spanish-American War out of combat in France. Only 42,000 blacks served in combat units in the main European theater of the war. About 89 percent of black soldiers therefore did in the service what most had done in civilian life: they cooked, washed dishes, cleaned latrines, shoveled manure, loaded trucks and ships, buried the dead, and carried out the most unpleasant chores the Army needed done. For the most part, African Americans in World War I served on a "military chain gang."

The two black combat divisions received poor equipment, poor training, and poor leadership by white officers. The Ninety-third Division served with the French because the U.S. commander, General John J. Pershing, had no place at the front for black troops. As one white officer put it, "Our great American general simply put the black orphan in a basket, set it on the doorstep of the French, pulled the bell, and went away."

The Ninety-third Division faced some of the best German forces in France, suffered 35 percent casualties, and received well over two hundred Distinguished Service Crosses and various grades of the Croix de Guerre, France's highest military honor. But this seemed all but forgotten as Army brass focused on the alleged failure of one or two battalions from a regiment of the Ninety-second Division. Exhausted and thrown into an impossible sector on the front during the great German offensive of 1918, some soldiers of the Second and Third Battalions of the 368th Infantry Regiment broke and ran. A court martial found five black officers guilty of cowardice and sentenced four to die, though the civilian-run War Department overturned all the verdicts after an investigation.

But the military establishment overlooked the fact that the Ninety-second suffered heavy casualties and most of its men fought well. Twenty-one of its soldiers won the Distinguished Service Cross. The Army also ignored the fact that some white units broke and ran under the German onslaught. The military establishment continued to insist that the Ninety-second was a complete failure that typified black combat units.

Most of the white officers in command of black troops were overtly racist, a fact that affected greatly the morale of black soldiers. General Robert Lee Bullard, an Alabamian who led the Second Army, exclaimed, "Poor Negroes! They are hopelessly inferior. . . ." Major J.

N. Merrill of the First Battalion of the maligned 368th Regiment called black soldiers "rank cowards." Colonel Allen C. Greer, Bullard's chief of staff, claimed that blacks were innate rapists and a danger to French women.

Predictably, black soldiers were deeply embittered by their experience during the war. They resented orders from their white superiors not to fraternize with French women. In August 1918, the Army supplied the French with a document on "Secret Information concerning Black American Troops." It advised the French people not to treat blacks as equals and falsely charged that African American troops had committed more rapes in France than all the rest of the Army. When blacks returned home, southern demagogues sounded the alarm about "French-women-ruined niggers."

Although sixteen blacks won the Medal of Honor during the Civil War, no African American received the highest military award in World War I, despite many documented cases of supreme heroism. Adding insult to injury, no American black military units were allowed to participate in the Allied victory parade in Paris. Furthermore, white officers such as Bullard and Greer continued to write and defame black troops throughout the 1920s and 1930s, leaving the U.S. Army prejudiced against the use of black combat troops in World War II.

During the war the Army and the Department of Justice questioned black loyalty and gathered copious intelligence under the label "Negro Subversion." Attorney General A. Mitchell Palmer drafted a 1919 report entitled "Radicalism and Sedition among the Negroes as Reflected in Their Publications." J. Edgar Hoover, who became head of the General Intelligence Division of the Justice Department in 1919 and the first Director of the FBI in 1924, began intense surveillance of African Americans because he found "a dangerous spirit of defiance and vengeance at work among Negro leaders." Hoover considered all civil rights activity tantamount to disloyalty, and he continued spying on black leaders until his retirement in 1972, most famously on Martin Luther King, Jr.

The power and the racial rhetoric of the Republican party during the Progressive Era gave blacks some hope that the federal government would support black rights. But the business-first Republicans who dominated the political landscape in the 1920s offered no such hope. After his inauguration in 1921, President Warren G. Harding made the now-customary Republican tour of the South and announced in Birmingham on October 26, 1921: "There shall be recognition of the absolute divergence in things social and racial. Men of both races may well stand uncompromisingly against every suggestion of social equality. . . . Racial amalgamation there cannot be."

Emblematic of the postwar racial scene was the dedication of the Lincoln Memorial in Washington, D.C., in 1922. Former president William Howard Taft, now the Chief Justice of the Supreme Court, headed the Lincoln Memorial Commission that orchestrated the dedication of the famous national symbol that has served as the backdrop for so many civil rights demonstrations over the years. The dedication turned into a segregated event, as military ushers herded blacks to the rear of the audience. The forty-one-page report of the Lincoln Memorial Commission to Congress referred to Lincoln twenty times as "the man who saved the Union" but only once as the "emancipator." National unity was the dominant theme of the many speeches given by dignitaries at the dedication ceremony. Taft failed to mention slavery in his long speech. Even Robert Moton, Washington's successor at Tuskegee, was compelled to fall in line with the unity theme when the commission heavily censored his original speech that protested against racial discrimination. In the nation's capital in 1922, it was as if the Civil War and Lincoln had nothing to do with race and civil rights—or broken promises.

By 1919 Du Bois looked back on his "Close Ranks" editorial with regret and shame. Thereafter he belligerently voiced his growing outrage at white America, speaking for thousands, if not millions, of blacks. In the May 1919 edition of *The Crisis,* he bellowed that America was "yet a shameful land" because "It *lynches*. . . . It *disfranchises* its own citizens. . . . It encourages *ignorance*. . . . It *steals* from us. . . . It *insults* us. . . ." Concluding the editorial, he thundered:

> We *return*. We *return from fighting*. We *return fighting*.
> Make way for Democracy! We saved it in France, and by the Great Jehovah, we will save it in the U.S.A., or know the reason why.

The spirit of the New Negro led to a rapid expansion of the NAACP during the war and thereafter. In 1913 the NAACP had 14 branches with only 1 in the South. In 1919 the black organization had

300 branches, with 155 in the South, and a membership exceeding 80,000. Nothing expressed the mood of the New Negro better than Claude McKay's poem, "If We Must Die," which first appeared in July 1919 and was later reprinted in many black journals.

> If we must die, let it not be like hogs
> Hunted and penned in an inglorious spot,
> While round bark the mad and hungry dogs,
> Making their mock at our accursed lot.
> If we must die, Oh let us nobly die,
> So that our precious blood may not be shed
> In vain; then even the monsters we defy
> Shall be constrained to honor us though dead!
> Oh, Kinsmen! we must meet the common foe!
> Though far outnumbered let us show us brave,
> And for their thousand blows deal one death-blow!
> What though before us lies the open grave?
> Like men we'll face the murderous cowardly pack,
> Pressed to the wall, dying, but fighting back!

Despite the fighting spirit of post–World War I African Americans, black rights advanced little in the next thirty years. But bigotry and white supremacy certainly did. The Ku Klux Klan, revived by *The Birth of a Nation* in 1915, reached its peak in the 1920s. It flourished not just in the South but also in the Northeast and Midwest, and its membership by some estimates soared to 5 million. Madison Grant and Lothrop Stoddard continued to write popular racist tracts and the cult of eugenics flourished as never before. In 1924 Congress, on the basis of racist research and eugenics, drastically restricted immigration and enacted racist quotas for southeastern European nations.

Amidst this racially repressive climate and the economic depression of the postwar period, African Americans searched desperately for an effective and uplifting course of action, but the quest proved difficult. By 1923 the NAACP had lost thousands of members and about two hundred branches. Its pet project, a federal antilynching bill, never became law.

Moreover, the black movement now seemed to divide even more along ideological, class, and color lines. Marcus Garvey, who emigrated from Jamaica in 1916, led a "race first," black nationalist, separatist crusade—until he was convicted of mail fraud and deported in 1927. The separatist Garvey led the first black mass movement in America and injected a healthy dose of self-esteem into African Americans with his black-is-beautiful theme. A. Philip Randolph, whom the Justice Department called the "most dangerous Negro in America," assailed capitalism, praised unionism, and stressed class over race. Du Bois continued his leadership at the NAACP until he was forced out of the organization in the early 1930s for allegedly abandoning integrationist principles.

Reminiscent of the Washington–Du Bois feud, the internecine quarrels between African American factions in the 1920s grew fierce and personal. Garvey, a full-blooded black, applauded Harding's Birmingham speech, cooperated with the Klan, and characterized the NAACP as a white-controlled, reactionary organization. He depicted Du Bois as a "lazy, dependent mulatto" who liked to dance with white women and "sometimes sleep with them." Du Bois called Garvey a "liar" and said he was "either a lunatic or a traitor." He described the Jamaican as an ugly "little fat black man" who was "the most dangerous enemy of the Negro race in America and in the world." Randolph characterized Garvey as "a clown and an imperial buffoon" and as a "Supreme Jamaican Jackass" who was "squat, stocky, fat, and sleek, with protruding jaws and . . . small bright pig-like eyes." Like Garvey, Randolph blasted Du Bois as an elitist ill-suited as the leader of a downtrodden people.

Still, blacks never gave up the fight for equality. African Americans gained a greater sense of themselves after the war, and they continued the protest movement against racial injustice that Du Bois had begun at Niagara in 1905. In addition, blacks made great cultural advances in the postwar period, as seen by the artistic flowering of the Harlem Renaissance. African Americans contributed significantly to all aspects of American artistic culture: painting, sculpture, opera, literature, theater, dance, and Broadway musicals. And their development of ragtime, blues, and ultimately jazz gave blacks a new sense of pride. After the war, jazz became the most popular music in the nation, and the black music of that era still heavily influences American—and the world's—music today. Black education also advanced in the 1920s, with more blacks attending college than ever before. And it was the generation of blacks who emerged from the military, the campuses, and the churches after World War I that provided a base from which the final and victorious assault on Jim Crow was launched in the wake of the next world war.

BIBLIOGRAPHICAL ESSAY

The following essay identifies some of the major sources for this book and suggests further reading for those who would like more information on the Progressive Era and race. Due to the constraints of space and the voluminous publications on the Progressive Era, not to mention those on Reconstruction and post-Reconstruction, this bibliography is necessarily selective. In the interest of space, long subtitles have sometimes been omitted when the main title is sufficient to indicate the content of the source.

Several surveys have placed postwar African American life in broad historical perspective, among them John Hope Franklin and Alfred A. Moss, Jr., *From Slavery to Freedom* (2000); Joe William Trotter, Jr., *The African American Experience* (2001); Darlene Clark Hine, William C. Hine, and Stanley Harrold, *The African–American Odyssey* (2000); Colin A. Palmer, *Passageways: An Interpretive History of Black America* (1998); August Meier and Elliott M. Rudwick, *From Plantation to Ghetto: An Interpretive History of American Negroes* (1970); and Arnold H. Taylor, *Travail and Triumph: Black Life and Culture in the South since the Civil War* (1976).

A good starting point for the subjects of Emancipation and Reconstruction is Eric Foner's comprehensive *Reconstruction: America's Unfinished Revolution, 1863–1877* (1988). Michael Perman provides a fine short survey of this period in the second edition of his *Emancipation and Reconstruction* (2003). Perman's bibliographical essay thoroughly evaluates the literature of the three schools of interpretation on Reconstruction: the Dunning school, the Revisionists, and the post-Revisionists. Three valuable historiographical articles that lend perspective to the passionate debate on Reconstruction are Bernard A. Weisberger, "The Dark and Bloody Ground of Reconstruction Historiography," *Journal of Southern History* (1959); John Hope Franklin, "Mirrors for Americans: A Century of Reconstruction History," *American Historical Review* (1980) and Eric Foner, "Reconstruction Revisited," *Reviews in American History* (1982).

The highly negative, racist views of Reconstruction held by the Dunning school of historians became deeply entrenched in America in the early twentieth century. Claude G. Bowers, *The Tragic Era* (1929) and George F. Milton, *The Age of Hate* (1930), popularized the Dunning view, and two of the most successful films ever made indelibly etched this jaundiced view of Reconstruction on the minds of Americans: *The Birth of a Nation* (1915) and *Gone With the Wind* (1939).

Revisionism flourished in the 1950s and 1960s in the midst of the civil rights movement or, as some have labeled it, the Second Reconstruction. The Revisionists virtually turned the Dunning orthodoxy on its head. They depicted the southern policies of Republicans as principled, far-sighted, and realistic. Furthermore, they debunked President Johnson and assailed southern "Redeemers" as reactionary, violent racists. The increasing acceptance of the Revisionist view was signaled in two early influential surveys: John Hope Franklin, *Reconstruction: After the Civil War* (1961) and Kenneth M. Stampp, *The Era of Reconstruction, 1865–1877* (1965).

In the 1970s, however, the post-Revisionists emphasized the shortcomings of Republicans, including Lincoln, and they, like the Dunning school, lamented the failure of Reconstruction. Scores of books and articles criticized Republicans for being too conservative and cautious—and often too racist—and for failing to secure land and lasting civil rights for blacks. Examples of this view are Michael Les Benedict, *A Compromise of Principle: Congressional Republicans and Reconstruction, 1863–1869* (1974); Richard H. Abbott, *The Republican Party and the South, 1855–1877* (1986); and William Gillette, *Retreat from Reconstruction, 1869–1879* (1979). Merrill D. Peterson analyzed Frederick Douglass's critical view of Lincoln in *Lincoln in American Memory* (1994).

Although post-Revisionism gained strength in the 1970s, Revisionism continued to augment its case. Leon F. Litwack's *Been in the Storm So Long: The Aftermath of Slavery* (1979) dissected the thought and behavior of the freedmen and lauded their initiative in pursuit of land, education, stable families, and equality. And Revisionists gave increasing attention to the role of black politicians during Reconstruction in such works as Charles Vincent, *Black Legislators in Louisiana during Reconstruction* (1976) and Thomas C. Holt, *Black Over White: Negro Political Leadership in South Carolina during Reconstruction* (1977).

As passions have cooled over the years, some historians have blended elements of the Revisionists and post-Revisionist schools. Although the Revisionist LaWanda Cox argued in *Lincoln and Black Freedom* (1981) that the martyred president was a sincere advocate of racial equality, she also emphasized the "limits of the possible" and doubted whether a successful Reconstruction (in the modern sense) could have been achieved given the tremendous social, political, and constitutional obstacles to racial equality in the 1860s and 1870s.

The impact of slavery on the black personality during Reconstruction and after became a controversial topic with the explosion of revisionist books on slavery after World War II. Kenneth M. Stampp argued in *The Peculiar Institution* (1956) that slaves were a rebellious and "troublesome property," but Stanley M. Elkins claimed in *Slavery* (1959) that the American system of slavery was so harsh that it produced docile workers with Sambo personalities. Black scholars in the 1960s and 1970s contended that African Americans emerged from slavery with healthy psyches because of the protective power of slave culture, a view found in John W. Blassingame's influential book, *The Slave Community: Plantation Life in the Antebellum South* (1972). The essays in *The Debate over Slavery: Stanley Elkins and His Crit-*

ics (1971), edited by Ann J. Lane, illuminated this touchy subject, and Peter Kolchin effectively countered the exaggerations of the "slave community" thesis in "Reevaluating the Antebellum Slave Community: A Comparative Perspective," *Journal of American History* (1983). Roger Wilkins, *Jefferson's Pillow Talk* (2001) and Nell I. Painter, *Southern History across the Color Line* (2002) also illuminated the topic, and Cornel West's *Race Matters* (1994) showed insight into the victimization of blacks under slavery and Jim Crow.

On the abandonment of Reconstruction, the Redeemer Era, and the rise of the New South and legal segregation, consult C. Vann Woodward's *Reunion and Reaction: The Compromise of 1877 and the End of Reconstruction* (1951); *Origins of the New South, 1877–1913* (1951); and *The Strange Career of Jim Crow* (1955, 1974). Woodward's thesis that the South tried more benign if "forgotten alternatives" before resorting to legal segregation was challenged by Howard N. Rabinowitz's *Race Relations in the Urban South, 1865–1890* (1978) and Joel Williamson's *After Slavery: The Negro in South Carolina during Reconstruction, 1861–1877* (1965) and *The Crucible of Race: Black-White Relations in the American South since Emancipation* (1984).

Several studies have updated Woodward's *Origins of the New South,* such as Edward L. Ayers, *The Promise of the New South* (1992); Howard N. Rabinowitz, *The First New South, 1865–1920* (1992); and Don H. Doyle, *New Men, New Cities, New South* (1990). Wilbur J. Cash, *The Mind of the South* (1941) and John David Smith, *Old Creed for the New South* (1985) stressed the continuation of Old South ideas and culture after the Civil War. The Lost Cause mentality was revisited in Rollin G. Osterweis, *The Myth of the Lost Cause, 1865–1900* (1973); Gaines M. Foster, *Ghosts of the Confederacy: Defeat, the Lost Cause, and the Emergence of the New South, 1865–1913* (1987); and Karen L. Cox, *Dixie's Daughters: The United Daughters of the Confederacy and the Preservation of Confederate Culture* (2003).

Several good studies traced the abandonment of blacks by Republicans, among them Vincent P. DeSantis, *Republicans Face the Southern Question: The New Departure Years, 1877–1897* (1959); Stanley P. Hirschon, *Farewell to the Bloody Shirt: Northern Republicans and the Southern Negro, 1877–1893* (1962); Heather Cox

Richardson, *The Death of Reconstruction: Race, Labor, and Politics in the Post–Civil War North, 1865–1901* (2001); and Xi Wang, *The Trial of Democracy: Black Suffrage and Northern Republicans, 1860–1910* (1997). Especially helpful on the defeat of the Blair Education Bill and the Federal Elections Bill was Thomas Adams Upchurch's *Legislating Racism: The Billion Dollar Congress and the Birth of Jim Crow* (2004). Nina Silber showed how reconciliation between the North and South dampened the abolitionist zeal in *The Romance of Reunion: Northerners and the South, 1865–1900* (1993).

Although C. Vann Woodward painted the Populists as friends of blacks in *Tom Watson: Agrarian Rebel* (1938), more recent studies have demonstrated pervasive racism in the agrarian movement. The best general study of agrarians and blacks is Gerald H. Gaither, *Blacks and the Populist Revolt* (1977). But see also Charles Crowe, "Tom Watson, Populists, and Blacks Reconsidered," *Journal of Negro History* (1970); Robert Saunders, "Southern Populists and the Negro, 1893–1895," *Journal of Negro History* (1969); Sheldon Hackney, *Populism to Progressivism in Alabama* (1969); and Gregg Cantrell and D. Scott Barton, "Texas Populists and the Failure of Biracial Politics," *Journal of Southern History* (1989). On Benjamin Tillman, the master demagogue and pseudo-Populist, see Stephen Kantrowitz, *Ben Tillman and the Reconstruction of White Supremacy* (2000) and Francis Butler Simkins, *Pitchfork Ben Tillman* (1944).

The horrors of the convict lease system were exposed in Matthew J. Mancini, *One Dies, Get Another: Convict Leasing in the American South, 1866 to 1928* (1996); Alexander C. Lichtenstein, *Twice the Work of Free Labor: The Political Economy of Convict Labor in the New South* (1996); Edward L. Ayers, *Vengeance and Justice: Crime and Punishment in the 19th-Century American South* (1984); and Mary Ellen Curtin, *Black Prisoners and Their World, Alabama, 1865–1900* (2000). Two important books by J. Morgan Kousser and Michael Perman covered disfranchisement. Kousser placed most of the blame for disfranchisement of blacks on upper-class, black-belt Democrats and showed that many poor whites also lost the vote in *The Shaping of Southern Politics: Suffrage Restriction and the Establishment of the One-Party South, 1880–1920* (1974), while Perman added more complexity and nuance to the story and stressed the desire for white mastery over blacks in *Struggle for Mastery: Disfranchisement in the South, 1888–1908* (2001).

Rayford W. Logan captured the worsening situation of African Americans after Reconstruction in *The Negro in American Life and Thought: The Nadir, 1877–1901* (1954) and its enlargement, *The Betrayal of the Negro: From Rutherford B. Hayes to Woodrow Wilson* (1965). Bess Beatty gauged black reaction to their plight in *A Revolution Gone Backward: The Black Response to National Politics, 1876–1896* (1987). Nell I. Painter looked at early migration in *Exodusters: Black Migration to Kansas after Reconstruction* (1977), and the rise of black nationalism and emigration to Africa was covered in Wilson Jeremiah Moses, *The Golden Age of Black Nationalism, 1850–1925* (1978) and Edwin S. Redkey, *Black Exodus: Black Nationalist and Back-to-Africa Movements, 1890–1910* (1969). On the early life of Booker T. Washington and the Atlanta Compromise speech of 1895, Louis R. Harlan's *Booker T. Washington: The Making of a Black Leader, 1856–1901* (1972) is unsurpassed. In a new and important book, *A Nation under Our Feet: Black Political Struggles in the Rural South from Slavery to the Great Migration* (2003), Stephan Hahn traced in great depth the political strivings of freed slaves up to World War I.

The literature on progressivism has grown tremendously in the last quarter century—much of it also covering the late nineteenth century and the period between the world wars. A good deal of this literature has tried to define the nature of the large and diverse Progressive Movement and to mark its beginning and end. In "An Obituary for 'The Progressive Movement,'" *American Quarterly* (1970), Peter Filene famously argued that the movement was so incoherent and contradictory that it did not deserve its name. But most historians, while admitting the paradoxes and contradictions of progressivism, have not buried the signifiance of the movement.

An excellent starting point for the historiography of the Progressive Movement is Arthur S. Link and Richard L. McCormick, *Progressivism* (1983). Other good historiographical works include John D. Buenker, John C. Burnham, and Robert M. Crunden, *Progressivism* (1977); Daniel T. Rodgers, "In Search of Progressivism," *Reviews in American History* (1982); Edward G. White, "The Social Values of the Progressives: Some New Perspectives," *South Atlantic Quarterly*,

(1971); Steven J. Diner, "Linking Politics and People: The Historiography of the Progressive Era," *Magazine of History* (1999); and Robert D. Johnston, "Re-Democratizing the Progressive Era: The Politics of Progressive Era Political History," *Journal of the Gilded Age and Progressive Era* (2002).

Several general studies of progressivism provide good introductions to the topic and deal at some length with race. Steven J. Diner offered a synthesis of the latest research in *A Very Different Age: Americans of the Progressive Era* (1998), as did Michael Gerr, *A Fierce Discontent: The Rise and Fall of the Progressive Movement, 1870–1920* (2003). Both books include a chapter on black-white relations. Other high-quality studies include John Milton Cooper, Jr., *Pivotal Decades: The United States, 1900–1920* (1990); John Whiteclay Chambers II, *The Tyranny of Change: America in the Progressive Era, 1900–1917* (1980); and William L. O'Neill, *The Progressive Years* (1975). Nancy Cohen's somewhat eccentric book, *The Reconstruction of American Liberalism, 1865–1914* (2002) starts progressivism well back in the Gilded Age but concedes the uniqueness of twentieth-century progressivism. Two studies on the left that dismissed progressivism as probusiness and conservative are Gabriel Kolko, *The Triumph of Conservatism: A Reinterpretation of American History, 1900–1916* (1963) and James Weinstein, *The Corporate Ideal in the Liberal State: 1900–1918* (1968).

Earlier general studies of progressivism, such as George E. Mowry's *Theodore Roosevelt and the Progressive Movement* (1947), Arthur S. Link's *Woodrow Wilson and the Progressive Era, 1910–1917* (1954), and Richard Hofstadter's *The Age of Reform* (1955) gave little attention to the race problem or exaggerated the problack sympathies of the progressive presidents. After World War II, however, historians began to document a record of conscious and unconscious racism and nativism in the Progressive Movement. Among the early works that exposed the blind spot in northern progressivism—it was unmistakable in the southern variety—were John Hope Franklin, *From Slavery to Freedom* (1947); Logan, *The Negro in American Life and Thought*; Oscar Handlin, *The Uprooted* (1951); Dewey Grantham, Jr., "The Progressive Movement and the Negro," *South Atlantic Quarterly* (1955); John Higham, *Strangers in the Land* (1955); James A. Tinsley,

"Roosevelt, Foraker, and the Brownsville Affray," *Journal of Negro History* (1956); Kathleen Long Wolgemuth, "Woodrow Wilson's Appointment Policy and the Negro," *Journal of Southern History* (1958) and "Woodrow Wilson and Federal Segregation," Ibid. (1959); Seth M. Scheiner, "President Theodore Roosevelt and the Negro, 1901– 1908," *Journal of Negro History* (1962); Idus A. Newby, *Jim Crow's Defense: Anti-Negro Thought in America, 1900–1930* (1965) and Newby, ed., *The Development of Segregationist Thought* (1968); August Meier and Elliott Rudwick, "The Rise of Segregation in the Federal Bureaucracy, 1900–1930," *Phylon* (1967); David W. Southern, *The Malignant Heritage: Yankee Progressives and the Negro Question, 1901–1914* (1968); Nancy J. Weiss, "The Negro and the New Freedom: Fighting Wilsonian Segregation," *Political Science Quarterly* (1969); Willard H. Smith, "William Jennings Bryan and Racism," *Journal of Negro History* (1969); Morton Sosna, "The South in the Saddle: Racial Politics during the Wilson Years," *Wisconsin Magazine of History* (1970); Richard Weiss, "Racism in the Era of Industrialization," in *The Great Fear: Race in the Mind of America,* edited by Gary B. Nash and Richard Weiss (1970); *Racism in the United States* (1972), edited by David M. Reimers; and Richard B. Sherman, *The Republican Party and Black America: From McKinley to Hoover, 1896–1933* (1973).

For an introduction to the European origins of scientific racism, see the essays in *Race and the Enlightenment* (1997), edited by Emmanuel Chukwudi Eze. Particularly insightful on race, racism, and intelligence tests are Thomas F. Gossett, *Race: The History of an Idea in America* (1963); Stephen Jay Gould, *The Mismeasure of Man* (1981); Audrey Smedley, *Race in North America* (1993); Jonathan Marks, *Human Biodiversity: Genes, Race, and History* (1995); Pierre Van den Berghe, *Race and Racism: A Comparative Approach* (1967); and Lewis M. Terman, *The Measurement of Intelligence* (1916). On the role of anthropology in the rise of scientific racism, see George W. Stocking, Jr., *Race, Culture, and Evolution: Essays in the History of Anthropology* (1968) and Lee D. Baker, *From Savage to Negro: Anthropology and the Construction of Race, 1896–1954* (1998). For the rise of cultural anthropology and antiracism, consult Franz Boas, *The Mind of Primitive Man* (1911) and Vernon J. Williams, Jr., *Rethinking*

Race: Franz Boas and His Contemporaries (1996). Above all, on American racism consult the classic, history-making book by Gunnar Myrdal, *An American Dilemma: The Negro Problem and Modern Democracy* (1944).

To see how Darwinism affected race thinking, see Richard Hofstadter, *Social Darwinism in American Thought* (1944); Carl N. Degler, *In Search of Human Nature: The Decline and Revival of Darwinism in American Social Thought* (1991); and Mike Hawkins, *Social Darwinism in European and American Thought, 1860–1945* (1997). Paul A. Kramer highlighted Anglo-Saxonism in "Empires, Exceptions, and Anglo-Saxons: Race and Rule between the British and United States Empires, 1880–1910, *Journal of American History* (2002), as did the progressive scholar Edward A. Ross in his *Foundations of Sociology,* which went through five editions from 1905 to 1915. Beatrix Hoffman explored the influence of Frederick Hoffman's thinking in "Scientific Racism, Insurance, and Opposition to the Welfare State: Frederick L. Hoffman's Transatlantic Journey," *Journal of the Gilded Age and Progressive Era* (2003). Madison Grant's *The Passing of the Great Race* (1916) and Lothrop Stoddard's *The Rising Tide of Color against White World-Supremacy* (1920) typified popular works in this vein. Two recent books illustrated how scientific racism permeated the world fairs: Robert W. Rydell, *All the World's a Fair: Visions of Empire at American International Expositions, 1876–1916* (1984) and Christopher Robert Reed, *"All the World Is Here!": The Black Presence at White City* (2000). Two excellent books have assessed American racism: Matthew Pratt Guterl, *The Color of Race in America, 1900–1940* (2001) and Gary Gerstle, *American Crucible: Race and Nation in the Twentieth Century* (2001).

Like scientific racism, the American eugenics movement continues to attract the attention of scholars. A few of the important publications are Donald Pickens, *Eugenics and the Progressives* (1968); Mark H. Haller, *Eugenics: Hereditarian Attitudes in American Thought* (1963); David J. Kevles, *In the Name of Eugenics: Genetics and the Uses of Human Heredity* (1985); and Edward J. Larson, *Sex, Race, and Science: Eugenics in the Deep South* (1995). Edwin Black's provocative *War Against the Weak: Eugenics and America's Campaign to Create a Master Race* (2003) tied American eugenics, and especially Lothrop Stoddard, to German Nazism. For the views of the major American eugenicists in the Progressive Era, see Charles Benedict Davenport, *Heredity in Relation to Eugenics* (1911).

For histories of antimiscegenation laws, see William D. Zabel, "Intermarriage and the Law," *Atlantic Monthly* (1965); Robert J. Sickels, *Race, Marriage, and the Law* (1972); David H. Fowler, *Northern Attitudes toward Interracial Marriage* (1987); Peggy Pascoe, "Miscegenation Law, Court Cases, and Ideologies of 'Race' in Twentieth-Century America, *Journal of American History* (1996); Peter Wallenstein, *Tell the Court I Love My Wife, Race, Marriage, and Law: An American History* (2002); and Charles F. Robinson II, *Dangerous Liaisons: Sex and Love in the Segregated South* (2003).

One cannot study race today without confronting a mountain of "whiteness" studies, which meticulously demonstrated that many groups and nationalities considered white today were not considered so before World War II. Notable among these studies are David R. Roediger, *The Wages of Whiteness: Race and the Making of the American Working Class* (1991); Theodore W. Allen, *The Invention of the White Race* (1997); Alexander Saxton, *The Rise and Fall of the White Republic* (1990); Michelle Brattain, *The Politics of Whiteness: Race, Workers, and Culture in the Modern South* (2001); Karen Brodkin, *How Jews Became White Folks and What That Says about Race in America* (1998); Grace Elizabeth Hale, *Making Whiteness: The Culture of Segregation in the South, 1890–1940* (1998); Noel Ignatiev, *How the Irish Became White* (1995); and two books by Matthew Frye Jacobson, *Whiteness of a Different Color: European Immigrants and the Alchemy of Race* (1998) and *Barbarian Virtues: The United States Encounters Foreign Peoples at Home and Abroad, 1876–1917* (2000). For a spirited critique of whiteness studies, see Peter Kolchin, "Whiteness Studies: The New History of Race in America," *Journal of American History* (2002).

Historians once seemed to assume that certain segments of the Progressive Movement, such as social workers, feminists, leftist muckrakers, and Social Gospel preachers, were more sympathetic to blacks than the average progressive politician. In his path-breaking book, *Spearhead for Reform: The Social Settlements and the Progressive Movement, 1890–1914* (1968), Allen F. Davis argued that settlement-house workers were mostly racial liberals. But more recent studies have contested his view. Thomas Lee Philpott demonstrated in *The Slum and the Ghetto: Immigrants, Blacks, and Reformers in Chicago, 1880–1930* (1991) that many social workers were more interested in assisting European immigrants than blacks and were often indifferent or racist in their attitudes toward African Americans. Elisabeth Lasch-Quinn reinforced Philpott's argument in *Black Neighborhoods: Race and the Limits of Reform in the American Settlement House Movement, 1890–1945* (1993). Louise Michele Newman's *White Women's Rights: The Racial Origins of Feminism in the United States* (1999); Laura E. Donaldson's *Decolonizing Feminism: Race, Gender and Empire Building* (1992); Edna C. Green's *Southern Strategies: Southern Women and the Woman Suffrage Question* (1997); and Glenda Elizabeth Gilmore's *Gender and Jim Crow: Women and the Politics of White Supremacy in North Carolina, 1896–1920* (1996) also proved that racism tainted the feminist movement.

As for muckrakers, only Ray Stannard Baker wrote extensively about race in *Following the Color Line* (1908). Baker had fairly stereotypical views of African Americans, according to Robert C. Bannister, Jr., *Ray Stannard Baker: The Mind and Thought of a Progressive* (1966) and John E. Semonche, *Ray Stannard Baker: A Quest for Democracy in Modern America, 1870–1918* (1969). On the racial shortcomings of muckrakers in general, see Herbert Shapiro, "The Muckrakers and Negroes," *Phylon* (1960). John R. Cooley also unearthed racism in the works of famous American fiction writers in *Savages and Naturals: Black Portraits by White Writers in Modern American Literature* (1982). Donnarae MacCann explored another factor that shaped the progressive mind in *White Supremacy in Children's Literature: Characterizations of African Americans, 1830–1900* (1998).

As for the Protestant Social Gospel movement, many white progressive preachers were paternalistic at best. David M. Reimers found much racism in the mainstream churches in *White Protestantism and the Negro* (1965), as did George M. Fredrickson in *The Black Image in the White Mind* (1971). More defensive of the Social Gospelers were Ronald C. White, Jr., *Liberty and Justice for All: Racial Reform and the Social Gospel* (1990) and Ralph E. Luker, *The Social Gospel in Black and White: American Racial Reform, 1885–1912* (1991). The defeatism of the Social Gospel leader Washington Gladden can be seen in "The Negro Crisis: Is the Separation of the Two Races to Become Necessary?" *American Magazine* (1907). The racism of the American Catholic church was amply demonstrated in Stephen J. Ochs, *Desegregating the Altar: The Josephites and the Struggle for Black Priests, 1871–1960* (1990); David W. Southern, *John LaFarge and the Limits of Catholic Interracialism, 1911–1963* (1996); and John T. McGreevy, *Parish Boundaries: The Catholic Encounter with Race in the Twentieth-Century Urban North* (1996).

Since many northern whites seldom saw African Americans, they got their images of blacks from minstrels and eventually from films, which were devastating for blacks. Robert C. Toll introduced minstrelsy in *Blacking Up: The Minstrel Show in Nineteenth-Century America* (1974). Eric Lott's *Love and Theft: Blackface Minstrelsy and the American Working Class* (1993) and W. T. Lhamon, Jr.'s *Raising Cain: Blackface Performance from Jim Crow to Hip Hop* (1998) added nuance and complexity to the subject, demonstrating that racist white performers in blackface were also attracted to black culture. On the racist content of early films, see Thomas Cripps, *Slow Fade to Black: The Negro in American Film, 1900–1942* (1977); Daniel J. Leab, *From Sambo to Superspade: The Black Experience in Motion Pictures* (1976); and Donald Bogle, *Toms, Coons, Mulattoes, Mammies and Bucks: An Interpretive History of Blacks in American Films* (1996). For more detail on the blatant racism in the 1915 film *The Birth of a Nation*, see the essays in the anthology, *The Birth of a Nation* (1994), edited by Robert Lang.

The topic of southern progressivism and race has generated voluminous literature. Dewey Grantham, Jr., *Southern Progressivism: The Reconciliation of Progress and Tradition* (1983) and William A. Link, *The Paradox of Southern Progressivism, 1880–1930* (1992) are two reliable works on southern reformers and their dilemmas. Woodward's *Origins of the New South;* George Brown Tindall's *The Emergence of the New South, 1913–1945* (1967); and Hugh C. Bailey's *Liberalism in the New South: Southern Social Reformers and the Progressive Movement* (1969) also provided essential context for the southern movement. On disfranchisement, segregation, and racial violence in the South, the pickings are rich. But start with the engaging volumes of Leon F. Litwack, *Trouble in Mind: Black Southerners in the Age of Jim Crow* (1998); Joel Williamson, *The Crucible of Race* (1984); Morton Sosna, *In Search of the Silent South: Southern Liberals and the Race Issue* (1977); Bruce Clayton, *The Savage Ideal: Intolerance and Intellectual Leadership in the South, 1890–1914* (1972); Lawrence J. Friedman, *The White Savage: Racial Fantasies in the Postbellum South* (1970); Jack Temple Kirby, *Darkness at the Dawning: Race and Reform in the Progressive South* (1972); and William Cohen, *At Freedom's Edge: Black Mobility and the Southern White Quest for Racial Control, 1861–1915* (1991).

Nothing enlivened southern politics more than racial demagogues. In addition to the already cited biographies of Ben Tillman and Tom Watson by Kantrowitz and Woodward, respectively, some of the best studies of race-baiters are William F. Holmes, *The White Chief: James Kimble Vardaman* (1978); Raymond Arsenault, *Wild Ass of the Ozarks: Jeff Davis and the Social Bases of Southern Politics* (1984); Oliver H. Orr, *Charles Brantley Aycock* (1961); and Dewey W. Grantham, Jr., *Hoke Smith and the Politics of the New South* (1958). On racial moderates in the New South, see Hugh C. Bailey, *Edgar Gardner Murphy: Gentle Progressive* (1968); John M. Cooper, Jr., *Walter Hines Page: The Southerner as American* (1977); and Raymond B. Nixon, *Henry W. Grady: Spokesman of the New South* (1943).

On the origins, practice, and effect of segregation, see Woodward, *The Strange Career of Jim Crow* (1974); John W. Cell, *The Highest Stage of White Supremacy* (1982); Bertram W. Doyle, *The Etiquette of Race Relations in the South: A Study in Social Control* (1937); and William H. Chafe, Raymond Gavins, and Robert Korstad, eds., *Remembering Jim Crow* (2001). For the black image in the white southern mind, consult Claude H. Nolen, *The Negro's Image in the South* (1967) and H. Shelton Smith, *In His Image: Racism in Southern Religion, 1788–1910* (1972).

For useful state and local studies that reveal the plight of southern blacks, see Lester C. Lamon, *Black Tennesseans, 1900–1930* (1977); John Dittmer, *Black Georgia in the Progressive Era, 1900–1920* (1977); Donald L. Grant, *The Way It Was in the South: The Black Experience in Georgia* (1993); Neil R. McMillen, *Dark Journey: Black*

Mississippians in the Age of Jim Crow (1989); James C. Cobb, *The Most Southern Place on Earth: The Mississippi Delta and the Roots of Regional Identity* (1992); Fon Louise Gordon, *Caste and Class: The Black Experience in Arkansas, 1880–1920* (1995); Margaret Law Callcott, *The Negro in Maryland Politics, 1870–1912* (1969); George C. Wright, *Life Behind a Veil: Blacks in Louisville, Kentucky, 1865– 1930* (1985).

The roots of agricultural hardship and poverty among African Americans has been thoroughly examined in Gavin Wright, *Old South, New South: Revolution in the Southern Economy since the Civil War* (1986); Jay R. Mandle, *The Roots of Black Poverty: The Southern Plantation Economy after the Civil War* (1978); Roger Ransom and Richard Sutch, *One Kind of Freedom: The Economic Consequences of Emancipation* (1977); Harold S. Woodman, *New South, New Law: The Legal Foundations of Credit and Labor Relations in the Postbellum Agricultural South* (1995); Nan Elizabeth Woodruff, *American Congo: The African American Freedom Struggle in the Delta* (2003); and Robert Higgs, *Competition and Coercion: Blacks in the American Economy, 1865–1914* (1980).

In *Black Property Owners in the South, 1790–1915* (1990), Loren Schweninger disclosed how difficult it was for blacks to acquire land. Charles S. Johnson gave an unvarnished view of black life in the South in *Shadow of the Plantation* (1934). Few sources are more revealing in regard to the tribulations and joys of a black farmer than Theodore Rosengarten, *All God's Dangers: The Life of Nate Shaw* (1975). Two fine works found extensive peonage in the South: Pete Daniel, *The Shadow of Slavery: Peonage in the South, 1901–1969* (1969) and Daniel A. Novak, *The Wheel of Servitude: Black Forced Labor after Slavery* (1978). Highly useful for economic and social statistics are three publications by the U.S. Department of Commerce: *The Social and Economic Status of the Black Population in the United States: An Historical View, 1790–1978* (1979); *Negroes in the United States,* (1915); and *Negro Population, 1790–1915* (1918).

The discrimination against blacks by unions is treated in Charles H. Wesley, *Negro Labor in the United States, 1850–1925* (1927); Sterling D. Spero and Abram L. Harris, *The Black Worker and the Labor Movement* (1931); William H. Harris, *The Harder We Run: Black*

Workers since the Civil War (1982); Herbert R. Northrup, *Organized Labor and the Negro* (1944); and Bernard Mandel, "Samuel Gompers and the Negro Workers, 1886–1914," *Journal of Negro History* (1955).

Although interracialism was strongest in the coal industry, even there much racial discrimination was evident—as shown by Brian Kelly, *Race, Class, and Power in the Alabama Coalfields, 1908–1921* (2001); Daniel Letwin, *The Challenge of Interracial Unionism: Alabama Coal Miners, 1878–1921* (1998); Joe William Trotter, Jr., *Coal, Class, and Color: Blacks in Southern West Virginia, 1915–1932* (1990); and David Alan Corbin, *Life, Work, and Rebellion in the Coal Fields: The Southern West Virginia Miners, 1880–1922* (1981). Henry M. McKiven showed in *Iron and Steel: Class, Race, and Community in Birmingham, Alabama, 1875–1920* (1995) that race trumped class in a basic industry. Eric Arnesen related the obstacles facing blacks in two major areas of employment in *Waterfront Workers of New Orleans: Race, Class, and Politics, 1863–1923* (1991) and *Brotherhoods of Color: Black Railroad Workers and the Struggle for Equality* (2001). Segregation gave black entrepreneurs opportunities, and some proved quite successful in business, as shown in Juliet E. K. Walker, *The History of Black Business in America: Capitalism, Race, Entrepreneurship* (1998); Robert C. Kenzer, *Enterprising Southerners: Black Economic Success in North Carolina, 1865–1915* (1997) and John Sibley Butler, *Entrepreneurship and Self-Help among Black Americans* (1991). But, overall, most sources show that the great majority of black businesses were undercapitalized and precarious.

Racial violence was pervasive in the South from 1865 to about 1970. Herbert Shapiro's *White Violence and Black Response: From Reconstruction to Montgomery* (1988) and James W. Clarke's *The Lineaments of Wrath: Race, Violent Crime, and American Culture* (1998) are general introductions to the gory topic. William F. Holmes investigated rural violence against blacks in "Whitecapping: Agrarian Violence in Mississippi, 1902–1906," *Journal of Southern History* (1969). The three investigations of lynching in the 1890s by the black crusader Ida B. Wells (later Wells-Barnett) have been reprinted in *On Lynchings: Southern Horrors, A Red Record, Mob Rule in New Orleans* (1969).

Other worthy treatments of mob murder are the NAACP's study, *Thirty Years of Lynching in the United States, 1889–1918* (1919); W. Fitzhugh Brundage, *Lynching in the New South: Georgia and Virginia, 1880–1930* (1993); Philip Dray, *At the Hands of Persons Unknown: The Lynching of Black America* (2002); Sandra Gunning, *Race, Rape, and Lynching: The Red Record of American Literature, 1890–1912* (1996); Dennis B. Downey and Raymond M. Hyser, *No Crooked Death: Coatesville, Pennsylvania, and the Lynching of Zachariah Walker* (1991); George C. Wright, *Racial Violence in Kentucky, 1865–1940* (1990); and Vincent Vinikas, "Specters of the Past: The Saint Charles, Arkansas, Lynching of 1904 and the Limits of Historical Inquiry," *Journal of Southern History* (1999). Two insightful sociological studies are Stewart E. Tolnay and E. M. Beck, *A Festival of Violence: An Analysis of Southern Lynchings, 1882–1930* (1995); and Jonathan Markovitz, *Legacies of Lynching: Racial Violence and Memory* (2004). The numerous photographs of lynchings in James Allen and others, *Without Sanctuary: Lynching Photography in America* (2000), are powerfully haunting.

On the problem of what constitutes lynching, consult Christopher Waldrep, "War of Words: The Controversy over the Definition of Lynching, 1899–1940," *Journal of Southern History* (2000). On gender and lynching, see LeeAnn Whites, "Love, Hate, Rape, and Lynching: Rebecca Latimer Felton and the Gender Politics of Racial Violence," in *Democracy Betrayed: The Wilmington Race Riot of 1898 and Its Legacy,* edited by David S. Cecelski and Timothy B. Tyson (1998); Linda Gilmore, *Gender and Jim Crow* (1996); and Martha Hodes, *White Women, Black Men: Illicit Sex in the Nineteenth-Century South* (1997).

Black migration out of the South was a major theme in the Progressive Era and World War I. An outstanding introduction to black migration is *The Great Migration in Historical Perspective* (1999), edited by Joe William Trotter, Jr. Other first-rate studies include James R. Grossman, *Land of Hope: Chicago, Black Southerners, and the Great Migration* (1989); Farah Jasmine Griffin, *"Who Set You Flowin'?": The African American Migration Narrative* (1995); Carole Marks, *Farewell—We're Good and Gone: The Great Black Migration*

(1989); Florette Henri, *Black Migration: Movement North, 1900–1920* (1975); Louise V. Kennedy, *The Negro Peasant Turns Cityward* (1930); Kenneth Marvin Hamilton, *Black Towns and Profit: Promotion and Development in the Trans-Appalachian West, 1877–1915* (1991); and Hannibal B. Johnson, *Acres of Aspiration: The All-Black Towns in Oklahoma* (2002).

For the formation of ghettos and class stratification, consult Gilbert Osofsky, *Harlem: The Making of A Ghetto, 1890–1930* (1963); Kenneth L. Kusmer, *A Ghetto Takes Shape: Black Cleveland, 1870–1930* (1976); and Joe William Trotter, Jr., *Black Milwaukee: The Making of an Industrial Proletariat, 1915–1945* (1985). The essays in *The Underclass Debate: Views from History*, edited by Michael B. Katz (1993) contain excellent information that accounts for the lack of black social mobility.

Two chapters in Stephen Grant Meyer's *As Long as They Don't Move Next Door* (2000) deal with segregated housing in the Progressive Era. Although Herbert G. Gutman exaggerated the stability of the black family in *The Black Family in Slavery and Freedom, 1750–1925* (1976), his work must be considered. For the central place of the church in black social life, see Carter G. Woodson, *History of the Negro Church* (1972). Fraternal orders played a role second only to the church in black social life and are illuminated in David T. Beito, *From Mutual Aid to the Welfare State: Fraternal Societies and Social Services, 1890–1967* (2000) and William A. Muraskin, *Middle-Class Blacks in a White Society: Prince Hall Freemasonry in America* (1975). The YMCA played an important role in the development of black leadership and black welfare, as shown in Nina Mjagkij, *Light in the Darkness: African Americans and the YMCA, 1852–1946* (1994),

For studies that deal with northern blacks during the Progressive Era, see David Gordon Nielson's *Black Ethos: Northern Urban Negro Life and Thought, 1890–1930* (1977); Joe William Trotter, Jr., *River Jordan: African American Urban Life in the Ohio Valley* (1998); David A. Gerber, *Black Ohio and the Color Line, 1860–1915* (1976); Emma Lou Thornbrough, *Indiana Blacks in the Twentieth Century* (2000); Constance McLaughlin Green, *The Secret City: A History of Race Relations in the Nation's Capital* (1967); Thomas C. Cox, *Blacks in Topeka, Kansas, 1865–1915: A Social History* (1982); Lillian Serece Williams, *Strangers in the Land of Paradise: The Creation of an African American Community, Buffalo, New York, 1900–1940* (1999); Albert S. Broussard, *Black San Francisco: The Struggle for Racial Equality in the West, 1900–1954* (1993); Mark R. Schneider, *Boston Confronts Jim Crow, 1890–1920* (1997); and James J. Connolly, *The Triumph of Ethnic Progressivism: Urban Political Culture in Boston, 1900–1925* (1998).

As blacks migrated to the cities after the Civil War, race riots became more common in urban areas of both the North and South. For books that covered urban riots from 1898 to 1919, see Leon H. Prather, Sr., *We Have Taken a City: Wilmington Racial Massacre and Coup of 1898* (1984); David S. Cecelski and Timothy B. Tyson, eds., *Democracy Betrayed: The Wilmington Race Riot of 1898 and Its Legacy* (1998); William Ivy Hair, *Carnival of Fury: Robert Charles and the New Orleans Riot of 1900* (1976); Brian Butler, *An Undergrowth of Folly: Public Order, Race Anxiety, and the 1903 Evansville, Indiana Riot* (2000); Mark Bauerlein, *Negrophobia: A Race Riot in Atlanta, 1906* (2001); Charles Crowe, "Racial Violence and Social Reform—Origins of the Atlanta Riot of 1906," *Journal of Negro History* (1968) and "Racial Massacre in Atlanta, September 22, 1906," ibid. (1969); Roberta Senechal, *The Sociogenesis of a Race Riot: Springfield, Illinois, in 1908* (1990); James L. Crouthamel, "Springfield Race Riot of 1908," *Journal of Negro History* (1960); Elliott M. Rudwick, *Race Riot at East St. Louis, July 2, 1917* (1964); Robert V. Haynes, *A Night of Violence: The Houston Riot of 1917* (1976); William M. Tuttle, *Race Riot: Chicago in the Red Summer of 1919* (1972); Richard C. Cortner, *A Mob Intent on Death: The NAACP and the Arkansas Riot Cases* (1988); and Grif Stockley, *Blood in Their Eyes: The Elaine Race Massacres of 1919* (2001).

Several recent studies cast damning light on the racial policies of the political parties and the federal government in the Progressive Era. Desmond S. King's *Separate and Unequal: Black Americans and the U.S. Federal Government* (1995) is an excellent introduction to federal discrimination. On the progressive presidents, see Kenneth O'Reilly, *Nixon's Piano: Presidents and Racial Politics from Wash-*

ington to Clinton (1995) and George Sinkler, *The Racial Attitudes of American Presidents: From Abraham Lincoln to Theodore Roosevelt* (1971).

The best book on Roosevelt and race is Thomas G. Dyer, *Theodore Roosevelt and the Idea of Race* (1980), but see also Gary Gerstle, "Theodore Roosevelt and the Divided Character of American Nationalism," *Journal of American History* (1999), on the complexity of Roosevelt's views. Only a few general biographies of Roosevelt are adequate on race. The revised 1975 edition of William H. Harbaugh's important biography, *The Life and Times of Theodore Roosevelt,* was much more critical of the Rough Rider on race than the 1961 edition. H. W. Brand's huge biography, *T. R.: The Last Romantic* (1997) was informed with the latest research on Roosevelt and race, as was Lewis L. Gould's *The Presidency of Theodore Roosevelt* (1991). Gail Bederman's *Manliness and Civilization: A Cultural History of Gender and Race in the United States, 1880–1917* (1995) deftly linked Victorian manhood to racism and Roosevelt's muscular values. Two well-researched books examined Roosevelt's biggest blunder concerning blacks: John D. Weaver, *The Brownsville Raid* (1970) and Ann J. Lane, *The Brownsville Affair: National Crisis and Black Reaction* (1971).

No one book on William Howard Taft or Woodrow Wilson matches Dyer's work on Roosevelt, but the already cited works of Wogelmuth, Grantham, Meier, Newby, Sosna, Sinkler, the Weisses, and others provide ample proof of the white-supremacist attitudes of these presidents. The glaring deficiencies of the Socialist party on race are exposed in Mark Pittenger, *American Socialists and Evolutionary Thought, 1870–1920* (1993); Ira Kipnis, *The American Socialist Movement, 1897–1912* (1952); Sally M. Miller, "'For White Men Only': The Socialist Party of America and Issues of Gender, Ethnicity and Race," *Journal of the Gilded Age and Progressive Era* (2003); and Upton Sinclair's influential novel, *The Jungle* (1906). Relatively speaking, the leftist Philip S. Foner tended to soft-pedal the racism of Socialists in *American Socialism and Black Americans* (1977). Donald Bruce Johnson and Kirk H. Porter performed a great service in supplying the platforms of all the major parties in *National Party Platforms, 1840–1972* (1973).

The relative indifference or hostility to blacks by leading progressive thinkers was evident in influential books published during the Progressive Era, most tellingly in Walter Lippmann, *A Preface to Politics* (1914); Herbert Croly, *The Promise of American Life* (1912); Frederic C. Howe, *The Confessions of A Reformer* (1925), and Albert Bushnell Hart, *The Southern South* (1910). George W. Norris's autobiography, *Fighting Liberal* (1961), reveals a typical lack of interest in the race problem on the part of northern progressives, though more concern for blacks can be seen in Walter Weyl's *The New Democracy* (1912). Nancy C. Unger, *Fighting Bob LaFollette: The Righteous Reformer* (2000) tended to make the Wisconsin progressive look better on race than he was, even though he was more racially sensitive than most progressive politicians. For the changed views of former abolitionists, see Lyman Abbott, *Reminiscences* (1911) and Charles Francis Adams, Jr., *Charles Francis Adams, 1835–1915: An Autobiography* (1916). James M. McPherson argued that some former abolitionists retained their appetite for the advancement of civil rights into the twentieth century in *The Abolitionist Legacy: From Reconstruction to the NAACP* (1975).

The generally baleful influence of the Supreme Court and lower courts on black rights can be seen in Loren Miller, *The Petitioners: The Story of the Supreme Court of the United States and the Negro* (1967); Michael Klarman, *Neither Hero Nor Villain: The Supreme Court, Race, and the Constitution in the Twentieth Century* (1999); and Donald G. Nieman, *Promises to Keep: African-Americans and the Constitutional Order, 1776 to the Present* (1991). On the best-known civil rights case after *Brown* v. *Board of Education,* see Charles A. Lofgren, *The Plessy Case: A Legal-Historical Interpretation* (1987) and Thomas Brook, ed., *Plessy v. Ferguson: A Brief History with Documents* (1997). Mark Curriden and Leroy Phillips, Jr., analyzed the much-neglected but significant case of *United States* v. *Shipp* (1909) in *Contempt of Court* (1999).

The best account of Washington and his feud with Du Bois is Louis R. Harlan's Pulitzer Prize winner, *Booker T. Washington: The Wizard of Tuskegee, 1901–1915* (1983). Pre-Harlan biographies of Washington were largely uncritical and not based on primary sources. Harlan also edited the *Booker T. Washington Papers* (1972–1987) in fourteen volumes. Washington's ghostwritten autobiographies, *Story of My Life* (1900), *Up From Slavery* (1901), and *Working with the Hands* (1904) are self-serving and not always factually reliable. The collection of essays, *Booker T. Washington and Black Progress* (2003), edited by W. Fitzhugh Brundage, reconsidered all aspects of the wizard of Tuskegee. For a look at the most important influence on Washington's thinking, see Robert Francis Engs, *Educating the Disfranchised and Disinherited: Samuel Chapman Armstrong and Hampton Institute, 1839–1893* (1999).

On Du Bois, David L. Lewis's two volumes on the black leader are essential. Both *W. E. B. Du Bois: Biography of a Race, 1868–1919* (1993) and *W. E. B. Du Bois: The Fight for Equality and the American Century, 1919–1963* (2000) won Pulitzer Prizes. Also available are three volumes of *The Correspondence of W. E. B. Du Bois* (1973–1978), edited by Herbert Aptheker. Du Bois generated autobiographies throughout his long life. He started his story in *The Souls of Black Folk* (1903) and continued in *Darkwater: Voices from within the Veil* (1920); *Dusk of Dawn: An essay toward an Autobiography of a Race Concept* (1940); and *The Autobiography of W. E. B. Du Bois* (1968). One can access much of Du Bois's work in *The Oxford W. E. B. Du Bois Reader* (1996), edited by Eric J. Sundquist.

Many pre-Lewis biographies of Du Bois offered insight into the black leader's mind. Highly critical of Du Bois's ideological inconsistencies were Francis L. Broderick, *W.E.B. Du Bois: Negro Leader in a Time of Crisis* (1959) and Elliott M. Rudwick, *W. E. B. Du Bois: A Study in Minority Group Leadership* (1960). Arnold Rampersad stressed Du Bois's creative writing in *The Art and Imagination of W. E. B. Du Bois* (1976). Other worthy studies of Du Bois are Jack B. Moore, *W. E. B. Du Bois* (1981) and Manning Marable, *W. E. B. Du Bois: Black Radical Democrat* (1986). For recent publications that throw light on various aspects of Du Bois's thought, see the essays in *W. E. B. Du Bois, Race, and the City: The Philadelphia Negro and Its Legacy* (1998), edited by Michael B. Katz and Thomas J. Sugrue; Shamoon Zamir, *Dark Voices: W. E. B. Du Bois and American Thought, 1888–1903* (1995); Richard Cullen Rath, "Echo and Narcissus: The Afrocentric Pragmatism of W. E. B. Du Bois," *Journal of American History* (1997); and Axel R. Schäfer, "W. E. B. Du

Bois, German Social Thought, and the Racial Divide in American Progressivism, 1892–1909," *Journal of American History* (2001). Daryl Michael Scott is critical of Du Bois's (and almost all liberal) ideas about race in *Contempt and Pity: Social Policy and the Image of the Damaged Black Psyche, 1880–1996* (1997).

A superior source on the Washington–Du Bois feud because of its primary research and objectivity is Raymond Wolters, *Du Bois and His Rivals* (2002). Jacqueline M. Moore also covered both leaders even-handedly and tended to minimize their differences in *Booker T. Washington, W. E. B. Du Bois, and the Struggle for Racial Uplift* (2003). Two other works that profitably compare and contrast Washington and Du Bois are Manning Marable, *Black Leadership* (1998) and Adam Fairclough, *Better Day Coming: Blacks and Equality, 1890–2000* (2001). Though rambling, unfocused, verbose, and sometimes vitriolic, *Reconsidering the Souls of Black Folk* (2003) by Stanley Crouch and Playthell Benjamin contains some useful insights into Du Bois and his critics.

Still an essential source on black thought in the Progressive Era is August Meier, *Negro Thought in America, 1880–1915: Racial Ideologies in the Age of Booker T. Washington* (1963). But see also the essays in Cary D. Wintz, ed., *African American Political Thought, 1890–1930* (1996) and August Meier, Elliott M. Rudwick, and Francis L. Broderick, eds., *Black Protest Thought in the Twentieth Century* (1971). On black views of whites, consult Mia Bay, *The White Image in the Black Mind: African-American Ideas about White People, 1830–1925* (2000).

For the story of the rise of the NAACP and Du Bois's troubled relations with white liberals, see Charles F. Kellogg, *NAACP: A History of the National Association for the Advancement of Colored People* (1967); B. Joyce Ross, *J. E. Spingarn and the Rise of the NAACP, 1911–1919* (1972); Mary White Ovington, *The Walls Came Tumbling Down* (1947); Carolyn Wedin, *Inheritors of the Spirit: Mary White Ovington and the Founding of the NAACP* (1998); Langston Hughes, *Fight for Freedom: The Story of the NAACP* (1962); Robert L. Zangrando, *The NAACP Crusade against Lynching, 1909–1950* (1980); and William B. Hixon, Jr., *Moorfield Storey and the Abolitionist Tradition* (1972). On the more conservative and economically oriented

National Urban League, see Nancy Weiss, *The National Urban League, 1910–1940* (1974) and Jesse Thomas Moore, Jr., *A Search for Equality: The National Urban League, 1910–1961* (1981).

Emma Lou Thornbrough has documented the influence of T. Thomas Fortune in "The National Afro-American League, 1887–1908," *Journal of Southern History* (1961) and *T. Thomas Fortune: Militant Journalist* (1972); Fortune's own *Black and White: Land, Labor, and Politics in the South* (1984, 1969) revealed how radical he had once been before falling under the sway of the Tuskegee Machine. On other important black leaders, see Stephen R. Fox, *The Guardian of Boston: William Monroe Trotter* (1970); Mark Perry, *Lift Up Thy Voice: The Grimké Family's Journey from Slaveholders to Civil Rights Leaders* (2001); Dickson D. Bruce, Jr., *Archibald Grimké: Portrait of a Black Independent* (1993); Kelly Miller, *Race Adjustment* (1908); Eugene Levy, *James Weldon Johnson: Black Leader, Black Voice* (1973); James Weldon Johnson, *Along This Way: The Autobiography of James Weldon Johnson* (1933); Calvin S. Morris, *Reverdy C. Ransom: Black Advocate of the Social Gospel* (1990); Leroy Davis, *A Clashing of the Soul: John Hope and the Dilemma of African American Leadership and Black Higher Education in the Early Twentieth Century* (1998); Torrence Ridgely, *The Story of John Hope* (1948); Ernestine Williams Pickens, *Charles W. Chestnutt and the Progressive Movement* (1994); Benjamin E. Mays, *Born to Rebel: An Autobiography* (1971); and Ann Field Alexander, *Race Man: The Rise and Fall of the "Fighting Editor," John Mitchell, Jr.* (2002). Ironically, one of the most brutally racist polemics against blacks, *The American Negro* (1901), was written by a mulatto, William Hannibal Thomas. John David Smith tried to explain Thomas's self-hatred in *Black Judas: William Hannibal Thomas and The American Negro* (2000).

Only in recent years have historians and biographers begun to give black women reformers their due. Jacqueline Jones Royster edited the antilynching writings of Ida B. Wells-Barnett in *Southern Horrors and Other Writings* (1997) and Alfreda M. Duster edited *Crusade for Justice: The Autobiography of Ida B. Wells* (1970). See also Patricia A. Schechter's *Ida B. Wells-Barnett and American Reform, 1880–1930* (2001) and Linda McMurry, *To Keep the Waters Troubled:*

The Life of Ida B. Wells (1998). Beverly Washington Jones portrayed another important black leader in *Quest for Equality: The Life and Writings of Mary Eliza Church Terrell* (1990) and recently reissued are Church's 1940 memoirs, *A Colored Woman in a White World* (1996). Jacqueline Anne Rouse told the story of one the most active black women in the Progressive Era in her *Lugenia Burns Hope: Black Southern Reformer* (1989). Two biographies followed the life of the black educator Anna Julia Cooper: Louise Daniel Hutchinson, *Anna Julia Cooper: A Voice from the South* (1981) and Leona C. Gabel, *From Slavery to the Sorbonne and Beyond: The Life and Writings of Anna J. Cooper* (1982). Karen A. Johnson dealt with the lives of two important reformers in *Uplifting the Women and the Race: The Educational Philosophies and Social Activism of Anna Julia Cooper and Nannie Helen Burroughs* (2000). Evelyn Brooks Higginbotham also stressed the contributions of Burroughs in *Righteous Discontent: The Women's Movement in the Black Baptist Church, 1880–1920* (1993).

For general studies of black women activists, see Cynthia Neverdon-Morton, *Afro-American Women of the South and the Advancement of the Race, 1895–1925* (1989); Dorothy Salem, *To Better Our World: Black Women in Organized Reform, 1890–1920* (1990); and Floris Barnett Cash, *African American Women and Social Action: The Clubwomen and Volunteerism from Jim Crow to the New Deal, 1896–1936* (2001). See also the provocative essays in *Gender, Class, Race, and Reform in the Progressive Era* (1991), edited by Noralee Frankel and Nancy S. Dye. Two studies that dealt with the suffrage movement and exposed the racism therein are Rosalyn Terborg-Penn, *African American Women in the Struggle for the Vote, 1850–1920* (1998) and Marjorie Spruill Wheeler, *New Women of the New South: The Leaders of the Woman Suffrage Movement in the Southern States* (1993).

The lives of working black women, menial and professional, are described in Tera W. Hunter, *To 'Joy My Freedom: Southern Black Women's Lives and Labor after the Civil War* (1997); David M. Katzman, *Seven Days a Week: Women and Domestic Service in Industrializing America* (1978); Darline Clark Hine, *Black Women in White: Racial Conflict and Cooperation in the Nursing Profession, 1890–1950* (1989); and Stephanie J. Shaw, *What a Woman Ought To*

Be and To Do: Black Professional Women Workers During the Jim Crow Era (1996). Beverly Guy-Sheftall pointed out the double burden of being female and black in *Daughters of Sorrow: Attitudes toward Black Women, 1880–1920* (1990).

In the 1990s several studies focused on the black elite and color consciousness, the first being Willard B. Gatewood, *Aristocrats of Color: The Black Elite, 1880–1920* (1990). Also subjecting the upper-middle class to scrutiny, much as the black sociologist E. Franklin Frazier had done in the 1930s and 1940s, were Jacqueline M. Moore, *Leading the Race: The Transformation of the Black Elite in the Nation's Capital, 1880–1920* (1999) and Lynne B. Feldman, *A Sense of Place: Birmingham's Black Middle-Class Community, 1890–1930* (1999). Kevin K. Gaines condemned the paternalistic attitudes of the black elite toward the black masses in *Uplifting the Race: Black Leadership, Politics, and Culture in the Twentieth Century* (1996). Stanley Liberson, *A Piece of the Pie: Blacks and White Immigrants since 1880* (1980) and Arnold M. Shankman, *Ambivalent Friends: Afro-Americans View the Immigrant* (1982) related the uneasy relationship of blacks and immigrants.

There are many works on the crucial subject of black education, many of them highly critical of the South's backward, separate and unequal public school system. Some of the better works on this topic are James D. Anderson, *The Education of Blacks in the South, 1860–1935* (1988); Adam Fairclough, *Teaching Equality: Black Schools in the Age of Jim Crow* (2001) and "Being in the Field of Education and Also Being a Negro . . . Seems . . . Tragic: Black Teachers in the Jim Crow South," *Journal of American History* (2000); Louis R. Harlan, *Separate and Unequal: Public School Campaigns and Racism in the Southern Seaboard States* (1958); Eric Anderson and Alfred A. Moss, Jr., *Dangerous Donations: Northern Philanthropy and Southern Education, 1902–1930* (1999); Donald Spivey, *Schooling for the New Slavery: Black Industrial Education, 1868–1915* (1978); and H. Leon Prather, Sr., *Resurgent Politics and Educational Progressivism in the New South: North Carolina, 1890–1913* (1979).

On black literature, especially on Paul Lawrence Dunbar and Charles Chestnutt, most helpful are Dickson D. Bruce, Jr., *Black American Writing from the Nadir: The Evolution of a Literary Tradi-*

tion, 1877–1915 (1989) and various anthologies such as *Dark Symphony: Negro Literature in America* (1968), edited by James A. Emanuel and Theodore L. Gross, and *Black Insights: Significant Literature by Black Americans, 1760 to the Present* (1971), compiled by Nick Aaron Ford. James Weldon Johnson, a poet, novelist, and musician as well as a political activist, told what it was like to be a black man on Broadway in his autobiography cited above, but see also Susan Curtis, *The First Black Actors on the Great White Way* (1998). On black dance, see Richard A. Long, *The Black Tradition in American Dance* (1989) and Lynne Fauley Emery, *Black Dance from 1619 to Today* (1988).

The Progressive Era saw the development of ragtime, blues, and jazz, which forever transformed American popular music. The literature on black music is massive, but for starters see Arnold Shaw, *Black Popular Music in America: From the Spirituals, Minstrels, and Ragtime to Soul, Disco, and Hip-Hop* (1986). On the origins and meaning of the blues, see LeRoi Jones (Amira Baraka), *Blues People* (1963); Clyde Woods, *Development Arrested: The Blues and Plantation Power in the Mississippi Delta* (1998); William Ferris, *Blues from the Delta* (1970); Paul Oliver, *Blues Fell This Morning: The Meaning of the Blues* (1963); William Barlow, *"Looking Up at Down": The Emergence of Blues Culture* (1989); and Jeff Todd Tilton, *Early Downhome Blues: A Musical and Cultural Analysis* (1994). For that unique American art form called jazz, consult Burton W. Parenti, *The Creation of Jazz: Music, Race, and Culture in Urban America* (1992). A still useful introduction to emerging jazz is Gunther Schuller, *Early Jazz: Its Roots and Musical Development* (1968). On the leading trumpet player of the early twentieth century, see Laurence Bergreen, *Louis Armstrong: An Extravagant Life* (1997) and James Lincoln Collier, *Louis Armstrong: An American Genius* (1983). For the life of one of the most fascinating early formulators of jazz, see the updated version of Alan Lomax, *Mister Jelly Roll: The Fortunes of Jelly Roll Morton, New Orleans Creole and "Inventor of Jazz"* (2001).

On sports, see Arthur Ashe's encyclopedic *A Hard Road to Glory: A History of the Afro-American Athlete, 1619–1986,* 3 vols. (1988). The story of black baseball is told in Robert Peterson, *Only the Ball Was White* (1992). On the controversial world heavyweight champion from 1908 to 1915, see Al-Tony Gilmore, *Bad Nigger! The National Impact of Jack Johnson* (1975); Randy Roberts, *Papa Jack: Jack Johnson and the Era of White Hopes* (1983); and Thomas R. Hietala, *Fight of the Century: Jack Johnson, Joe Louis, and the Struggle for Racial Equality* (2002).

For further information on blacks in the military during World War I, Arthur E. Barbeau and Florette Henri, *The Unknown Soldiers: Black American Troops in World War I* (1974) is the best starting point. The story of one of the most noted black combat units in France is dramatically told in Stephen L. Harris, *Harlem's Hell Fighters: The African American 369th Infantry in World War I* (2003). Also useful on the military and the discriminatory draft are Bernard C. Nalty, *Strength for the Fight: A History of Black Americans in the Military* (1986); Robert B. Edgerton, *Hidden Heroism: Black Soldiers in America's Wars* (2001); Jeanette Keith, "The Politics of Southern Draft Resistance, 1917–1918: Class, Race, and Conscription in the Rural South," *Journal of American History* (2001); and James Mennell, "African Americans and the Selective Draft Act of 1917," *Journal of Negro History* (1999).

One can follow the debate on whether blacks should have supported the war and deferred civil rights activity in William Jordan, "'The Damnable Dilemma': African-American Accommodation and Protest during World War I," *Journal of American History* (1995); Mark Ellis, "'Closing Ranks' and 'Seeking Honors': W. E. B. Du Bois in World War I," *Journal of American History* (1992); and William G. Jordan, *Black Newspapers and America's War for Democracy, 1914–1920* (2001). The obsession with black subversion during the war is treated in Mark Ellis, *Race, War, and Surveillance: African Americans and the United States Government during World War I* (2001) and Theodore Kornweibel, Jr., *"Investigate Everything": Federal Efforts to Compel Black Loyalty during World War I* (2002).

On the rise of Marcus Garvey and black nationalism during World War I and after, see Tony Martin, *Race First: The Ideological and Organizational Struggles of Marcus Garvey and the Universal Negro Improvement Association* (1976) and E. David Cronon, *Black Moses: The Story of Marcus Garvey and the Universal Negro Improvement Association* (1955). Paula F. Pfeffer dissected the other radical black leader who competed with Du Bois for the leadership of African Americans in *A. Philip Randolph, Pioneer of the Civil Rights Movement* (1990), as did Jervis Anderson in *A. Philip Randolph: A Biographical Portrait* (1973). To trace the thought of Washington, Du Bois, Garvey, and Randolph and some of the interaction between them, see the primary sources in *African American Political Thought, 1890–1930: Washington, Du Bois, Garvey and Randolph* (1996), edited by Cary D. Wintz.

Adam Fairclough's "Civil Rights and the Lincoln Memorial: The Censored Speeches of Robert R. Moton (1922) and John Lewis (1963)," *Journal of Negro History* (1997) and Scott A. Sandage's "A Marble House Divided: The Lincoln Memorial, the Civil Rights Movement, and the Politics of Memory, 1939–1963," Journal of American History (1993) illustrates how completely white America had disconnected Lincoln from the issue of race by 1922, yet another sign of the continuing nadir for African Americans.

INDEX

White Supremacy (Kantrowitz), 27–28
Berea College v. *Kentucky,* 131
Berger, Victor, 123
Beveridge, Albert J., 37, 46
Bilbo, Theodore G., 28, 91
biological determinism, 2, 11–12, 151
  See also scientific racism
The Birth of a Nation (film), 70–71, 128, 132–33, 170
Black Codes, 14–15, 16, 54
black identity, 152, 156
The Black Image in the White Mind (Fredrickson), 65
black press
  approach of, 175
  on black participation in wars, 182–83
  on Brownsville affair, 118
  Du Bois on, 167
  Manly affair, 32–33
  Niagara Movement and, 161
  uses of New Negro, 181
  Washington's control of, 143, 158
Black Rage (Grier/Cobbs), 10
Black Reconstruction in America (Du Bois), 20
blacks. *See* African Americans
Blair bill, 22, 34
Blease, Cole, 28, 91
Blight, David, W., 126
Boas, Franz, 55
Boston Confronts Jim Crow, 1890–1920 (Schneider), 56–57
Boston riot, 158–60
Bourbons. *See* Redeemer Era
Boyle, James, 60
Brattain, Michelle, 77
Brawley, Benjamin, 178–79
Brown, Henry Billings, 29
Brown, William Garrott, 117
Brownsville affair, 118–19, 122, 171
The Brownsville Raid (Weaver), 119
Bruce, John Edward, 178–79
Bryan, William Jennings, 89, 121
Buchanan v. *Warley,* 132, 171

Buffalo Soldiers, 32
Bulkley, William L., 173
Bullard, Robert Lee, 188
Bull Moose party, 123–24
Burgess, John W., 54
Burleson, Albert Sidney, 127
Burns, Tommy, 68
Burroughs, Edgar Rice, 68
Burroughs, Nannie Helen, 179–80
Bushee, Frederick, 62
businesses, 44, 46, 85–87
Butler, Matthew C., 18
Butt, Archie, 121

capitalism, 51
Carnegie, Andrew, 41, 51, 142
Carrington, E. C., Jr., 124
Carroll, Charles, 52
Cash, W. J., 18
caste system, 72, 93, 99, 109, 133
Catholic church, 64
chain gangs, 107
Chamberlain, Daniel, 36
Charles, Robert, 95–96
Chestnutt, Charles W., 38, 174, 178
Chicago race riot, 185
Chisum, Melvin J., 161
Christianity and the Social Crisis (Rauschenbusch), 65
Church, Robert, 86
churches
  advancement of race through, 172
  black civil rights and, 63–66
  color prejudices in, 87
  establishment of schools during Reconstruction, 16
  segregation of, 17, 20, 64, 100–101
  social work in black communities, 179–80
  white supremacists of, 92–93
citizenship, 15, 16
Civil Rights Act of 1875, 16, 17
civil rights bills of 1866, 14
civil rights movement, 20, 136, 180, 181
Civil Service Commission, 128

The Progressive Era and Race: Reaction and Reform, 1900–1917
Developmental editor and copyeditor: Andrew J. Davidson
Production editor: Lucy Herz
Proofreader: Claudia Siler
Indexer: Pat Rimmer
Printer: Versa Press, Inc.